ANVIL!

THE STORY OF ANVIL

STEVE 'LIPS' KUDLOW
AND ROBB REINER
WITH ROBERT UHLIG

CORGI BOOKS

TRANSWORLD PUBLISHERS
61–63 Uxbridge Road, London W5 5SA
A Random House Group Company
www.rbooks.co.uk

**ANVIL! THE STORY OF ANVIL
A CORGI BOOK: 9780552159692**

First published in Great Britain
in 2009 by Bantam Press
an imprint of Transworld Publishers
Corgi edition published 2010

A CIP catalogue record for this book
is available from the British Library.

Addresses for Random House Group Ltd companies outside the UK
can be found at: www.randomhouse.co.uk
The Random House Group Ltd Reg. No. 954009

The Random House Group Limited supports The Forest Stewardship
Council (FSC), the leading international forest certification organisation.
All our titles that are printed on Greenpeace approved FSC certified paper
carry the FSC logo. Our paper procurement policy can be found at
www.rbooks.co.uk/environment

Typeset in 11/16 Life by
Falcon Oast Graphic Art Ltd
Printed in the UK by CPI Cox & Wyman, Reading, RG1 8EX

2 4 6 8 10 9 7 5 3 1

From Lips to Robb
From Robb to Lips

It takes two men to make one brother

ISRAEL ZANGWILL

Foreword
by Slash

I grew up in the LA of the early eighties. It was a pretty exciting place back then. Punk had killed off the dinosaur bands of the seventies with their bombastic stage shows and concept albums. Rock music, which my friends and I were into, had changed because of it, and just like American kids had in the sixties, the new generation was looking across the pond to England for what the new wave of music was going to be. We all loved the Sex Pistols, but when bands like Motörhead started to break, we were completely absorbed. They were fast, furious and raw. Totally brilliant stuff.

So the last thing we were expecting was an album by four completely unknown young dudes from Toronto, Canada to blow us all away. But it did. We'd never heard of Anvil before 1982, but when my friends and I heard *Metal On Metal* for the first time, we all got goosebumps. Here was the intensity and speed that we loved from those new British bands, but there was also this crazy blend of melody and heaviness – it was the first time any of us had heard that *rat-a-tat-a-tat-a* rhythm – kick drums and bass guitar firing eighth notes in unison like some sick thunderous machine gun!

Anvil's music would turn out to be the bridge between that first wave of British metal and the new wave of American speed or thrash metal that would spawn bands such as Metallica, Anthrax and Slayer.

At the time, we all just assumed Anvil were going to be huge stars. And not just because Robb Reiner's drumming and Steve 'Lips' Kudlow's guitar playing were harder and faster than anything we'd ever heard before. The band also had this sick name – what could be more heavy metal than 'Anvil'? – and their live shows were legendary. Lips would appear onstage in a bondage harness playing his Flying V with a dildo and singing these insane lyrics. At an Anvil show you were always laughing as hard as you were banging your head. That was what was completely refreshing about them and completely different to anything we had ever seen before.

Though *Metal On Metal* was a huge influence on anyone who picked up a guitar at that time and inspired numerous bands, in the end a lot of people ripped off Anvil's licks – as well as the way they dressed and their stage antics – and made them their own. That's how it goes, of course, sometimes. But somewhere along the way Anvil got left behind in all the dust those other bands kicked up. I always thought they really should have made it a lot bigger than they did and I could never understand why they didn't. Sometimes it's just down to dumb luck or being in the right place at the right time. Either way, I don't think Robb and Lips ever really got the respect they deserved. It taught me that talent and a huge statement aren't always enough to guarantee that an influential band will be remembered.

For years I wondered what had happened to Anvil. And then my English friend in LA, Sacha Gervasi, told me Anvil were still going, still recording albums and touring. I was amazed. When Sacha told me he wanted to make a movie about them – he'd known them since he was a kid – I decided I wanted to be part of it. It wasn't just because of my respect for their music, but because of the struggle I realized Lips and Robb had endured for more than thirty years. It's pretty amazing when you think about it. Every year some new hot band appears on the scene and sells millions of records, but how many of them can say they'll stay together for one or two years, let alone thirty?

You've got to give Lips and Robb credit. Keeping that bond going, getting through the ups and the downs, dealing with the egos, the loss of band members, the stress from their families and everything else that the music industry throws at you, no matter how many or how few records you sell, is in my opinion the ultimate proof of integrity and commitment to a dream, to the pact they made as kids to rock together for ever.

It's hard enough to keep up the passion and the interest when you're doing really well. Even then, a simple argument can be enough to split a band, but Robb and Lips didn't quit, even though they never had the chance to experience the pleasures of multi-platinum success like so many of the bands they had influenced.

They decided that, no matter what, they had to keep playing, keep coming up with new material and keep making new albums. They always believed that if they did, one day Anvil would achieve the recognition that had eluded them for so long. It wasn't an easy road. But these guys just hung in there, stuck to what they believed in and simply refused to admit defeat, even in the face of a sometimes disinterested world. When they were sitting on the edge of the precipice, they leaned on each other instead of pushing each other over the edge. They truly kept the fire going. That's a lot harder than it looks, trust me.

To me, Robb's and Lips's tale of unending devotion is deeply humbling and I hope it inspires anyone in any profession, let alone rock music. I hope they stick it out for another thirty years. But more than that, I hope they get the credit they've been denied for so long and emerge as one of the most successful metal bands ever. After all these years, that would be truly awesome.

Long live Anvil!

Slash

Los Angeles, 14 February 2009

1 ON THE BRINK

ROBB: Walking off stage at the Civic Centre at Glens Falls, I punched the air. We'd smoked them. An Aerosmith audience that had come to see their classic rock heroes had been turned over by Anvil, an obscure heavy metal band from Toronto. They'd never even heard of us, but we'd won them round. We'd fucking triumphed.

Backstage, a tall slim guy, very Jewish with big hands, brown eyes and a scrambled way of speaking, was waiting: David Krebs, the man who discovered AC/DC and Aerosmith. The manager of Ted Nugent, Def Leppard and the Scorpions. The man we needed to impress.

'How d'you boys think it went?'

'Amazing, man!' I was stoked. 'Fucking unbelievable. The people loved us. We kicked ass.'

Krebs appeared blown away. 'You were hot, but you

might have had good luck tonight. I'm gonna come and see you tomorrow night.'

Twenty-four hours to prepare to blow Krebs out of the arena for a second time. Then he might come good on the deal he'd been promising since he first made contact. A fortnight earlier, we'd been working in the studio on *Forged In Fire*, our third album. I'd taken the call.

'Hey, man, I hear you guys are the real deal.'

At the time, I couldn't believe it. *David Krebs*. Mr Mega. From New York. Spitting words down the line like a machine gun firing bullets. Fuck.

'I hear you guys are the future of metal.'

I turned to Lips, standing beside me, guitar in hand. 'Brother, it's the big boy.' I cupped the phone. 'It's Krebs. Leber and fucking *Krebs*, man.'

Lips's eyes widened. Leber and Krebs was the biggest music management company in New York. 'Man . . . no way.'

To say I was stoked to hear from Krebs would be an understatement. I was fucking awed. A powerful big-time manager interested in us? We were Anvil, four young guys from Toronto who were gaining a reputation as the heaviest rockers – and hardest party animals – on the metal circuit, but to most of the world we were unknown. Maybe our years of playing five sets a night, seven nights a week, in the bars and clubs of Quebec,

Ontario and New York would now pay off. Maybe the buzz on the street and our rise over the last year – playing the Monsters of Rock festival at Donnington and the Marquee Club in London, blowing Iron Maiden and Motörhead off the stage on support tours – had at last caught the attention of a man who could really make it happen on a global scale for us. Maybe.

'I want to see your band. Ross Halfin and Doug Thaler tell me you're the next big thing. They say I should check you guys out. They say you're fucking great.'

Ross was a legendary heavy metal photographer and Doug was a well-known manager who had just signed Mötley Crüe. Cool endorsements indeed.

'How can I see you? Where are you playing? I want to meet you guys.'

Looking at Lips in the hope he might have an answer, I hissed an urgent request. 'Dates?'

Lips shrugged. No luck.

'Mr Krebs, sir. We don't have any dates lined up.'

This didn't sound good. We had no gigs because we had no management and because we were in the middle of recording.

'You know what?' said Krebs. 'I'm going to give you guys a week with Aerosmith. You can open for them. And I'll come and see you.'

The bad boys from Boston were the biggest band in

America. Although on the slide from their 1970s peak, Aerosmith in 1983 were still an amazing live draw with an awesome front man in Steven Tyler. I was blown away.

'You can open for my boys here in America at the Spectrum in Philly and in Canada at the Forum. I want to see you guys on a big stage and then we'll talk.'

The line went dead and I told the band – Lips, Dave 'Squirrely' Allison our rhythm guitarist and Ian 'Dix' Dickson our bassist – the news. They went mad.

'This is it,' said Lips. 'Like . . . fuck.'

We'd been building up to this moment for six years with Squirrely and Dix. Lips and I had been playing together for longer, ever since the day more than a decade ago when as young teenagers we'd vowed we'd rock together for ever. And now the Big Opportunity had come.

That night we walked on to the stage at the Civic Centre in front of thousands of Aerosmith fans. Few of them knew us and even fewer wanted to hear our set. We knew it was going to be tough. These guys had come to see a classic rock band and we were a heavy metal act. Barely a murmur of applause greeted the end of our first song, but at least we hadn't been booed off the stage. Dressed in a bondage harness, Lips worked a storm at the front. Squirrely, the Kevin Bacon of metal, performed his usual role of flaunting his pretty-boy looks and leaving his trousers undone to catch the attention of the chicks. Dix was Dix, reliable and hard-working on his bass. And I was at the back: Robbo, the greatest drummer of my generation.

By the end of our half-hour set, the audience had come around. They didn't love us, but they didn't hate us and we got an awesome cheer as we took our bow. It was enough to convince Krebs we'd got promise, but he wanted to check tonight's performance wasn't some flash in the pan.

The next night we played the Broome County Arena, a large ice-hockey venue at Binghamton, New York. We were just as good, if not better. Krebs was there again and we smoked him. We were living up to the legend of Anvil.

'You guys could have been lucky again tonight.' Krebs was checking us out and he liked what he saw, but guys like him don't make hasty decisions. 'I'm gonna come and see you one more time. This time it'll be in Philly.'

We played two more dates with Aerosmith. The War Memorial Auditorium at Syracuse went well and the Forum in Montreal was almost a home crowd for us. Then we travelled to Philadelphia, where we had two nights off before the big one at the Spectrum. With two nights to kill, we did what every self-respecting metal band would do. We partied. Big time.

In those days we had a pretty full entourage. Roadies,

friends, a few fans and of course the groupies. Chris Tsangarides, who was producing our album in Toronto when the call came from Krebs, came along for the ride and to help sell our merchandise at the gigs. As usual we were staying in some cheap shithole hotel, all of us squeezed into two double rooms, me and Squirrely in the party room, Lips and Dix in the quiet room. Meanwhile, Aerosmith were jetting in a few hours before the gig and arriving in limos. They were rock stars on a whole other plateau. We were dreaming of becoming them.

I was sitting with CT, drinking, talking and partying in Lips's room with a bunch of people. Every now and then our nice quiet party would be disturbed by a bunch of guys and chicks getting up to go into the other room. We all knew what that meant, but CT was oblivious. He had produced albums for Judas Priest, Black Sabbath and Thin Lizzy, but he had never been out with a band like Anvil before. This quietly spoken Greek-Cypriot Brit had never seen road antics.

'CT.' I got up and gestured at the door. 'I am going to show you the shit that happens on the road.'

Me and Lips took CT into the other room. It was dark, but we could still kind of see what was going on. Two girls were naked on the bed and there were guys all around, maybe five or six. It was an orgy.

'You like it when I finger you, doncha, bitch,' said a male voice from among the heap of bodies.

There was a short pause while the chick in question emptied her mouth. 'Yeah . . . you bet.'

Beside me, CT was losing it, giggling uncontrollably because he was so uncomfortable. I took him out into the corridor to cool down.

'I've never seen anything like this before.' CT was shaking. 'Maybe in the movies, but certainly not in real life.'

For Anvil, it was business as usual. The party ended after the sun came up on the next day, when we were scheduled to play the biggest North American gig of our career in front of nearly twenty thousand Aerosmith fans at the Philly Spectrum.

For Aerosmith, it was a return to their heartland. They'd played the same venue a fortnight earlier. Both dates had sold out, but things were not entirely good in the Aerosmith camp. Joe Perry, the founding lead guitarist, known with Tyler as one of the Toxic Twins because of their fondness for stimulants and heroin, had left the band and been replaced with Jimmy Crespo. Brad Whitford, the longtime rhythm guitarist, had recently followed Perry out of the door during the recording of their latest album, *Rock In A Hard Place*. After ten years of international fame and recognition, Aerosmith's fast-paced life of touring, recording and monumental drug use had caught up with them. Most of the band was pretty distant, but we'd met Tyler when he came to our changing room a couple of times to say hi. Still recovering from a serious motorcycle accident a few years earlier, he didn't look well.

As we made our way to the Spectrum stage, their tour manager took us aside.

'Tonight it's no thirty-five-minute set. You're playing for an hour and a half.'

'What?' Lips was freaking out. Nearly twenty thousand Aerosmith fans were waiting to see their idols. They'd tolerate us for half an hour at most, but then the trouble would start. 'An hour and a half? You must be fucking joking.'

The tour manager said Tyler was in a bad way because of his motorcycle accident. He was on painkillers and they couldn't get him up. 'Aerosmith can't make it on time and Steven can only do a shorter show tonight. You're playing for ninety minutes.'

So we went out and we kicked ass. We had more than enough material to play for longer and the extra time on stage gave us a chance to win the crowd over. I could tell they were wondering what the fuck had happened to Aerosmith, but we put on a good enough show to make an arena full of Aerosmith fans stop yelling for their band. Fortunately they hadn't noticed Squirrely, who as always had partied harder than anyone else, puking behind the Marshalls between songs. And the rest of us had put on a smoking show. We'd pulled it off. It felt awesome.

When we came off stage Krebs was waiting with his wife and Dee Snider, front man of Twisted Sister. He wasted no time in getting to the point.

'What we gotta do is get your stuff out down here in the United States. Get people aware of your music. We gotta get you a global record deal.'

Our first two albums, *Hard'N'Heavy* and *Metal On Metal*, had been released by Attic, a Canadian heavy metal label. Elsewhere they were available only as imports. A global deal would change our fortunes dramatically. At last we might get the recognition we deserved and make some money from our recordings.

Krebs turned to Lips. 'You're like Ted Nugent, but even more fucking metal, man. Sign with me and your band will go all the way to the top.'

The break we'd been hoping for had finally come. We'd got a manager. And not some little guy but the biggest of the biggest. He hardly knew our music and he'd seen us perform only three times, but he could see we were the future of metal. The fucking real deal. The next big thing. Everything I'd dreamed of was about to happen – recognition, fame, wealth and adoration – and it could only get better.

LIPS: A few months later, we'd signed with Krebs and we were booked to support Motörhead on a six-week tour of Britain. But on 21 May, a week before the

Motörhead tour, we travelled to Bruges in Belgium to play the Heavy Sounds festival.

Gary Moore was headlining and there were eight other bands on the bill including Uriah Heap, Ostrogoth and 'Surprise'. That surprise was Anvil. No one in the crowd of ten thousand knew we were playing.

We'd been to Europe before. In 1982 we played the Monsters of Rock festival at Donnington followed by two nights at the Marquee Club in London at which we'd staked our reputation as one of the heaviest, fastest metal bands around. But this was our first time on the European mainland and we were still relatively unknown outside the community of hardcore headbangers in Canada and New York. We'd have to work very hard to win over this crowd.

The festival was being held in a dilapidated old football stadium. It was damp and overcast and we were exhausted. Money was too tight for hotels, so we'd travelled all night in a beat-up old van with our equipment. Any hope of catching up on sleep disappeared when we arrived at the stadium. Our accommodation was a trashed changing room, but the biggest obstacle to rest and recuperation was a rock star flying in a hot air balloon over the festival. Lemmy, lead singer and founder of Motörhead with a legendary appetite for doing speed and playing loud, was throwing towels down to the crowd.

We'd supported Motörhead in Canada in 1981 and I'd met Lemmy several times since then. A few months earlier, at about the same time Krebs called us in the studio, Motörhead's manager Doug Smith had contacted me.

'Can you come and play for Motörhead? We need a guitar player. Our guy's gonna walk out.'

'Fast' Eddie Clarke had quit in a hissy fit when Lemmy had proposed recording a cover of Tammy Wynette's 'Stand By Your Man'. He thought it went totally against Motörhead principles.

Most metal guitarists would have grabbed the opportunity with both hands. Motörhead was one of the best bands in the business. *Ace Of Spades*, their recent album and single, was a headbanger classic. But we were in the middle of writing and ready to go into the studio. I had a simple answer.

'What you saying, man? We gotta go and record *Forged In Fire*. I gotta stick with my brothers. No. Can't do it, man. Not possible.'

Now, making my way towards our changing room, I was passing a caravan when I felt somebody attempt to snatch the scruff of my neck from behind. Ready to punch whoever had grabbed me, I turned around. Lemmy was standing in the doorway of a caravan, grinning and holding the collar of my jacket.

'Get the fuck in here. I want to have a word with you.'

Oh no. Even without his gravelly voice, mutton chops and moles, Lemmy could be a fright. Everything about him said one thing: Don't mess with me.

'I want you to listen to this.' Lemmy passed me the headphones to his Walkman. 'This is the album you should have done.'

I listened. It was very good.

'Why didn't you do it?'

'Lemmy, I had to record our own album. I've got my band and I've got to try to make it with them. It wouldn't have been right.'

'I can respect that. That's all right.' Lemmy nodded. With him, that was as good as a smile. 'Have a listen and tell me what you think.'

I listened for a while. 'Fucking cool, man. I like it.' I really did. And I still do.

'You take care,' said Lemmy. 'I'll see you next week.'

We were the next act due on stage and we needed to get ready, so I left Lemmy's caravan and headed down to the cesspit of our changing room, where I washed my hair in a cracked sink. Then I heard it.

'Anvil! Anvil! Anvil!'

It was the crowd. How did they know we were here? We weren't even named on the bill, yet they were yelling for us. No one ever chanted like that for Anvil. Maybe a few tens of people in a club in Toronto, but not ten thousand voices shouting as one.

'What the fuck is going on?' It was Dix. His bewildered look summed up all our feelings.

Robb, Squirrely, Dix and I walked up to the stage. We could see the crowd and they were freaking out. The roadies had uncovered Robb's drum kit and the crowd could see the Anvil logo on the front of each of his two bass drums. Presumably that had set them off. A few months earlier we'd played in front of thousands of Aerosmith fans, few if any of whom had known who we were even though we were close to home. Now we were thousands of miles away – in the middle of Belgium, for fuck's sake – and thousands of headbangers were demanding we come on stage. Win the crowd over? What?

It was a real shock.

We ran on stage and the audience went wild. I felt the fire. Catching Robb's eye, I knew what he was thinking: Let's go! Fucking yeah. We kicked into the first number and the place went nuts. I mean it went fucking nuts.

A cold shiver went down my back as I realized we'd found our audience. I'd dreamed of the show when everyone was chanting our name and now, about to release our third album and go on tour with Motörhead, it had actually happened for us. The crowd wanted one thing and one thing only – Anvil – and that afternoon they got it full fucking blast.

We were going over. We were rocking. And the people were loving it. They were flipping out totally. At the end of the set we got encored. As we came off stage I knew we'd taken the show. Backstage we were the sensation of the festival. Everybody was talking about Anvil. This day would go down in heavy metal legend.

That night I got back to my hotel room, sat down and wrote a letter to Lee, my girlfriend in Toronto. I tried to put into words what had happened that day, how I was so blown away by the response we'd got from the crowd.

My future is assured, I wrote. *There's no doubt in my mind that I can now do this for the rest of my life because today I saw my fan base. It is real. It's not just hoping. It's actually there.*

Today I made a difference and the people who saw me revered me as something very special. Now I know I will always have an audience. I didn't have to win them over today. They were already there. They've got our albums and they know who we are. We have a future.

It was a turning point in the rise of Anvil. For the first time I felt confident that I was going to be able to make music for ever. The fans had shown me. I'd reached the heartland of metal in Europe and struck an almighty chord.

Robb believed that a mega-manager was the vital cog in the machine. Without a manager, Anvil would always struggle, he said. But I didn't agree. I felt the people were the key. And I knew that day that this part of the world was my stronghold. Every metal musician knew in their heart of hearts that Europe was the secret to long-term success because it wasn't a place of trends. Fans there were fans until the day they died. That simple fact was going to make my career go on for as long as I wanted it. These people would venerate me as an important commodity. I'd seen it in their eyes and now I felt it in my soul.

2 TWO GOOD JEWISH BOYS

LIPS: I was totally correct in my prediction on that day at the Heavy Sounds festival in 1983. That hardcore fan base – we called them woodworkers because they appeared to come out of the woodwork whenever we toured Europe – stuck with us for the rest of our careers. The trouble was they were the only ones.

After Heavy Sounds, things took off for us. We released our third album, *Forged In Fire*, a metal classic that inspired dozens of bands which went on to sell tens of millions of records – just ask Slash or Lars Ulrich, drummer and co-founder of Metallica, or Scott Ian of Anthrax. They'll tell you how important *Metal On Metal* and *Forged In Fire* were to them. And we toured Europe, North America and Japan several times. But after that things changed. I suppose you could say our market fragmented and our music became more exclusive.

What the hell. It didn't matter because Anvil kept going. Robb and I stuck together for the simple reason that we're brothers and we both knew one day success would come and the world would truly appreciate the awesome majesty of Anvil.

For almost twenty years we kept touring and recording albums, most of them self-financed. By mid-2005 there were twelve of them, the most recent being *Back To Basics*, and we had just returned from playing a metal festival in Italy when an email arrived on my computer.

Hi! It's Teabag, the email said. *Haven't heard from you guys in years. How have you been? If anybody – Lips, Robb or anybody – is there, please email me back.*

I immediately called Robb.

'Hey, Gaze, man . . .' Robb's middle name is Géza; it's Hungarian. If it's real official shit I'll call him Robb. If it's happy-go-lucky stuff then it's Robbo. And if it's the real-love brother thing, then it's Gaze. That's how we are. 'You'll never guess who fucking emailed me.'

'Jethro? It wouldn't be Maddog.' I guess Teabag wasn't the first person on Robb's list.

'Fuckin' Teabag, man!'

'What?' Robb sounded profoundly blown away. 'Sacha?'

'Yeah, man. He emailed me, man. I just got it.'

'No way, man.'

'You better believe it, Gaze, man. It's Teabag. It's fuckin' beautiful. Little Teabag has returned.'

Teabag was Sacha Gervasi, an English kid we'd met at the Marquee Club in London in 1982. He'd become a friend and even roadied for us in his school holidays. Then he'd disappeared – it was complicated and messy – and we thought we'd never hear from him again. Now he was back on the scene.

'What's Teabag doing, man?'

'I don't know.'

'Well fuckin' email him back and ask him. Don't you wanna know?'

I emailed Teabag straight away.

Hey, Teabag, I wrote. *What the fuck. I thought you'd either died or become a lawyer.*

That was a fair assumption. Teabag was very clever and very well educated. The son of an American professor of economics at Oxford and a Julliard-trained concert pianist, he lived on Abbey Road in London two blocks from where the Beatles took that famous photo on the zebra crossing. You could even see his house on the album cover. He also had a self-destructive streak that had played a big part in his disappearance from our lives.

Teabag's reply arrived a few hours later. *Both are true,* it said. *I almost died and I almost became a lawyer.*

The email explained that Teabag had gone to law

school, and then dropped out. A few years later he'd gone to film school and now he was a successful screenwriter in Hollywood. He'd written *The Terminal* for Tom Hanks and Steven Spielberg. At the end of the email was a phone number. Beside it were four words: *Give me a call.*

'Hey, Lips. How are ya?' From the moment he picked up the phone Sacha sounded exactly the same as when we'd first met.

'Man, I'm good. It's been a long time. How are you?'

Teabag told me that he'd seen some very rough times but had somehow managed to overcome them and now found himself living a pretty incredible life. I told Sacha that Anvil was still going.

'Holy fuck. You're still a band? That's amazing.'

'Still Robbo and me. Still going strong. Still rocking.'

'I want to see you. Can you come down to LA?'

'Yeah . . . well the money's a bit tight . . .'

'Don't worry, man. I can take care of it. You don't have to pay to come and see me. And what about Robb? How's Robbo doing?'

'Robb's doing OK. But he can't travel because shit happened a few years ago and he's not allowed into the States right now.'

Sacha suggested I came on my own. I phoned Robb – he was blown away when he heard Sacha was making movies – and a few days later I was picking up a ticket at the airport and boarding a plane. Sacha met me at LAX in an old silver convertible Aston Martin that looked like it belonged in a Bond movie. He had a scruffy beard but otherwise he was no different from the Teabag I'd loved twenty years ago. Bubbly, full of energy and very special.

'What happened, man . . .' I didn't know what to say. I was overwhelmed.

'Hey . . . man . . . you look just . . .'

We looked into each other's eyes, the years fell away and it all tumbled out. What Robb and I had been doing, how worried we'd been about Sacha the last time we saw him and all the other shit we'd been through. The good years and the bad years. When we arrived at his house – and it was some awesome fucking house – Sacha turned to me in the kitchen.

'How's my friend Robb?'

'Not good.' I tried to hold it together. 'Not good at all, man.'

I started to cry. When the sobs had subsided, I told Sacha about my recurring nightmare. Robb is on a metal gurney surrounded by police. There are needles in his veins and tubes all around him. The police are giving Robbo a lethal injection and I'm begging them to give my brother another chance.

'I have it all the time. The same fucking nightmare. And I'm begging everyone: Please don't do this.'

Sacha leaned forward. 'You think he's going to die? You think Robbo's going to kill himself?'

'Yeah, man. I do. I think my brother's gonna go.'

'Wow. How did it all start?'

A good question. How did me and Gaze get here? And where did it all start?

ROBB: Looking for a fresh start in life, my father William arrived in Toronto at the tail end of the 1950s. He was in his late twenties, but he'd already seen more than most of us experience in a lifetime. His father, a Jewish refugee from revolutionary Russia, had settled in Hungary and then, when German troops occupied Hungary in 1944, the family was among the four hundred thousand Jews deported to Auschwitz concentration camp.

In January 1945, Auschwitz was liberated by the Red Army. My father was very sick and only days away from death. He was only fifteen years old. Who knows what would have happened if the camp had been liberated two or three weeks later? Most likely, my father would have gone the same way as his father, who died three days before the Russians arrived.

Having survived such terrors, my father returned to Hungary and normality, until one day he went to the horse races with a girlfriend and met my mother, Eniko. Chatting as the races ran behind them, William fell for

Eniko that afternoon and after a whirlwind romance, they married on 21 October 1956, two days before the start of the Hungarian Revolution. For years, the Soviet-appointed government had oppressed, tortured, executed and deported tens of thousands of its country-men. Now the revolution was claiming the lives of thousands more. More than two hundred thousand Hungarians became refugees, among them my parents, who left Budapest with England in mind.

With only the belongings they could carry, my parents walked from Hungary to Austria, arriving cold and soaked to the skin by rain. They were given train tickets to England and soon crossed the Channel, my mother coughing and wheezing all the way. On arriving in Dover, my mother collapsed and was admitted to hospital. She had pneumonia. Meanwhile, my father made contact with a cousin in Wokingham, a small town in southeast England, and handed over to a local newspaper journalist photographs he had taken of Russian tanks invading the streets of Budapest. He was reported in the press as Mr X and regarded as some kind of hero. But England did not appeal to my parents. Fed up with the English climate, they emigrated to Canada a few months later, when my mother had recovered, their passage paid for by the Canadian government. Their first stop was Edmonton, and then they moved on to Toronto, where I was born in 1958.

For all his colourful and dramatic past, my father rarely talked about his experiences. He wanted to shelter my sister and me from that world. 'You children,' he would say, 'should know nothing but good. All I want is for you to be happy.' And although all my friends were Jewish and we lived in the Jewish middle-class suburb of Bathurst Manor in northern Toronto, religion played no role in our family life. My mother wasn't Jewish, so when it came to my bar mitzvah, my father asked me: 'Which way do you want to go with it?' It didn't matter to me at all, so I shrugged and went back to what by then had become my true passion: the drums.

By the late 1960s, I'd discovered the music of Jimi Hendrix, Cream, the Beatles, the Who and the Rolling Stones. But it was an episode of *I Love Lucy* that turned me on to being a musician. On 5 October 1970 I watched open-mouthed as Lucy tricked Buddy Rich into giving Little Ricky drumming lessons. In one scene, Buddy Rich performed a drum solo that lasted nearly two minutes. Transfixed, I pestered my mother: 'I want to be a drummer. I want to learn drums.'

Initially my parents were sceptical. Thinking I'd grow out of it, they refused to buy me a drum kit. Instead they sent me to a drum school. Within a few weeks, the teacher was telling them I was doing good. A few months later, the teacher was saying I had a natural talent. That Christmas my parents gave me my first drum kit.

For about six or seven years, I studied. Then I outgrew the teacher and the books and the real education began. By the time I was fourteen I'd given up on school. Every morning I'd go in to school, register, and then return home to practise for eight hours a day in a room in the basement. My parents approved – my father's philosophy was that I should do whatever made me happy – so they did my homework while I bashed the skins.

I studied the drumming styles of all the greats and practised relentlessly until I could copy all of them. Ian Paice of Deep Purple was a huge inspiration and is still a god to me. John Bonham, Ginger Baker and Mitch Mitchell were all deities in my world.

Eventually the school authorities realized I hadn't attended school for months. I was summoned to the principal's office, where I was told I would be failed for the eighth grade.

'I don't care,' I said. 'I'm gonna be a drummer and that's it. I know I got it in me and I don't care about your school system. I don't care about anything.'

The principal didn't look happy. 'Reiner, we're going to get your parents involved.'

'Go ahead. My parents are totally supportive of me becoming a great musician. They know I'm gonna be a rock star.'

My parents knew I had magic in my hands. I was just a little kid, but they could see I had real talent and that I was obsessed with drumming. Nothing else in my life interested me. I had no time for girls. I didn't drink, smoke or take drugs. I cut myself off from my friends to practise as much as possible. My only aim was to get good enough so that when the day came for joining a band, I would be the one choosing the band, not the other way round.

The school phoned my parents frequently and asked them to send me to school, but my parents shrugged it off every time. 'We understand Robb is too young to quit school,' my dad would say, 'but all he wants to do is drum.'

No child could have asked for more encouragement or better support than I received from my parents. 'Go on and do it, man,' my father would say. 'You're doing great. Sounds great. You're awesome. Everybody tells us you're awesome.'

I was.

LIPS: Bathurst Manor, where Robb lived, ran along the side of a large Canadian Air Force base. I lived in a neighbourhood on the other side of the airfield that had somewhat less expensive property. The only difference was that the houses where I lived didn't come with paved driveways. Instead they had loose gravel that local children would throw around, a difference of a thousand dollars to which my dad's response was: 'Who the hell cares? Let the kids throw stones; we'll deal with it when we can afford to get it paved.'

Whitburn Street, where I lived, was a mix of Jews and working-class Italians. Four doors down from me lived Eddie Schwartz, the guy that wrote 'Hit Me With Your Best Shot' for Pat Benatar. It was a good place to live, but my dad always regretted moving to Whitburn Street, mainly because of the heavy traffic to downtown where he owned a tailoring shop. Like many a tailor's son, I was always in rags. And when I wasn't in rags, I was dressed in clothes that I didn't want to wear. In first grade, my father made me some dress trousers for school when all the other kids were wearing jeans. And then in 1966, when all the other kids were wearing drainpipe jeans, Dad made me some bell bottoms. Maybe that's why when I was fifteen years old, inspired by the album cover of *Goodbye Cream*, I would walk round Yorkdale Shopping Centre wearing tails and green fluorescent striped pants.

I was close to both my brothers, but it was my sister Rhonda, six years older than me, who dragged me at five years of age to Tommy Commons's record store to hang out and listen to music by Elvis or Duane Eddy or Lesley Gore, who had just scored a hit with 'It's My Party'. A few years later, when I was eight, I heard the first Beatles and Dave Clark Five singles on the radio. By the time I was ten, the Stones were in ascendance. 'Satisfaction' and 'Route 66' were blasting out of radios and record players everywhere, and there was nothing I wanted more than a guitar.

My father, who was so direct at times it was painful, eventually caved in to my demands and returned from his shop one day with an electric guitar under his arm. Jeffrey, my elder brother, was electronically adept and hooked it up to a Grundig stereo we had in the living room. I slung the guitar on a strap over my shoulder, strummed it and gazed at myself in the mirror. I thought I looked like Keith Richards.

'You know what? I'm gonna do this for ever. I'm gonna be like the Stones. I wanna be a rock star. I'm going to make a group.'

Gary, my younger brother, shook his head. 'You can't mean that.'

'Yeah I do. I'm going to do this for ever.'

I knew in my heart that I meant it. I was only ten years old but I'd found my calling.

Two years later and I was getting good at the guitar. Like Robb, I'd practise every day, but my schoolwork was suffering and I was getting into a lot of trouble. Determined to be a rock star, I had little respect for authority and I'd become the class clown. I'd incite other kids to play around and to be obstinate with the teachers. Because of my attitude and disruptiveness, most of the teachers had little time for me, all except Mrs Brisbane, a gorgeous leggy blonde with whom, like most of my friends, I was smitten.

Mrs Brisbane knew that my mother had been badly injured in a car accident and had been recuperating for many months at home, struggling to cope with four kids. She felt sorry for me and I knew it, so I exploited her sympathy. One of my stunts was to walk out of Mrs Brisbane's class and to keep walking right out of the school. I'd done it several times before, but this time Mrs Brisbane chased me all the way through the park and finally caught up with me. I don't know how she didn't lose her temper.

'Listen, you can't do this.' She held me by the shoulders. 'You've got to come back. We can sort it out. We can talk it through. Please come back.'

But I was stubborn. 'It doesn't matter, Mrs Brisbane. School's only going to be an insignificant, short period of time before I can do what I really wanna do. I'm going to be in a rock band.'

'You can't think that you don't need school,' she pleaded. 'It's difficult to make it in music. You can't just run away from school.'

'Look at what I can play after two years. I'm only twelve and I'm playing Hendrix stuff. I'm meant to do this. It's a talent from God, so who are you telling I can't do it?'

Mrs Brisbane was very understanding. Over the next months she looked after me. We'd take packed lunches to a ravine near the school, where we'd sit on the log and Mrs Brisbane would listen to my dreams and talk to me. She could see that most of my rebellion was a cry for attention because my mother couldn't give me what I needed. If it hadn't been for Mrs Brisbane, I might have spun completely out of control.

Fortunately I had two elder siblings at home. Jeffrey, who was eight years older than me, couldn't have been more supportive. He taught me my first guitar chords and would bring back records from university. Thanks to him I heard Hendrix the week it came out, not years later, like the rest of the kids I knew. Jeffrey built my first guitar amplifier from a mail-order kit and he always indulged me on my birthday. Thanks to Jeffrey, I learned that knowledge was the most valuable thing in life and that material possessions didn't lead to happiness. But most of all, Jeffrey was the first person to take my dreams of becoming a rock star seriously. 'Why not?' he'd say. 'Anything's possible.' And when I played Jeffrey a bunch of stuff I recorded as a kid, he was impressed. 'You put that together? That's your song? You made that?' It was what any aspiring artist needed to hear.

Meanwhile my parents were trying to get me to go to synagogue, something that to my mother's distress I didn't take at all seriously.

'How are we going to get this kid to go to Hebrew school?' she'd say. 'All he can do is talk about and think about guitars.'

Jeffrey stepped in. 'We want to get him a Fender guitar for his bar mitzvah. Then he'll go.'

That was the ticket. 'Yeah, I'll go to Hebrew school for that,' I said.

I did the bare minimum to pass through the school. I learned to read but not to understand Hebrew lettering. The only bit that interested me was learning how to read the cantillation signs over the top of each word in the Torah, the Hebrew Bible. Each little symbol signified a melody, like a riff on a guitar, and by learning how to read it I achieved the bare minimum required to survive a bar mitzvah. Sitting on the podium while the Rabbi yakked on after I'd read the Torah at my bar mitzvah – some sermon about the state of affairs and shit – I caught the eye of Jeffrey, smiling in the congregation. Leaning back, I fingered an air-guitar solo and mouthed my relief to my brother. 'I got it. It's happening. I did it.' That Fender guitar was all I could think about. I was completely obsessed.

The next day I called every music store in Toronto. A pawn shop called Henry's was selling Fender guitars that were a couple of years old. Dad gave me three hundred dollars of my bar mitzvah money and kept the rest to pay for the party. A few days later, on my thirteenth birthday, I got my Fender Telecaster and set a precedent in our neighbourhood. I'd already started playing with my friend Gary Greenblatt, who also lived on Whitburn and whom I'd known since the age of three, but we needed a drummer. A kid across the street called Jay Weiss was a wannabe drummer, so we suggested he should ask for a kit for his bar mitzvah. Two weeks later he had himself a set of Trixon drums. Now we had ourselves a three-piece band for rehearsing. That lasted a short while, then I put together another band with some buddies including Bruce Hartley, a bass player who lived down the street.

We started playing junior high school dances, our set comprising mainly of Grand Funk Railroad tracks. I organized all the gigs, did all the promo, made all the posters and stuck them up. Most junior high dances started at 3.30 p.m., so I'd get my mother to write me a note to leave school early so that I could prepare. 'I don't know if this is right,' she'd say, but she never said no.

I wanted to put on a gig at my junior high. Realizing that things weren't working out with Bruce and the guys, I put my own band together for the gig. I called in this kid Steven Franklin who played drums. Gary moved from acoustic guitar to bass and I called the band Truck. We wrote our own material – the first composition was 'Lola' about a little frozen treat that we liked – and we played some covers, such as 'A Little Help From My Friends' in the Joe Cocker way, 'Jumping Jack Flash', 'Johnny Be Good' and 'Midnight Hour', but all of them really heavy with a grinding beat. For that gig I got twenty dollars, but Gary and Steve both wanted five bucks each, so that left just five for me and five for expenses. Ridiculous shit, but a start. My whole life I'd been wanting to do this and now it was happening.

While I was improving my licks and riffs, Robb was drumming on the other side of the airbase. Oblivious to each other, it took a woman to bring us together.

It was the dead of February, freezing cold outside and my parents were in Mexico when two friends and I, Allan Bagelman and Danny Ursa, decided to hold a party. Allan already had a girlfriend and Danny had asked a girl to the party. As for me, for some time I'd had my eye on a girl at school called Lee, the sister of a girl in Bruce Hartley's class. The first time I'd seen Lee was in the lobby of a friend's apartment block. She was something else – dark brown hair, green eyes, very thin and very well endowed – and I was smitten. Somehow I got hold of Lee's phone number, but I was too shy to invite her, so Danny made the call, pretended to be me and asked her.

On the night of the party, I picked Lee up from her house. The ground was covered with snow and ice as I took her back to my house, a few blocks away, and led her into the basement. By my later standards, the party was very tame. We didn't even have pot in those days. We might have had some beer, but nothing more. After a while I led Lee into my bedroom where in the dull glow of blue light bulbs, Lee and I got better acquainted. From that day on, I was head over heels for Lee, which soon freaked out my parents.

'This is not good,' my father would kvetch. 'Your mother keeps asking why you can't meet a nice Jewish girl. And I think you're too young to be so serious about this young lady.'

But I was not going to give up on Lee, so my parents hatched a plan to move across the airbase to Bathurst Manor, where Dad had always wanted to live. It might sound like an extreme reaction to teenage love, but that's the way my parents worked, although I suspected it might have been a way for my dad to justify the better driveway and easier commute to his tailoring shop that he'd always wanted. I moved to a new high school and a few weeks later Lee joined me, catching the bus each morning to the school in Bathurst Manor. My parents hadn't considered bus routes when they put the family through our sudden move, or that Lee and I were determined that nothing would stand in the way of our relationship.

Within a few weeks of starting at my new school I'd

met another guitar player called Marty Hoffman in my biology class. He was in a rock 'n' roll band called Goliath and we'd play together after school. Then one day Marty asked me if I wanted to come to a jam at the weekend.

'Hey, I know a drummer,' he said. 'We'll get him to come along.'

'Anyone I know?'

'He's the kid who plays in the house on the corner of Yeomans and Yorkdowns.'

'The *kid*? That house with the yellow garage door? Holy fuck! That guy's a *kid*? I thought he was about twenty-five years old.'

Every day on the way home from school I'd hear a load of heavy music blasting out of that basement – Sabbath, Grand Funk and a lot of Cactus – and whoever was playing to that music was playing tight. This drummer was knocking sick shit out of his kit.

'No. He's younger than me, man. So are you gonna get the fuck up and come along, yeah?'

ROBB: Marty called me. 'Hey man, what're you doin' on Saturday? You want to come over? I've got this guitar player. We can have a jam. Come on, we need a drummer.'

So I showed up. The guitar player – Lips was his name – was already there, a nervous, wired kind of kid, but also kind of cool. He looked very young; although I later found out he was in fact two years older than me. I immediately dug him.

I'd brought just my snare drum and my hi-hat cymbals. As I put them together with a bass drum and some other drums that Marty had in his basement, Lips walked over.

'Oh man, Marty told me that you're the crazy drummer guy, the guy that can really play drums.'

'Yeah.' I knew I already had a reputation.

We started to jam blues songs and rock 'n' roll tunes, standard stuff but kind of boring and generic. Then Lips stopped playing. 'Hey, man, you know I'm really into Sabbath and Grand Funk.'

I freaked. Like, what? Those were the bands that I loved. And Deep Purple, Hendrix and Cream. At that time, the biggest bands in Toronto were the Bee Gees, the Eagles, Peter Frampton and other lame shit. On the bus to school, I'd have battles with other guys over who's better – Grand Funk or Emerson, Lake & Palmer? Hardly anyone was into the kind of hard rock bands that I liked, but this kid dug them all.

Lips and I started to jam some Sabbath. Immediately it sounded good. Everyone was like, 'Right on.' Marty stepped out of the jam because he wasn't up on any of this heavy stuff. He was a bluesy rock 'n' roll guy. And here was Mr Lips with the heavy shit, the same stuff that I was into. We just made magic there between us. It felt awesome.

We finished playing. 'What was that?' said Marty.

Lips smiled. 'I don't know. We just made it up.'

'Fuck off, man. You guys are full of shit.'

Sitting behind my drums, I shrugged. 'We made it up.'

'No way, man. What are you telling me? What were you just fuckin' playing?'

'We were just jammin',' said Lips. 'I just made up some cool riff and Robb was playing and I was playing.'

Marty grinned. 'Hey, that's fuckin' cool.'

It was the first time I'd felt in total harmony with another musician. I wanted to jam some more, but Lips had other plans.

'I gotta go. My girlfriend . . . I gotta run.'

I could tell Lips felt awkward. He wanted to jam some more, but he also wanted not to let his girl down. It was obvious he was torn between the two demands on his time. Watching him, I thought there was some pretty weird stuff going on. But other than that, I liked everything about Lips. He seemed really cool. And it felt like he dug me too.

After the jam, we were walking towards our homes, me carrying my snare and hi-hat, Lips holding his guitar case and kicking the snow. Then he suddenly stopped.

'Hey, man, you know what? Let's make a band.'

I'd known Lips only a couple of hours but I immediately said yes. I knew already that Lips and I had something special. Two metal warriors brought together by our love of heavy rock? Like . . . fucking yeah. A true binding in brotherhood.

It was like a dream that had come true. Really cool. But also totally straightforward. I'd met a guitarist who played as fucking heavy as I hammered on the drums. That was pretty well it. A simple thing.

3 THE ANGEL THAT GOT AWAY

LIPS: Within a few weeks of meeting and founding our band, Robb and I were rehearsing for our first gig. Marty, who had got the booking at the local Jewish community centre, was on guitar and my old friend Bruce Hartley was on bass. All we needed was a vocalist. We'd rehearse in Marty's parents' garage. As we arrived one day for a jam, Marty made an announcement.

'I got us a vocalist. You're really going to like this guy,' he said. 'He can really sing.'

Slim, tall and with long hair, the dude that walked in reminded me of Jim Morrison of the Doors. Pretty decent looking; just what we needed in a front man. His name was Ashley Jarnicki. And when he sang, he had a wonderful voice with really good pitch. He was extroverted and charismatic. We'd found our vocalist.

It didn't take long for Ashley to integrate into our

band. He was a lot of fun and he and I would hang out together, smoking pot. Robb didn't join in at this point as he was still totally focused on his musicianship to the exclusion of everything else. He studied, rehearsed, jammed and gigged. That was it. He didn't have girl-friends, he didn't fuck chicks, he didn't do drugs. People thought he was crazy, but he was just single-minded. All his focus was on his drums.

As we got to know Ashley, we realized his friendliness was the result of an intense need to be liked. Ashley didn't have a happy home life. There was a sense of turmoil in his house, which was huge and beautiful, but with mattresses on the floors and very little furniture. In time we came to realize that Ashley's father, who was a developer, maybe wasn't doing so well.

Ashley was always questioning things. One night we decided to walk the seven miles from his place to my place. It was three o'clock in the morning and all the buses had stopped. As we crossed the main street at the top of Ashley's street, Ashley paused at the edge of the graveyard.

'Hey, man, makes you think . . .' Ashley nodded at the graves. 'What do you think this is all about?'

I had as many questions and as few answers as Ashley, so we stood there for forty-five minutes, talking about life and what it meant, those existential questions about why we are here and how does it all end. Until that night I'd always carried with me that sense of invincibility and immortality that most teenagers never question. But something changed that night. Maybe it was too much pot, but for the first time I realized why I was alive.

'Ashley, man, all I know is that we have a journey to make before we get here.' I pointed at the gates of the graveyard. 'We have a lot to go through and we shouldn't be wondering why we're standing here looking at a graveyard. It should be the last thing on our agenda. All that matters is that we realize we're lucky to be alive.'

I knew then and there that it was my destiny to make music and entertain people. At the age of ten I'd told my little brother that I was going to rock for the rest of my life. Even as an innocent child, I'd been aware of my calling and I'd known what I wanted to do. That night I realized that I'd have to fight for my art – the heavy metal fight – but provided I never gave up, one day I would overcome all the negativity I'd encounter along the journey. In the meantime, every obstacle would be part of my training for the day I achieved success.

The day of the gig at B'nai Brith House, the Jewish community centre on Hove Avenue, came and we each chipped in ten dollars to rent a PA system from Steve Shapiro, a local guy who played in a weddings and bar mitzvahs band. I can't remember how it went. All I remember is that immediately after the gig, Marty, Bruce and Ashley left the band. It was no big deal. In our neighbourhood, young bands like ours formed and broke apart on a weekly or even daily basis. A few guys would get together to play a gig or two, and then split. Maybe they got bored, maybe they fell out or maybe they just had something else to do the next week. Marty, Bruce and Ashley leaving was no different. All it meant was that Robb and I were on our own again.

ROBB: Determined to maintain metal momentum, Lips recruited this bass player called Mike Mayer that he knew from Whitburn Street; we formed a three-piece and called ourselves Gravestone.

We played a few gigs at synagogues, a buddy called Les Brown taking the singing duties, but it wasn't the same without Ashley, so we contacted him and after some persuasion, he rejoined the brotherhood.

From the first day, we were determined to write and perform our own material. Most of the other bands in Toronto were cover bands gigging in bars and clubs in which the crowd would be disappointed if it didn't recognize every song that was played. And these bands had no respect for bands that wrote their own songs. 'How good can you be?' they'd say. 'Are you playing those songs because you can't copy? I guess you can't play "Highway Star".'

Playing a Deep Purple classic such as 'Highway Star' was something that we'd mastered a long time ago. I'd learned a lot from studying Ian Paice's drumming on the track, but we didn't want to measure our musicianship by how well we copied. It bothered Lips deeply, especially in these formative years, and made him stubbornly resist any requests to play cover versions.

'Man, I don't care what anybody else says,' Lips would insist whenever we had a request to play a cover. 'I'm going to write and play my own fuckin' songs and I don't fuckin' care if other people give us a hard time. We'll overcome it. Our music will be our legacy. No writing, no legacy, no integrity.'

A few months after forming Gravestone, we replaced Mike Mayer with Gary Greenblatt, another friend from Lips's days in Whitburn Street. Like Mike, Gary was often uncomfortable when we insisted on playing original material, but Lips never gave way. I'd watch as Lips would argue at gigs and rehearsals.

'I'm not fucking doing it. It's weird, man. The first thing most musicians want to do is play what everybody else plays, not something that comes from inside. But if you play other people's music, your originality as a musician is forever in question. All I know is that I am a writer. I must create regardless of what anybody else says.'

For many musicians, it was cool to play something as

good as they'd heard their heroes play it. But to Lips, the most awesome thing was to play something and then say: 'I made this up.' It took mega confidence but we learned more by writing our own music than we ever did by copying.

Already at seventeen Lips was an extremely original guitarist. Having learned all kinds of chord progressions from books, he started experimenting. I'd spent five years studying the best drummers and trying to incorporate their techniques into my own playing until my own unique style had evolved from a synthesis of what I'd learned and what I had inside me. Later on we picked up half a dozen classic songs and made them heavier so that they fitted the style of our own music, but in those early days of Gravestone we stuck stubbornly to our philosophy of originals only. And it worked. The band got stronger quickly, so that we were soon recording our first demos of original material in the basement of our friend Chemo's house.

LIPS: The legendary Chemo tapes still sound good to me when I listen to them now. The music is quite like Sabbath, Purple or Zeppelin. The lyrics of one of the songs, 'Dreams End', were about Ashley, who was extraordinarily imaginative but lived virtually in a dream state. They were about me urging Ashley to wake up because life is not a dream.

Even as a teenager, Ashley acted as if we were really rock stars but we just didn't know it. He thought he was like Robert Plant, I was really Jimmy Page and Robbo was John Bonham. I was much more realistic and I let Ashley know it.

'We're just a bunch of kids,' I'd say. 'What are you on about, man?'

But Ashley dreamed it and lived it as if it really was true. I couldn't cope with Ashley's fantasies and it was reflected in the lyrics that I had Ashley sing: *My two dreams, one's escape, face reality with no red tape.*

One day, while we were rehearsing 'Dream's End' in Gary's garage, Ashley stopped the song and turned to me with a strange look in his eyes. 'You and Robb, man, you know you are the greatest?'

Thinking Ashley was going off on one of his dreamy monologues, I smiled. 'Ahhh, man . . .'

But Ashley looked deadly serious this time. 'You guys are as great as the greatest there is in the world. Gary and me, we're just having fun. But you and Robbo, you really are like professionals. You're the real thing. You're gonna go all the way.'

Ashley was the first person that recognized Robb's and my talent but unfortunately his dreaminess started to take over. Instead of Robert Plant, he began to think he was Peter Gabriel and he became interested in progressive music, which Robbo dismissed as 'pseudo shit'. Realizing Ashley no longer had the same heavy vision as Robbo and me, we reluctantly told him the time had come for him to leave Gravestone.

After Ashley left, I again assumed the mantle of vocalist. With several gigs booked, I was nervous about singing, but Robb assured me that we'd be OK. 'The nucleolus is intact,' he said. 'It's already forging itself, you know, man, our nucleolus.' I knew Robbo meant nucleus and thought he was right. As long as Gaze and Brother Lips were together, everything would be cool. And it was. We played several outdoor gigs and hockey rinks, working on our stage show and incorporating special effects. Inspired by old Frankenstein movies, Chemo built homemade Jacob's Ladders that we'd place on our speaker stacks. He also made some light organs that responded to the music. And we started experimenting more with our sound. I was playing my guitar with a violin bow to make cool sounds. Meanwhile Robbo combined his drum kit with some of the drums belonging to his friend Tom Smith. With a second bass drum, more tom-toms and extra cymbals, he was starting to create the drum sound for which Anvil later became famous.

ROBB: On 22 April 1974, I turned sixteen. I celebrated by going into school and asking to see the principal.

'This is it, man. I'm quitting.' The principal looked at

me like I'd lost it. 'I'm outta here. All I wanna do is play drums and I can't get it at school now.'

It shouldn't have come as a surprise to the authorities. A few years earlier I'd asked to join the school music program, so they'd given me an audition. Unfortunately I blew it. Not by underperforming, but by playing a drum solo non-stop for five minutes like a professional musician.

'Reiner,' the music teacher said, 'what you've just done is not a fair thing. What you are doing is wrong.'

What the fuck? I didn't know what this teacher dude was on about. 'Like . . . what, man?'

'Reiner, if we let you join the music class, you will be taking something away from somebody who would really benefit from it. You don't need music lessons.'

'Are you fuckin' telling me I can't join your class because I'm too fuckin' good?'

'No, I'm telling you that you are being selfish.'

'You're sayin' I'm cheatin'? You're gonna give me the rap?'

'You cannot play drums. OK?'

I went fucking crazy. 'I can't fucking believe this. I do what the class requires and it's *too good*? Right . . .'

That was it for me. I walked straight out of the school. A few days later I returned with my father and waited outside the principal's office while he spoke to the chief. When my father came out, it was sorted. I was allowed into the music program. But I told the principal how I felt: 'I'm just waiting for that day when I no longer have to count how many days it is until I can stay at home and keep playing for good.'

So when I told the principal on my sixteenth birthday that I was quitting, what did he do? He asked me my fucking plans.

'Listen, I'm not a school person. I'm going full time. I want to rock!'

The next day I saw Lips. 'School's over for me, brother. I'm gonna go get a band. I am gonna go full time. Like, I am doing it. I am going somewhere with this, man.'

But Lips wasn't ready for the big step. His parents wouldn't allow him. Anything but that goddam guitar, they'd say. Go get an education, they insisted. And Lips wouldn't break away.

'Listen, man, I gotta stay at school . . .'

It was the first time that our brotherhood was under threat, but I had to tell Lips straight. 'I've no choice, man. I'm gonna move on. I gotta do this. I am not gonna get a job. I am gonna go play.'

A few weeks later, we had another heart-to-heart outside Panzers, a Jewish deli in Bathurst. I'd heard that a band called Whalebone was auditioning for new members, including a drummer.

'I am going to do it,' I said. 'Are you with me or aren't you?'

'I can't, Gaze. You know I can't, man.'

'Then that's it, Lips. I gotta cut it dry now. That's it, brother.'

Only adults could join bands because you had to be at least eighteen to enter a bar. Although I was only sixteen, I could pass for eighteen, so I took a chance. When I walked into their rehearsal room, two guys were waiting, Trevor Horsefall, a guitarist from Blackpool in England, and John Burkitt on bass. Both were in their mid-twenties. We jammed for a few songs, mainly Free and Wishbone Ash numbers. Progressive, pretty cool music. I sunk the audition. They gave me the job straight away. I was a member of Whalebone.

Almost immediately we went on the road, playing bars and clubs. At every venue, I had to lie about my age, but no one questioned anything once they heard my drumming. And by the time they realized I was under age, it didn't matter. They could see I was no trouble and that all I wanted to do was play. As for Trevor and John, they had no qualms. I was fully integrated into the band and they knew they'd look a long time before they found another drummer as good as me.

I felt bad about leaving my brother behind and I knew Lips was heartbroken, but I also knew I couldn't wait until he persuaded his parents to let him rock. He just needed to wake up as a human being. And whenever Whalebone came back to Toronto, Lips and I would get together and he would rehearse on Trevor's gear.

Over the next two years I gained invaluable experience. I saw what it meant to be in a band. The money, the travel and everything that went with it. In many ways, I learned all I needed to know. I was travelling on the road, living out of a suitcase and surviving on sixty dollars a week with two guys that had nearly ten years' experience on me.

I learned to go without a lot of things and to concentrate on the essentials. We made money stretch out and we starved. A single Lipton Cup-a-soup would last us all day.

There were other tricks like hustling pool games in hotels for money, smooth-talking guys at the bar into buying us drinks or dinner, or hanging out with strippers. The kind of venues we played usually had peelers stripping all day and bands playing all night. And peelers usually had much more dough than the bands, so if you could find one to take care of you for a bit then that's what you did. It might sound exploitative and evil, but it was totally cool. In return for looking after us, buying us food and drink and smokes, we looked after the peelers, making sure no one took advantage of them. A lot of these chicks were lost in life and stripping had become their only option. They were young and hot and they knew how to dance, so it was a way of making some quick money. Most of them were alcoholics or drug addicts who were lonely and wanted attention, and that's what we musicians provided. It was a mutually supportive culture, a gypsy existence in which friendships and alliances were quickly formed and just as rapidly abandoned when we moved on to the next venue.

For a kid who'd led a sheltered existence for his first sixteen years, locking myself away to focus entirely on my art, it was extremely exciting. I cut loose. I was meeting people and seeing the real scene of humanity. The bars were full of cool-looking people with long hair. Wild, loose and crazy people who gave me attention, but people who could also cause trouble, so I learned how to take care of myself if things turned dark. I went from a kid who never touched drugs to a young adult who was totally comfortable hanging out with strangers, smoking pot and drinking all night. And watching Trevor and John struggle with the temptations that any married musician faces also taught me a lot about how to cope with the conflicts of commitment and freedom.

I was like a sponge sucking up everything around me, but it was only when I got home that I fully realized how much life on the road had changed me. When we weren't gigging I'd go back to living and rehearsing in the basement of my parents' house. To the people I'd left at home, I must have seemed quite exotic now that I was a travelling musician. I was now getting calls all the time from girls.

Shortly before midnight one night, as I was lying on my bed in the basement, a call came from a girl that I knew who had two sisters. 'Hey, what are you doing, man?'

'Whaddya mean, what am I doing?'

'Why don't you come over? My parents are sleeping but you could come on over and bang us.'

'OK. For sure, sounds like fun.'

'Hey, you can come and fuck my sister. We're all here, man. We can party.'

It sounded good to me all right. In fact it sounded pretty helpful. I had no girlfriend, so there was nothing to worry about.

I walked over to where they lived in an apartment a couple of streets away, but it was two storeys up, so I climbed on to some garbage cans and they unfurled some sheets. I grabbed hold of the sheets and yanked myself up eight feet to the window of their bedroom as quietly as I could manage. With the girls' parents asleep down the corridor, we partied for a few hours. Then I split. Walking home, I couldn't believe what I'd just been through. I'd got a call, walked over, climbed in a fucking window, had this wild sex session with two sisters and now I was walking home without anybody ever knowing what had happened. It was an experience on which I would later draw when Lips and I started to write more sleazy lyrics.

As for the music with Whalebone, we'd play originals and covers, but the covers were obscure Wishbone Ash and Thin Lizzy tracks. The fact that we played only one Led Zeppelin song at a time when everyone was into Zeppelin kind of said it all. As for the original material, it was bluesy rock in the vein of Deep Purple. For at least six months each year we followed the club and bar circuit, playing Quebec, north Ontario, Fort Frances, Sioux Lookout, places like that. All that playing totally improved my drumming. It turned more real, more serious, more demanding, more precise, more seasoned and more confident. It was more of everything.

Those years were a young man's dream, only I was living them long before anyone else I knew back home. And they were a time of no worries. I didn't care about making money as long as I could survive to play drums every night.

After two years on the road, the most recently recruited vocalist, Rob McArthur, left the group and very soon Whalebone dissolved. The drive that had kept Trevor and John going simply melted away. Maybe it was because I had matured, but I felt like my ambition had overtaken their commitment. They were dedicated to everything else – their wives and their jobs on the side to earn money to support their families – except wanting to be a rock star. I'd come to realize that if you wanted to be something, you had to live it. You had to think, feel it and be it. And these guys were just pretending. To them being a rock star was a hobby. These guys were never going to amount to anything, I figured. They didn't have the same commitment to rock as I did, so I didn't hang around to see if something new would emerge from the ashes of Whalebone. It was time for me to move on.

I'd learned as much as I would ever from Whalebone. I now felt I could be running the whole thing, only I would do it differently. I had ideas and it was time to put them into practice.

LIPS: While Robb was on the road with Whalebone, I was at college, studying how to be an audio-visual technician, and working with Ashley for his father. They'd pick me up at seven o'clock in the morning and we'd drive out to a housing development where Ashley's and my job was to clean all the debris off the floors, dig ditches or haul refrigerators and stoves up stairs into the homes. Working with Ashley, I realized his father's aggression came from a deep unhappiness and a lot of anger. While we were labouring, Ashley's father would yell at us, driving us like slaves. It would go on end-lessly, even when we were driving back home, but Ashley would always stay calm and gentle with his father. It was a very difficult relationship to witness.

Whenever Robb was playing near Toronto, I'd go to watch. It wasn't easy seeing my brother doing what I wanted to be doing. 'Hey, man, good band, man,' I'd say. 'But you're the best thing in the band. It's obvious. These guys are good, but you shine, man.'

I was missing my buddy, so when Robb told me he'd left Whalebone, I seized my chance. I'd heard a band called Kickback were losing their drummer and guitar player, so I went to see them play, still with the original drummer and guitarist. After the gig, I went ballistic on them.

'I want to join your band. I can do that gig in my fuck-ing sleep. You've got to hire me.'

I didn't hear from them. A week later, they got Robb over and were impressed. For a kid of eighteen, he was an amazing player and they immediately recruited him.

'You need a guitar player as well?' Robb said. 'Why don't you let me get my buddy? You should see him. He's fucking heavy, man.'

But the guys in Kickback were reluctant. Robb pressed them, telling them I was an awesome guitarist. After much persuasion, they agreed to give me a kick at the can. Within a few minutes of starting to jam, we'd left them for dust. They were shocked as we rocked out with a barrage of original material.

'OK. I guess you were right,' one of them said to Robbo. 'We thought you were just giving us shit because he's your buddy. But he's fucking awesome.'

Kickback was a Zeppelin tribute band and even though I was not really into Zeppelin, they wanted me on board, they said, because they wanted to expand their repertoire and I was a songwriter who wrote awesome riffs. I was just happy to be back jamming with my friend, brother Robbo. But it didn't last long.

Kickback had three gigs lined up, all of them week-long residencies, so I quit college and spent a solid week learning their set, cramming more than thirty Led Zeppelin songs. The singer, a six-foot-four guy who thought he was a cross between Mick Jagger and Robert Plant – he had Plant's curly long blond hair and Jagger's chops – had a severe attitude problem. We'd played one week in Northern Quebec and to be honest I'd struggled as I was still getting to grips with the new material. Our second gig was in Toronto at a bar called the Yonge Station. On the first night I was on stage, not jumping around as much as usual because I didn't know the songs that well. I was being one of those guitar players who spend most of the gig looking at the neck of their guitar rather than playing the guitar with their teeth. The place was packed but we weren't whipping up a storm. Frustrated that he wasn't getting the reaction he wanted from the crowd, the singer started to blame me for not putting on a good-enough show. Then, out of nowhere, he walked over to me and punched me in the kidneys while I was in the middle of a solo. I couldn't breathe. Fucking bastard.

As soon as we finished the set, I walked off stage and out of the door. We had another set to play but, quite frankly, I didn't care. Anyone who punched me during a show didn't deserve the time of day and I didn't give two shits what happened next.

'That's it, Gaze.' I was furious and Robbo knew it. 'We're not playing with other guys who wanna run the fucking show. We're gonna make our own band.'

Robbo smiled. He'd been waiting for months, if not years, for me to say this.

Then reality sunk in. 'How are we going to get a PA? How are we going to get lights? Where are we going to get this shit?'

'Shut the fuck up, Lips. Don't worry about it. We'll make it happen, don't worry.'

Robb was right. There was no looking back. We'd reached a critical turning point: the time to go for it on our own. My sister's husband, who was working as a property manager, lent us an empty building for rehearsing. We put an ad in a Toronto newspaper. *Supergroup of the Future*, it said in bold lettering at the top. *Supergroup for the 80s seeks bass player and second guitarist to complete line-up. Original material only.* And then we waited.

We had dozens of calls. Every single musician for miles around seemed to call us. The first guy we recruited was Don Woods, an old American draft-dodging hippy who boasted he had been Storm's original bassist. After jamming with us for a while, we asked him to join the band on bass.

After auditioning several other musicians, a guitarist called Dave Allison invited us over to his place. After a powwow, he auditioned by jamming a few tracks with us and immediately fitted in better than any of the other guys we'd auditioned. It worked. It felt good. It felt special. Dave became the fourth member, but only very briefly because Don was soon back out of the door after starting on Robb one day at rehearsal. For a while, Robb didn't say anything. He just let Don say his piece. Then he broke his silence.

'If you don't like it, get the fuck out. Pack up your shit and get the fuck out.'

'OK.' And Don packed up his shit and out the fuck he went. The smell had been there, but the sizzle wasn't. Now we were back to three – me, Dave and Robbo.

Rehearsing in the same building as us was another band led by Bill, the first Whalebone singer. Although he bugged the shit out of me, forever bragging about how he was going to become a superstar, we hung out with his band, watching them jam. What Bill didn't realize was that we were watching only for one reason. We were eyeing his bass player, Ian Dickson. He just did not fit in with these guys. With his long curly light brown hair, he looked more like one of us. We started to drop hints whenever the bass player was in earshot, but he was loyal to his band. When he came over to our rehearsal room, we'd smoke with him and ask if he'd ever thought of leaving his band, but he didn't take the hint. Then one day Bill walked into our room.

'I'm going to fire Ian after our gig this weekend.'

'Oh yeah?' This sounded interesting. 'OK, cool.'

Robb tried not to show his interest 'So . . . where are you playing?'

'The Oakdale Tavern.'

'Cool. Maybe we'll be there.'

That weekend we watched as Ian was handed an envelope as he came off stage. We knew what was in it and watched as he read the note inside. Ian frowned, but before he could say anything I went up to him.

'Don't say anything you might regret. We want to talk to you. Come outside.'

Standing in the parking lot, I put it to Ian. 'We know that you got fired. Don't worry about it. You're too good for them and we want you to join our band.'

'Let me think about it.'

'Listen, dude. When you drive your equipment back, just put it in our room and then have a think about it.'

'Oh. OK . . .' Ian looked baffled. He was a very easy-going, bubbly kind of guy. A follower rather than a leader and a yes person who rarely questioned anyone's devious motives. These kinds of recruitment tactics were a surprise to him, but he was just what we needed. He wasn't particularly innovative or imaginative as a musician, but he was totally solid and reliable. And, most importantly, he had long hair.

A few days later, Ian turned up in our rehearsal room. 'I'm in,' he said.

'Fucking yeah.'

We immediately started jamming. The seed of Anvil was sown.

ROBB: All we now needed was a vocalist and the obvious choice was Ashley, particularly as me and Lips had already recorded base tracks for Ashley to sing on. We approached Ashley and gave him tapes of songs such as 'School Love', which would later be recorded for our first album. Ashley promised us he'd work on his vocals and that we'd get together in a few days, but first he had to go to Detroit to buy some vacuum cleaners for a cleaning business he was starting with his dad.

A couple of days later, the phone rang. It was

Grossey, a friend I'd known since childhood. 'Ashley's dead.'

For a moment I didn't know what to say. 'What happened?'

Having arrived at the US border on the way to Detroit, Ashley had realized he'd left his identification behind and got in a cab back to Toronto, leaving his two friends waiting for him at the frontier crossing. It was a crazy idea, an eight-hour return trip, but without his papers he would never get to Detroit.

Not long after leaving the border, the taxi was on the ramp climbing up to the 401, the main highway through Ontario, when an articulated tandem truck flipped off the highway above and landed on the cab. Ashley was crushed. He survived for a few hours, but died in hospital.

That was it. One moment Ashley was there. The next gone.

I told Lips. He was devastated. 'Two years, man. Two years with Ashley. And now, over. A nineteen-year-old. It's not fair, man.'

None of us found it easy, but Lips remains bothered to this day by Ashley's death. It affected him very deeply.

As for the tapes we'd given Ashley, we never got them back. For a while, they didn't matter much to us. Ashley's death closed that door. But it also raised the question of who should be the vocalist. I thought there was an obvious answer.

'Lips, man. You should sing.'

But Lips was reluctant. He'd sung in the first incarnation of Gravestone, but had never overcome his lack of confidence in his ability. 'Man, I'm just not good enough. I don't think I can do it, man.'

But eventually I persuaded him. It made sense as he wrote a lot of the lyrics. And it made things simpler. Lips and I would always be together – it was now five years since we'd made the pact to rock together for ever – and as long as I had Lips, I'd have a vocalist.

4 LIPS RISES

ROBB: Lips's and my momentous decision to form our own band wasn't the only new relationship in my life at that time. After several years of being very footloose and very fancy free, I'd met the first chick who made me want to spend more time with her.

I'd gone to the Forum in Toronto to see some local bands with Lips, Dave and our buddies Bess and Chops. We were just hanging out, doing what kids do. Smoking dope, hiding from cops and all that. We were cool with long hair. I was already a rock star.

Then we spotted two girls across the hall. One of them was short with dark hair. Her taller, slimmer friend had really cool blonde puffy curled hair. She immediately did something to me deep inside. She had high shoes on, a real rocker chick. Even from a distance, she was fucking appealing.

'Hey, man, look at those hot fucking babes,' I

murmured to Chops. 'Look at that chick with the red pants.'

'I see her.' Chops looked approving. 'Whoa! Big Red. Hot chick.'

I held Big Red's eye as she walked across the room, but that was all. Then she disappeared out of sight.

A week later, the Eagles were playing the exhibition centre and Chops had a bright idea.

'Hey, let's go down, hang out and meet some chicks.'

It was something we did quite often. Rock concerts attracted thousands of cool chicks, especially girls' bands like the Eagles. If we hit on enough of them we'd get ourselves a date for the night. So we were down there and guess who comes walking out of the exhibition centre in the distance? I couldn't believe it. I was in shock. I was totally blown the fuck away.

'Chops, man, there's Big Red, that fucking chick with the red pants.' I was pretty excited and ran straight up to her. 'Hey, man . . . are you the same girl? I saw you last week at the Forum.'

'Yes, honey. I thought that was you.'

I offered Big Red and her friend, Sylvana, a ride home in Chops's car. As we drove, talking about music and surface stuff, I could tell she liked me and I thought she was super hot. It felt good. And it also felt like it was meant to happen. We'd seen each other the week before. A week later, we met again by chance and now I was in the car driving her home.

As I dropped Big Red off at her house, I asked for her number. She gave it to me, then I split, feeling totally buzzed up and thinking, Fuck! This is great, man.

I'd never had a proper girlfriend before because I'd never been interested in being committed. I was like everyone's boyfriend, but not really anybody's boyfriend. That's the kind of kid I was. But Big Red was different. The next day I didn't phone her, I just went over and called on her. I had an instant crush.

Big Red's mother answered the door and I could guess what she was thinking from the look on her face: Wow, who the hell are you? To her, I was just some long-haired rock and roll freak.

'Hey, is Jane here?'

A minute later Jane came out and I was like: Wow. It felt quite overwhelming. Jane looked all up for it, totally excited that this guy she'd met really came back. We went for a walk, talking non-stop, firing questions at each other to find out everything.

'So what do you do?' she asked.

'I'm a drummer. I play in bands and I'm putting together a new supergroup.'

'Wow. That's really cool. I like guys in bands. I'd love to see you play. Are you good?'

Jane was into the same kind of music. Man, we were in sync with everything. The next day I came back and we went for another walk. Within a week we were dating and soon we were totally committed to each other. It's been like that ever since. Because Jane was there when Lips and I formed the band, I've always regarded her as the third member of Anvil, part of its whole conception, there since the absolute beginning of the journey that me and Lips started.

LIPS: While Robb was getting together with Jane and we were forming the band, I was having trouble at home. One door opens and another closes, I suppose. Unlike Robb's folks, my parents had never been particularly supportive of my music. Their indifference had become a big part of what fuelled me, even though they didn't realize it. But with the band taking shape, I wanted to quit college. Robbo was right: it was time to make a commitment to the music. But now I had to tell my parents.

'You what?' Dad was not pleased. 'You've got to think of your future, not that goddam guitar.'

'You can't stop me,' I yelled. 'I am twenty. Fuck you. I can do what I want.'

'Not while you're living in this house.'

Fortunately I had a girlfriend. And part of the attraction of Lee was that she could be my ticket out.

'If you don't want me to do it when I'm living in this house, I'm moving out.'

It didn't take long to find an apartment with Lee. It was just around the corner from my parents' home. Les Brown, a buddy from the Gravestone days, got me a job polishing jewellery at a jeweller's where he was working. Now I could afford to make a go of it with Lee. Dad was not impressed.

'Is that all there is, Steven?'

'Whaddya mean? Is that all there is?'

'Don't you know the song by Peggy Lee – "Is That All There Is?"'

'No.'

'Because I don't know where you're going, but what I do know is that the day will come when one of you is going to ask: Is that all there is?'

'So?'

'Think about it, Steven. Ask yourself: Is that all there is?'

I knew what my dad meant. I was too young to be shacking up with a girl. But I wanted to quit college and the only way I could do that was by moving out. I felt ready.

Lee and I were really happy in our little apartment, although the job didn't last. I got laid off, which was wonderful because I could collect unemployment insurance. Now everything was totally cool. I was living with my girlfriend. I didn't have to go to work and I was still getting paid. And I could rehearse with the band every day; although I still hadn't made a buck from it.

Me and Lee hadn't been long in the apartment when there was a knock at the apartment door. It was Robbo.

'Lips, I need to move in. I had a big blow-up fight with my dad.'

'Gaze . . . what happened?'

Through a contact in the jewellery business, Robb's father had arranged a job for his son as something to fall back on if he didn't succeed in his music career. Robb started an apprenticeship making jewellery, for which he was paid a small wage. But somehow Robb had discovered that his father was paying for his apprenticeship and paying his wage. He went fucking nuts.

'I can't live with this,' Robb told his father. 'I am doing this on my own merits. You are taking my fucking credibility away.'

It was heart-wrenching to see Robbo's disappointment in his parents, who had always been highly supportive of his music career. Now he needed somewhere to live, so he moved in with Lee and me for a few months.

In that time we went on a road trip to see Black Sabbath – me, Robbo, Dave Allison, and two buddies, Bess and Pop McGuire – on the American side of the Niagara Falls. Bess had worked with Black Sabbath as Tony Iommi's guitar roadie and with Van Halen, who were opening for Sabbath, on their recent European tour.

Bess was quite a legend among Sabbath roadies. While on tour in England, Bess had been persuaded to hide inside a road case packed inside a truck because he'd forgotten his passport and he'd been told they were about to cross the 'border' into Scotland. The other roadies and band members even persuaded the police to stop the truck, search it, arrest Bess and take him to the police station until they told him there was no official border between England and Scotland.

Bess had made a call to Sabbath's road manager, Albert, who had said to come down and hang out backstage. We were totally freaked out. This was the chance to meet our idols, the Sabbath boys. As for Van Halen, having just recorded their first album, they were the up and coming band of the moment. And according to the rumours, Van Halen was blowing Sabbath off the stage. Sabbath was nearing its end. Ozzy was cooked, Tony had had enough and their morale was rock bottom.

We all crammed into Bess's mother's green Oldsmobile Cutlass, our first road machine that later drove us all around Quebec on tour. Bess was driving, we were smoking pot and Dave had three or four joints stuffed down the back of his cigarette pack. At the border into the States, we all got pulled out of the car and the cop had a look through things in the car.

'Ah one, ah two . . .' With his finger cocked like a gun, the cop jerked his hand in our direction and fired off a string of imaginary bullets at the five of us standing in a line. 'Three, four, five. You're all under arrest. Get over there.'

How stupid could we have been? The first thing they'd looked in was Dave's cigarette packet and they'd found our stash in a matter of seconds. The most elementary profiling would have picked us out. Five young guys with long hair squeezed into a car and on the way to a rock concert. We were so dumb.

Knowing we could all be detained for three days, Dave owned up to it. It was his shit anyway. The rest of us put up a big fight, really giving the cops the song and dance. We told the cops that Bess had worked with Black Sabbath and that we'd always loved the band.

'Man, we're dying to go. Please let us go.'

'OK, the car's impounded for trying to import contraband,' the cop said. 'We want fifty bucks to free it. It's a fifty-dollar fine.'

'Fuck, man,' we said as one. The border guards wanted the fine in American greenbacks and we were carrying only Canadian dough.

Each of us put in fifteen Canadian bucks and then we walked back across the border to the Canadian side, where there was a bank. We got the money changed and returned to pay the cop his fifty bucks. He confiscated the joints, but before he'd let us all go to the concert, he asked Dave for his details.

'Listen, you know . . . I've got a whole future, man,' said Dave. 'We're just putting the band together. I need to travel. Please have a heart, man. I'll never do this again, I swear.'

And to our amazement, the border guard went, 'OK, no problem.' He intentionally wrote down all the wrong information so that the next time Dave got to the border there'd be no record of him ever having been busted. 'Have a good time at Sabbath, boys,' he said as he waved us off.

We were blown away, whooping as we drove off and shouting to each other. 'Can you believe it, man, they actually caught us with drugs and they let us in. Can you fucking believe it?'

After the border incident, we were excited as hell when we got to the concert. Albert was true to his word and ushered us into the building just after the sound checks had finished. With backstage passes round our necks and Bess leading the way, we went into the Van Halen dressing room. The party was in full swing.

'Hey . . .' A few steps behind us, David Lee Roth walked through the door, threw his jacket across the room and spun his cowboy hat straight on to a hook on the hat rack. 'Brothers, what're your names?'

Bess introduced us to Dave and the rest of Van Halen. We hung out for a while with them. The room was filled with an overwhelming sense of a band that had really arrived, Dave Lee Roth especially. It was like all their dials were turned up to eleven.

'All right. Get out of here.' Dave grinned. We'd been with them a half-hour or so. 'We've got shit to do, man.'

We left the room. Right opposite it was Black Sabbath's room. The door opened and the first person I saw was Tony Iommi. I was like: Fuck, man. I couldn't believe it. Bess stepped forward.

'Hey man . . .' Bess started yapping away to Tony and before I knew it we were all in the Sabbath dressing room. The inner fucking sanctum. It was too much. I walked around, totally blown away. Bess introduced us to each guy in Sabbath, all except Ozzy, who was sitting on the floor, looking very sick.

'How's it going, man?' I said.

'Baaah . . .' Ozzy's voice was a hoarse whisper. One of the band explained that Ozzy had flu.

After the vibrancy, the feeling of energy and love, the sense of rock 'n' roll and excitement in the Van Halen dressing room, the Sabbath room felt dead. It was very subdued. Everyone was talking quietly and it felt very laid back. Maybe that was the difference between an English band and an American band, I thought. It was nothing like I'd expected. Nevertheless, I thought it was totally cool. There was Tony, man! I was losing it. Geezer Butler came over and started on Bess: 'Eh, you fucking Canadian cunt. You fucking colonial cunt, you.' Bill Ward was sitting to one side, tapping a table with his drumsticks, oblivious to us even being there. We all talked a bit about Keith Moon, who had died the previous day, then we headed up to the stage, where Bess started going through Tony's road case. He showed us how he used to set up Tony's equipment, and then he pulled out a little black box. Inside it were the finger tips for the middle and ring fingers of Tony's right hand, which he'd lost in an industrial accident in a sheet metal factory.

'Fuck man. Wow. Holy shit.' For a heavy metal guitarist, this was like seeing the Holy Grail. With Jimmy Page, Tony was one of the two pioneers of heavy metal riffs.

'Different tips give him different sounds.' Bess held up five or six pieces of plastic and leather.

'Holy fuck, man. Really?' I was totally blown away. Then Bess showed me Tony's distortion unit. 'Wow. Is that the real shit, man?'

I'd been listening to this guy play since I was fourteen. And here I was at twenty-two right in front of all his gear. It was too much. 'My fucking God, I don't believe I'm fucking looking at this.'

'Man, look at this.' Bess was going through all of Tony's drawers, pulling out pick-ups and showing me all the gear that was there.

We watched the gig from the side of the stage. First

Van Halen, who blew us all away. Totally so. Eddie Van Halen was an awesomely sick guitarist and he looked pretty cool playing his guitar bent over backwards.

Then it was Sabbath's turn. Remembering how sick Ozzy had been and the subdued atmosphere in the dressing room, I was expecting Sabbath not to match up to Van Halen. But from the moment he walked out on stage, Ozzy kicked ass like I'd never seen.

'Fuck, man. Look at that, Gaze.' I looked at Ozzy with awe. 'That's what it means to be professional, man.'

From that moment on I understood how important it was to give your audience what they'd come to see, no matter what was going on before you came on stage. I'd never seen such passion and dedication in a man as I did that night in Ozzy. It totally changed my outlook. It made me realize what my new venture required.

The whole band – Geezer and Tommy in particular – were wonderful to watch. Once they got on stage, all the sadness and tension we'd experienced in the dressing room evaporated as they did what they still enjoyed doing. Between songs, Geezer would come over to the side of the stage and carve on us, calling us fucking colonials. Standing side stage, it was the Sabbath we'd always loved. No one in the audience would have guessed at the backstage atmosphere. Seeing Black Sabbath was not only hugely inspirational; understanding that they were real people impressed on me the level of professionalism that was needed. It opened my eyes to what it meant to be in a real band. We'd witnessed the death throes of Sabbath – Ozzy was fired from the band after the tour – but it made no difference because once they were on stage they were the Black Sabbath that I knew and loved. But as soon as they'd played their last encore, they split. They were gone fast, like it was painful for them to be there.

As we drove back to Toronto, Bess dug into his pocket and pulled out a small silver box. It was one of Tony Iommi's pick-ups, hawked from one of Tony's flight cases. He gave it to Dave, who used it on all the albums he recorded with Anvil. As for Robb, he got a pair of Bill Ward's sticks.

ROBB: Watching and listening to other bands honed our idea of how we wanted our new band to be. We knew we were going to write and perform our own material, and we'd decided the musical direction when we were still playing with Kickback. As Lips described, it was a simple formula: 'We got to write really really fast speedy shit. No one does that, man.' In those days, speed metal hadn't been devised, let alone defined. But turned on by Deep Purple's fastest material, we were intrigued by the idea of a high-energy version of hard, heavy rock with technical challenges and odd time signatures.

As for lyrics, like any artists, we were inspired by the world that we knew. Having written a handful of songs with which we were happy, we decided to follow the pattern established so far: blatant overt in-your-face sex. While still in Whalebone I'd written 'School Love', which was inspired by some of the lesbian chicks I knew at school. I'd written it to a drum beat, which made the lyrics very staccato:

> *Out in the school yard little Peaches play*
> *Rubbing their beavers, they got a lot to say*
> *Never doing work, teachers are mad*
> *Really don't care 'cause they're never sad*
> *Little school Peaches take a word from me*
> *Got to do your work and that's the way to be*

The idea for another song came from those two sisters that I'd screwed one night as a teen, while 'Bedroom Game' was about this chick that I was hanging out with who just couldn't get banged enough. In true artistic fashion, the band that Lips and I were building was a product of its environment.

We also needed a name. Lips had acquired his nickname several years earlier from my father, who had heard a friend called Barney joking that my buddy had 'luscious lips'. From that moment on, my father always called him Lips or Lipsomatic. If we were going to build the band around our Ted Nugent-like front man then, I suggested, we should name the band after him. And so the band was christened Lips.

Before we could start touting for gigs, we decided we needed a promo photograph. At that time, Lips was really into the first album by Captain Beyond, so Lee made him a suit similar to that worn by the character on the cover of that album. She also made me a leather body suit. Dave wore his leather jacket and Dix wore his dad's smoking jacket. Lee also made a wild satin backdrop, then used Lips's camera to take a picture of us in her bedroom. To fit with our lyrics, we wanted our image to be very sexual, but thinking about it now, we just looked like we were in our Hallowe'en costumes.

Like any band, we were easy prey for the pond life and scum that surrounded the music business. Few clubs or bars would accept direct bookings from bands if they didn't know them. We had to go through an agent and therefore we had to entertain their approaches. Take Gary. He was the ultimate hustler; he even dressed like one in a fur coat. A total manager.

We were jamming at our usual rehearsal space when Gary came scouting for bands of which he could take advantage. He knew we were good. The other bands at the rehearsal place had tipped him off. There was a knock at the door and in walked Gary.

'You guys are never going to get anywhere.' For such

a short, pudgy guy, he had a fucking cheek. 'You're trying to get out there playing originals, but you're gonna have to learn that you can't do that. You mark my words.'

We tolerated Gary's whine for a while, then we asked him if he could book us some gigs.

'I'm not going to book you. I told you fucking before you've got to start picking up some cover tunes or you're going nowhere. You'll never make it in the music business playing originals.'

Sitting on the drum riser, I was listening to this guy yap on and on. Then I fucking had it. Before you get Robbo angry, you've got to really go against the grain of my beliefs. And this fucking shit was striking hard at our music. That was it. It was like he'd just flipped my switch.

I stood up. 'You listen to me, you fucking piece of fuck. Get the fuck out of my room.'

Gary looked shocked, but I hadn't finished.

'I'm gonna fucking make it and I don't need your fucking help. Get the fuck out of here. I never want to fucking see your ass in here again.'

I started moving towards him.

'OK, goodbye.' The door slammed and we heard footsteps retreating rapidly down the corridor.

A few days later, Gary phoned. He'd booked us for the Yonge Station, a rock bar in downtown Toronto on

Yonge Street, the main strip. You could get a steak there and a beer and watch a band. It was a good venue. The only problem was that it didn't pay much, but because it was in Toronto, we could afford to play it as we could live at home.

And as for Gary, as long as he got his ten per cent he was happy, I guess. And to some extent, he was not completely wrong. He was trying to help us get our foot in the door, but that was difficult if he had to tell club owners that we played originals. Club owners would greet the phrase 'These guys play originals' with a simple question: 'What the fuck is that?'

Our problem was that we were trying to change the scene. This was the height of the disco era and we were determined to play heavy metal. And to make matters worse, it was all our own material at a time when we didn't have a recording contract, so there was no way anyone could hear it before coming to see us.

To help us find more bookings, we recorded a demo of three songs – 'School Love', 'Ooh Baby' and a new number, 'Oh Jane Can You Wait' – in the Sound Kitchen, a cheap Toronto studio. Then with the demo in hand, we approached a management company called Franklin House to book us gigs. These guys were keener than Gary, but pointed out that we had one major missing part: a lighting and sound rig. Lips approached his father.

'Look, I want to, I wanna . . .' Although he'd seen his siblings squeeze their old man for cash on many occasions, Lips had never asked his father directly for money. 'We got a . . . you know, we wanna make . . . do a bank loan.'

'What for? And how are you going to pay it back?'

'Well, we've got a booking agent and everything. He's gonna make sure that we work.'

'I'd like to talk to him.'

'OK, no problem.'

Lips took his dad to Franklin House, where he sat down with Barry Cobus, as archetypical a small-time manager as you could hope not to meet.

'Your son is a very, very talented young man.' Barry laid it on thick. 'He's gonna go really far in the business, so anything you can do to help would be really in your best interest.'

When Lips's dad got home the smile on his face could have lit up the room. 'You must really have something. They wouldn't just say that to me, so, OK, I'll go sign the loan. No problem.'

My dad didn't need anything. As soon as I asked him he nodded. 'Robbo, you want a loan guaranteed? No problem. I'm sure you'll pay it back.' Done.

With sound and lighting equipment bought, and armed with a stack of glossy colour promo photographs of the band with the name Lips printed in the corner and our demo tape, we went in search of fame and fortune.

Our dads' backing of our equipment loan reaped rewards almost immediately when Franklin House booked us to support Zon, a Toronto prog rock band they managed, at the Ontario Place Forum, which had a rotating stage at the centre of a huge amphitheatre. It was only our sixth gig as Lips and we would be playing in front of more than ten thousand people. It was a big step up from playing small bars in front of a couple of hundred people and we were crapping ourselves.

Lips was dressed in a leopard-skin outfit while I was wearing a white jumpsuit with rhinestones, both of them made by Lee. Dave and Ian were in their usual outfits, in Dave's case as tight and slutty as ever. Because it was such a big gig for us, we'd invited all our friends and family along to root for us. When my father saw the size of the crowd, he almost flipped. I think it was the first time he realized the profound and awesome power that we commanded.

'Don't ever fucking pack this in,' he said shortly before I went on stage. 'You're the fucking best. You know that, don't you? Don't ever give up on this.'

A few minutes later we walked out in front of the crowd. It was really fucking scary and the nerves didn't subside when we started playing. For some reason, our sound engineer Luke had put the fucking bass microphones at the back of the drums. The sound was all wrong. And Lips couldn't hear anything from his monitors. Not his voice nor his guitar nor my drums. We all huddled together to hear each other's instruments. It wasn't the best way to showcase our act, but we survived. I was relieved we'd got through it.

Within a few weeks of playing the Ontario Place Forum, our management deal at Franklin House fell apart. The two partners had a big bust-up and split. We were back on our own again, arranging most of our gigs ourselves or relying on small-time booking agents to land us an occasional residency. Seven days a week for forty weeks of the year, we pounded the pavement, playing any club or bar that would have us. We needed to earn enough money to pay off the loan that our fathers had guaranteed. We'd start playing at eight o'clock and would rarely finish before three in the morning. Most clubs wanted at least three sets a night, but it was five sets of forty-five minutes every night in Quebec, where we spent most of our time. And some clubs demanded six half-hour sets. With this much playing, we soon built up our reputation, developed our repertoire and improved our craft. Playing a venue for seven nights a week meant we had to kick ass like you wouldn't believe on a Monday night as the crowd would often come in for free to check out the band. If they liked us, they'd tell everyone and return at the weekend, when they'd usually be charged entrance. And when we didn't have a club or bar gig, we'd take whatever was going. Schools, social clubs, country clubs, private parties, weddings, bar mitzvahs: we played them all.

Initially we went out all original and, from the very first gig in Quebec City, the audience response was awesome. We had a very powerful, overwhelming, progressive style with a highly animated front man. The whole thing was like: Wow. People were going: Holy Christ.

But towards the end of every night the crowd would yell out for tunes they knew. They wanted Jimi Hendrix and Led Zeppelin – we'd hear calls for that kind of stuff in every venue – and soon the bars and clubs stopped booking us because we didn't please the punters. At that time we were taking advice from a booking manager by the name of Bruce Wilson. When he told us that he could get us work all the time provided we picked up a few cover tunes, we caved in and learned some crowd favourites. Because we had quite a similar look to Ted Nugent, we learned about seven or eight of his songs, which we'd intermix with our own compositions. One Nugent cover, two of our own and one more from Nugent, and so on. We were still predominantly original but we used Ted Nugent as our launch pad to get us gigs. We also developed our own heavy arrangement for some other songs, such as '(I'm Not Your) Steppin'

Stone' by the Monkees, 'Born To Be Wild' and 'Jumping Jack Flash'.

Most venues gave us rooms upstairs to live in while we were the resident band. For a week-long residence we'd get paid $1,000 to $1,200. But after paying commission to a booking agent, loan instalments for the sound and lighting equipment, truck rental and gas money, we'd be left with maybe $100 to split between the four of us. For three years we had very little money. Laundry would always be done in the sink, using soap from the venue's toilets, and we'd look forward to the winter because we wouldn't need to refrigerate our food and could save on electricity bills. And although it was not allowed by the club owners, we'd smuggle hot plates into our rooms to cook our own meals – mostly macaroni cheese three times a day – to save money.

LIPS: Playing four to six sets a night for 280 nights a year meant we clocked up more than 1,400 sets in our first twelve months. Our stagecraft advanced at a furious pace, but because we were playing in front of predominantly French-speaking audiences in Quebec, we needed to develop ways of transcending the language barrier. It forced me to be a lot more creative in my stage antics. I'd get on tables and play in the crowd. I'd dive into the crowd at the front or run through the audience. I'd hang my guitar on a noose.

But my biggest stage gimmick was the prop for which I'd later become famous: the dildo.

I'd started playing my guitar with a vibrator even before we got out of the rehearsal studio. For $1.97 I bought one as a joke at Consumers Distributor, a catalogue store that sold everything from bicycles to toasters. In later years I'd have to buy vibrators there in bulk, often getting strange looks when I asked for half a dozen dildos at once, which I'd need just to keep up with the inevitable losses and thefts on the road, but the first one was bought for the sheer hell of it. It was only when I got it back to the studio that I discovered I could use it to get an unusual sound out of my guitar – a different type of cock rock, I guess – and from that moment it became part of my stage act.

The visual show was a very important part of the Lips experience and, as far as we were concerned, the more outrageous the entertainment, the better the show. I would pick the prettiest girl in the room, go up to her, play a guitar solo right in front of her so that she could see just how fast my fingers were moving. And then, as the song would reach its climax, I would pull out my dildo, use it to finish the last few bars, then thrust the vibrating pink plastic into her drink and swirl it around with a filthy grin on my face.

It was entertainment pure and simple. I became known as a crazy prolific performer, but because we were good musicians it wasn't like I was jumping around and being an idiot. I was performing with total sincerity and integrity. For example, we'd written a song called 'Bondage' that later appeared on our first album and which in the early days we'd use most nights to close our final set. I'd be dressed in my bondage harness and dog collar, and at the end of the song we'd segue into what we called the bondage session. Dix and Dave would stop playing, leaving just Robbo and me on drums and lead guitar. Depending on how inspired I was feeling and the mood of the crowd, I'd do all kinds of things, such as playing long intricate jams or running around the audience. We'd change time signatures and improvise, but the dildo would always play a part.

On some nights, I would paint a pair of lips on my ass. Then at the climax of the bondage session, I'd climb up on to the drum riser and grab Robb's microphone.

'This is why we're called Lips,' I'd bellow as I pulled down my zebra-striped pants and moon at the crowd, flashing the lips on my ass at all the chicks.

And the chicks loved it. One night in Quebec City, I was up on the drum riser, doing the moon, when I felt a hand around my vitals. A girl had climbed up on stage and was now grabbing me from below. Struggling to pull free, I continued my guitar solo, which admittedly went a bit free form with wailing feedback, while trying to pull up my pants and get her hands off my balls. A hairy encounter for both of us.

On another night, we were coming to the end of our third set when we noticed our sound man shouting at someone at the side of the stage. 'What the fuck are you doing, buddy?'

Someone drunk in the crowd had got hold of the noose I used as part of my stage act and was trying to hang himself. There was a scuffle as the sound man attempted to liberate my stage prop from the drunk, but other than that it was just a standard night.

Whatever happened, we never allowed these antics to detract from the music. It might have been a drummer and a guy playing his guitar with a dildo going completely apeshit, but because we were entertaining people and making them smile, it was done with integrity. Nobody was putting on this kind of stuff except us, so we got known for it. We were known as the heavy, heavy band with the crazy dildo-wielding singer.

In early 1979 we decided to take our stage show up a level. Our lyrics were kind of sexy and we were gaining a reputation for having a sleazy stage show – albeit an honest form of sleaze, we believed – so we thought we should decorate our stage accordingly. While playing Quebec City, we went down to a fabric store and bought dozens of bras, hankies, feather boas and items of women's underwear to drape over our microphone stands and speaker stacks. In a way, it was like the kind of thing the New York Dolls were doing, but without the make-up. Or the puffy hair. And in a very strong heterosexual fashion. We were not aiming for a glam look, but for a shocking sleazy sexual feel. Definitely from the harder metal end of the spectrum.

It definitely worked. When I came off stage at the end of our final set, it was like being backstage at a Van Halen show. The corridor was wall to wall pussy. I had to stand in line to get back into my own changing room. The girls were queueing up to get at us all, but most of all they wanted Dave. With his pretty-boy looks and our new even sleazier stage show, Dave had at last hit the jackpot for which he'd been waiting so long. They wanted him so bad. So very very bad. And for the rest of us in Lips, things would never be the same again.

5 BANGS AND BANGING

ROBB: Coming off stage to find a corridor full of chicks all wanting to meet us was totally exciting. But it wasn't just about the promise of easy no-strings sex, awesome though that was. I'd experienced enough of that when touring with Whalebone. The sight of all these chicks just wanting to party with us confirmed to me that we were now a proper band. Groupies only turn up when you're a band worth knowing. I'd always wanted to know what it felt like to be David Lee Roth and now I had some idea.

There was something magical about the way in which it happened. We'd go to a gig and before the show our dressing room would be empty. After the show it would be full of people, all of them strangers united in their mission to party with us. Likewise hotels, if we were lucky enough to be staying in one. When we arrived at the hotel, there'd rarely be anybody waiting for us. But within a few hours, the groupies would have found us. We never had to go looking for them. It was like bands were magnets and they were the iron filings. And the biggest, most powerful magnet of all was Dave Allison, or Squirrely as we called him by the time the groupies started taking an interest in us.

It was not difficult to work out why Squirrely was such a babe magnet. With long blond hair, blue eyes and a slender frame, he had a very cutesy feminine look that chicks found irresistible.

But more than his looks, it was the way Squirrely acted that made him such a total ladykiller. Playing his guitar on stage with his pants undone, Squirrely presented himself as a full-on slut. And off stage he reinforced that image. As Lips said, 'If we had any questions about Squirrely's motivation for being in the band in the early days, holy Christ by the time we came off stage at Quebec City we knew the answer.'

Squirrely played up to his slutty image because that was where his heart lay. Lips and I were in a band to rock and roll. Anything else was a fringe benefit. As for Dix, I never knew why he wanted to rock, but I guess it was probably because it beat having a proper job. But for Squirrely there was only one reason to be in a band. Chicks.

'You guys' – Squirrely looked at me and Lips – 'bring in the guys. I bring in the pussy.'

We heard that line a lot and every word of it was true.

Exactly when Squirrely acquired his nickname has been forgotten, but there were several good reasons for it. He had a habit of noisily sucking his teeth to release scraps of food that had got caught in gaps between them, which we thought sounded like a squirrel. He also had enormous nuts that we'd joke would attract squirrels if he sat still for long enough. But the way that I remember it is that he first picked up the nickname after relating his exploits with a groupie to us.

'I was rubbing her so hard,' he said, 'that she went squirrely.'

Lips started to laugh. 'Squirrely? You made her go *squirrely*? What the fuck?' And from that moment the name stuck.

Whenever there was a party, Squirrely was at the centre of it. Sometimes it would be Squirrely and me who went off and did crazy shit. Other times it would be Squirrely and Dix. But it didn't seem like a proper party if Squirrely wasn't there, so it was never just me and Dix or me and Lips. And if Lips partied, he tended to do it on his own. As for our roadies, they had a simple rule. They partied whenever, wherever and with whomever they could. We'd made sure our roadies were pretty cool-looking guys with long hair, just like us rockers, and they played it to the hilt. And because they were part of the expenses deducted from our fees, the roadies got paid before we did and usually had more money to show groupies a good time than we did.

LIPS: When the groupies started hitting on us, my initial response was one of complete shock. I'd heard tales of what went on when bands went on the road and I'd seen a little of it when we'd toured with Kickback. But this was a far cry from those relatively innocent days. This was nuts. Crazy, crazy, crazy nuts.

Girls would literally throw themselves at us and I struggled to understand why they wanted to do it. In some cases it was simple competitiveness. These girls wanted to be with the guy that all the other girls were eyeing. For other girls we were mere notches in their belts. They wanted to score a particular guy or maybe they'd always wanted to fuck a guy in a band. But often the girls just ended up backstage – it might be the first time they'd been to a rock show – and in the excitement of meeting the band, an innocent flirtation could quickly turn hardcore. Shit like that happened a lot.

But what really shocked me was the attitude of the groupies to each other. There wasn't a badmouthing we didn't hear.

'Don't fuck her,' groupies would yak, freaking out because one of us had started talking to one of the other chicks. 'Fuck me. She's got the clap and she doesn't suck cock. I do.' We heard it all, and often the carving on each other and calling each other names like whore and slut would escalate from a bitch-fest into a full-on fight.

When we could afford hotels, I usually shared with Dix and Robb would share with Squirrely. Their room would always be the party room and our room would be the waiting room. One night, while the usual craziness was going on in Squirrely's room, I was sitting on my bed with eight or ten girls in a line along the edge of it. I was partying, but it was tame stuff compared with what was going on next door and the line of girls waiting patiently to be invited next door began to intrigue me.

'Why are you here?'

No response. It wasn't a question they wanted to answer.

'What exactly are you here for?'

Still no reply. Then one of the girls spoke while the other chicks remained hostile. 'We're just here to hang out with you guys.'

'But you know what's going on in the other room so why are you here?'

That got a penetrating stare, like how dare I ask such a question.

'Is your reaction like that because you wish you were in the other room?'

'No.'

'So why are you here?'

'We're not groupies.'

'OK, but I'm trying to get a handle on this. I'm just trying to understand why you're here because if you're not interested in what's going on in the room next door, why are you carving on your girlfriend who's in the other room with the guys? You sound like you're jealous of them. What the fuck is this?'

Another blank response. Not one of them would admit that they wanted to have sex with someone in the band, but none of them had any other good reason for being there. And later, when the opportunity arose, they happily headed into the party room next door.

Surrounded every night by groupies and their antics, I was starting to understand why bands had such dismissive – and at times abusive – attitudes to women. It didn't excuse the musicians' and roadies' behaviour, but it helped to explain it.

We started to realize that the girls who came to see us were the same girls who had been to see every band that had come through town over the previous few months. When we met up with other bands we'd compare notes over who had passed whose dose of the clap on to whomever. It didn't make us feel any better about the groupies.

For a great deal of the time I was an observer because I had a girlfriend to whom I intended to remain vaguely faithful. I was forever going to bed with girls but not sleeping with them. Robb could never understand it, but the way I looked at it, I would rather blow the chicks away with what I could play on my guitar than with my dick. Most of the time, I didn't give a shit about the groupies, but that often meant I'd sit in the room, drinking and smoking, while all kinds of perverse shit was going on around me, the participants not caring if anyone was watching. I can't say I didn't enjoy the view, but at times it got a bit much. Sometimes I'd go to sleep with a couple screwing in the bed beside me and I'd wake up in the morning and they'd still be at it.

On one occasion, we had played a biker convention in a club that provided accommodation for the entire band and the roadies in a single room above the club. While we were all in little single cots in a row with the lights on, Squirrely was in bed with a girl, on top of her and having a good gig at full pelt. The rest of us wanted to sleep, so none of us was really paying attention, not least because the girl was totally drunk and really fucked up. Then she puked. Her vomit erupted straight up into the air, and then dropped on Squirrely and her.

The loving couple didn't break their stride, but we were out of our cots, jumping over each others' beds to run out of the room as fast as we could move. The stench was unbelievable.

'Geyser Chops.' Bess was disgusted. 'That's her fucking name now. Geyser Chops!'

Meanwhile Geyser Chops and Squirrely were still in the bed, fucking while they marinated in her stomach acid.

At around the same time, we were playing a club at Elliott Lake in Ontario. As usual, Robb was sharing a room with Squirrely. And as usual, Squirrely was in bed fucking a groupie. Midway through Squirrely's session, our lighting man broke into the room – to this day I don't know why except that like many roadies, he liked to always push things a step too far – and started to insult the girl, calling her a pig and a slut.

Upset by the dissing, the girl snatched a sheet around herself, grabbed her clothes and split. A short while later, there was a knock at the door. It was the groupie again, now dressed and looking for her watch, which she'd left behind. Fortunately for the girl, the roadie had found her watch. Unfortunately, he'd then chosen to whip it against the wall. Bits of watch and glass were all over the floor. The girl flipped out and ran out of the room, cursing at us and vowing revenge.

That night, when we got to the club we were playing, we found a posse of twenty local guys waiting, swinging baseball bats and wanting to settle with us. The chick had told them we'd raped her – an outrageous and untrue accusation – and the posse wanted our blood.

We barricaded ourselves inside the club and called the Mounties. The cops turned up in a matter of minutes and questioned the girl while the posse stood nearby, shouting threats and calling for our skins. The chick admitted she hadn't been raped and confessed that she had told everyone otherwise. Realizing they couldn't defuse the situation, the Mounties guarded our truck while we loaded it with our equipment, then gave us a full police escort out of town and down the highway for nearly 100 miles.

Escapades such as these were a regular part of the shit that went on when we were on the road. When things went well, we had some of the best times of our lives. But often we were dealing with strangers and girls who were unpredictable at the best of times. Throw in industrial quantities of alcohol and drugs, and anything could happen. In fact it often did. But as often as not, it was our roadies that got us into trouble, not us. One particular roadie, let's call him Roadie X, had a notorious ability for attracting shit. After one gig he slept with the wrong girl and got himself a urinary infection.

'Look at this, man.' Roadie X pulled down his trousers. His testicles were hugely swollen. 'They hurt like fuck.'

'You've got Mexican big balls. It's a medical condition.' I don't know from where I plucked the term, but he fell for it.

'Shit. Whatta I do?'

'You need to get it checked out by a medic.'

We took him to a hospital and watched as he walked off bow-legged down a corridor with a nurse. A while later he returned, red-faced and fuming.

'What happened?'

'I took my pants down, man, and then I go to the nurse: "I've got Mexican big balls." So she takes them in her hands and she goes: "They don't look too big to me."' We cracked up as he told the rest of the story. 'When the fuckin' nurse had fuckin' stopped laughing, she gave me some tablets and told me to be more careful next time.'

But Roadie X's medical encounters weren't always so funny, at least not to him. We were booked into a club for a week's residency and every day we'd go to a restaurant right across the street to eat. At the best of times Roadie X was a very rude guy – he'd never leave a tip and he could be totally nasty to the waitresses – but during this week his mood was even worse than usual.

'Hurry up, ya bitch.' Roadie X thumped the table as a waitress passed by. 'I've been waiting for fucking ages. Whaddya think's fuckin' keeping ya, ya lazy whore?'

Then his food arrived. It was poutine, a Quebec speciality of French fries with cheese, meat and spaghetti sauce. It was cheap and filling. We ate it all the time.

A couple of hours later, he was vomiting everywhere. And I mean everywhere. That afternoon we took him to hospital. By then, he had acute diarrhoea and was throwing up black bile. Although we didn't mention it, we all suspected that the waiting staff at the restaurant had put something in his food. Whatever it was, its effect was fast and violent.

The next day, Robb and I went into hospital to visit our trusty roadie. He was still making an awesome fuss, hammering a bell by the side of his bed to call the nurse. 'Where the fuck is the fuckin' nurse, man? I'm in total fuckin' pain.'

We heard footsteps approaching fast. A male nurse appeared with a look of anger on his face. Without saying a word, he walked over to Roadie X's bed, grabbed the bell and ran out. We couldn't blame him.

ROBB: At the same time as the parties were taking off backstage, we were trying to improve our stage show to attract the attention of the agents who booked the larger clubs. With all our expenses we were struggling to survive on fees of $800 to $1,200 a week we earned from the B-club circuit. If we could move up to A-clubs, we'd immediately double our takings.

To take our stage show up a gear we decided we needed to set off smoke bombs at the climax of our set, but being Lips, we couldn't afford to buy commercial pyrotechnics. Instead we made our own primitive homemade bombs using a recipe devised by Ken MacNeil, one of our roadies.

Professional pyrotechnics use flash powder, but that was not easily obtained, so we substituted gunpowder, which was available in hunting and camping shops. Working at Lips's kitchen table, we measured a large tin of powder into dozens of plastic 35-mm film canisters. To make fuses, we wrapped two pieces of wire around each canister, and then we wrapped the devices in black electrical tape. An electrical battery would provide the charge to set off the explosion and we'd encase everything in a metal mesh cage to contain the inevitable shrapnel.

For several performances the bombs went off like a dream, the only problem occurring when we hit upon the brainwave of adapting our charges to make sparkle bombs for a gig at a high school. We'd heard that if we mixed tea leaves with the gunpowder, the tea would be scattered by the explosion and drift slowly to the ground, sparkling in the air as it descended.

But it didn't turn out as planned. The leaves caught light all right, but they failed to sparkle and instead of smelling like burning tea, they had an unexpectedly exotic odour. The teachers at the high school freaked out.

'You're blowing up marijuana bombs.'

'No. It's just tea leaves,' Lips insisted.

But it was too late. The police were called and we were detained for half an hour until we could prove that our sparkle bombs contained nothing more than the best Darjeeling leaves.

Our next mishap came at a club, when, at the climax of our show, Bess threw the switch to trigger an explosion and the bomb didn't go off. Hammering out the beat behind my drum kit, I watched as Bess crawled across the stage, intent on connecting the bomb so that he could make a second attempt at detonation. Just as he reached the bomb, the fucker blew up right in his face. As the smoke cleared, Bess's face slowly emerged. Like Wile E. Coyote after being fried by an explosive in the Road Runner cartoons, he was totally coated in black soot and all his hair was standing on end, burned to a cinder. Our next number was 'Ooh Baby' and as Lips reached the chorus I spotted Bess back at his lighting board, singing in an Al Jolson voice, the whites of his eyes and his teeth the only visible features in the darkness at the side of the stage. By the time we reached the end of the song, all four of us had spotted Bess and we were all struggling to contain our laughter. But it wasn't that funny for Bess when his shock wore off and the pain kicked in.

'I can't fucking see, man.' We smeared cold cream all over Bess's face until his totally white face stood in stark contrast to his burned black hair. 'I still can't fucking see.'

Looking closely at Bess's eyes, I noticed his eyelashes

had fused in the heat of the explosion. 'Oh fuck. Sit down man.' With a pair of nail clippers, Lips removed all his eyelashes, restoring Bess's sight. Another typical Bess escapade. And another typical band fuck-up rescued at the last moment.

By the end of 1979, it seemed like our efforts on stage were starting to pay off. A street buzz was building around the band, powered as much by the heaviness of our music and the spectacle of our stage show as by our backstage partying antics. Then we got notice that Ralph Jolivet, a big-time agent in Toronto, wanted to see the band. If we could secure his services we might be able to make the leap up to larger clubs.

At that time we were playing regular gigs at the Yonge Station in Toronto, but that didn't stop us wanting to play the Gas Works, a much larger club down the street. Our booking manager, Bruce Wilson, had approached the owner of the Gas Works on our behalf several times but we couldn't find a way in, even though the Gas Works would be empty whenever we were playing the Yonge Station. There was something about us that the owner didn't like.

But now Jolivet, who booked the Gas Works, had wised up to the fact that there were queues outside the Yonge Station when we were playing while the Gas Works was empty. He had no choice but to start entertaining the idea that he'd better check us out.

On the night that Jolivet turned up, Lips was leaping off the stage, swinging on the chandeliers, down on his knees, making his guitar wail and the girls wet their knickers. We were playing like demons. We knew we were the hottest of bands. And when we came off stage, Jolivet was by all accounts clearly impressed. Bruce Wilson told us that he was totally fucking blown away.

'Jolivet said I better come and see him. He said to make an appointment with his secretary for the day after tomorrow.' With Jolivet beyond himself on the whole deal, we thought we had it cracked.

Two days later Bruce turned up at Jolivet's swanky offices, and then he came back and told us the deal.

'So what did he say, Bruce, man?' I was desperate to know. 'Have we got a booking?'

Bruce took his time. 'As soon as I got there Jolivet immediately hyped you up, guys. He said you were the most exciting act he'd seen for a long time.' Then Bruce dropped the bombshell.

'He said: "I can't handle your band because your singer's hands were dirty."'

We couldn't fucking believe it. 'What?'

'He said Lips's hands were dirty. He said you don't have the class to play the Gas Works.'

The only reason Lips's hands had been dirty was that he'd been down on his knees, rocking out. When he'd got up, he'd dusted down his pants and a little of the dust had remained on his hands. It was fucking unbelievable.

'Come on, man.' I wasn't going to stand for it. Jolivet's reason didn't make sense. 'Like he just told you we're fucking happening, man. And then he tells you that it don't matter because his hands were dirty. He just doesn't want to book us . . .'

'I'm sorry. That's the way it is, guys.'

'That's fuckin' ridiculous.'

Bruce shrugged.

'So whaddya say to him, Bruce?'

'Well, I told him he was wrong and then he said: "Listen to me, you little cocky . . ."'

Jolivet apparently lost his cool. I thought I could see what was playing here. I felt he was looking for any reason not to book us. It seemed as if he didn't like the idea that we were drawing big crowds away from the Gas Works and he wanted to put us in our place. He didn't like it that we were taking custom away from other bands he represented, like a Zeppelin tribute band and other lame-ass musicians.

Bruce turned to me. 'And he said: "I don't know about your drummer. He overplays."'

'Holy Christ, man, who the fuck is he?' I was raging. 'Jolivet don't know yet who I am, but he's going to fuckin' soon. And I'm going to leave him with an impression that he'll never fucking forget . . .' Before I said too much, Lips told me to be quiet. There was no point in wasting our energies talking about him.

I was convinced Bruce had got the brush-off because we were ahead of our time and jerks like Jolivet didn't recognize it. Yes, we were cocky about it. But that was because our attitude was like: We're already rock stars, just watch us play and you'll see.

LIPS: We decided it was time to record our first album. If we could get some tracks down, we could press a record and then we could sell it at gigs. A record would spread our music to a wider audience and that ought to lead to bookings at larger venues. We found a recording studio that was prepared to sell us a block of cheap time. With eight hundred dollars we'd saved from gig fees, we bought enough time to record at least ten tracks.

By this time, Robb was back living in the basement beneath his parents' home. The fight with his dad had lasted only a few months and now he was back in the bosom of his family. They certainly put up with a lot while we were writing the songs for the album. We already had more than a dozen tracks written but we needed to narrow them down to a core of ten to twelve to put on the album. With Robbo and me writing songs in the basement, the house above would often vibrate. Ornaments on the shelves would shake and Robb's dad would say that we put cracks in the walls. But Robbo's parents never really complained. Except, that is, when we were trying to write the riff to one song and spent hours playing it over and over again.

'If you guys don't know how to play that song by now, I'm going to . . .' Robbo's father was standing at the entrance to the basement looking totally pissed off. 'If I hear it one more time, I'm going to wring both your necks.'

Robbo and I had written all our earliest tracks, such as our first song, 'Thumb Hang', the inspiration for which came from learning about the Spanish Inquisition at school. We thought the idea that non-Catholics would be hanged from the ceiling by their thumbs would make a good subject for a song. 'Thumb Hang'? That sounded like a pretty cool title to us, so we wrote a song.

But after Lips was formed, we wanted the entire band to collaborate on the songs. The song titles and their general direction would come from me, but we all played a part. I would oversee the writing of lyrics, although Robbo had a big input as well. Squirrely also contributed, when his mind wasn't distracted by the prospect of getting laid, and would sometimes write whole songs on his own. Dix made less of a contribution to the content of the lyrics, but as the only one in the band who could spell reliably, his contribution was just as useful. The music for the song could come from anyone. If someone had a good riff or if Robbo had a good beat, we'd go with it and see what happened.

By the time we'd finished at the studio we had enough tracks to compile our first album, Hard'N'Heavy. Several tracks dated back to before Lips, but most were written for the album.

'School Love', the first track, was an older Robbo composition about lesbian love among his former class-mates. 'AC/DC' came from the chord sequence in the chorus of the song (A-C-C-C-D-C-C) and I wrote the lyrics with Lee, playing on the double meaning of the song title: electricity and bisexuality.

'At The Apartment' was about the romantic escapades of a buddy. Our buddy had gone through a pretty tough time. He'd been arrested on a drugs charge and tortured by the police. They pulled down his pants and took a mechanic's claw to his penis. Then they'd beaten him with a phone directory. It resulted in a court case, the police officers were fired and our buddy went free, but in a sense he'd already paid for his crime. He also had a son who had brain cancer, so he had been through a lot, but after breaking up with his wife he found happiness with a girl that lived in an apartment and that's where the song came from.

'I Want You Both With Me' was a Squirrely

composition, inspired by meeting Robb's sister, Andrea, and Sylvana, the chick who'd been with Jane at the Forum when Robb first set eyes on her. In typical Squirrely fashion, he had the hots for both of them. Although Squirrely was seeing Andrea, he couldn't leave Sylvana alone and believed the attraction was mutual. In the last verse Squirrely laid out his dilemma.

Well Syl she's nice but she's so hard to know
And she puts me down
The other loves me and she lets it show
So she's hanging around
I guess I'll make the most
And I'll see them both
'Cause they suit me fine you know, honey
That I lay them all the time

Robb and I wrote 'Bedroom Game' after I heard Robb carrying on with a girl. They were in the bedroom above where I was hanging out in the basement of her house and the noise of it went on and on and on. When they finally emerged, Robbo told me they'd made a bet over how many times they could do it in succession. They hit their target, but it went downhill real quick after that as they realized that what they had was nothing more than lust. So I wrote:

I said I'd go ten so did you
But in the end you were the loser too
You went crazy after that night
Just making trouble wanting to fight
I'll pack you in 'cause you're not for me
It's hard to understand but it's got to be

The next song, 'Ooh Baby', was built around a riff
that sounded good. Again the lyrics were about sex –
there was a theme building here – while the next track,
'Oh Jane', was about Robb's love for Jane.

Oh Jane can you wait
I'm coming home, but I'm running late
Just playing one more town
You know I miss you and I want you around
Oh Jane I'm alone
On the road but I'm coming home
I feel your love in my heart
And I hope that we will never part

Squirrely wrote the lyrics to 'Hot Child' about some
chick he was fantasizing about, while I'd written the
lyrics to 'Bondage' several years previously when I was
working for my uncle in a shoe warehouse. Bored by the
job, I sat down in a corner of the warehouse one day
and attempted to write something really sexual because

I thought it would be cool. It was very innocently done – I had no experience of bondage but thought it sounded heavy – and it was my attempt to cut close to the edge. The music came from a tune we'd jam at club sound checks. We also recorded a heavy cover of the Stones track 'Paint It Black'.

In the midst of laying down the tracks in the studio, Van Halen came to town and Bess suggested we went to check them out as he could get us backstage. In the year or so since we'd seen them support Sabbath at Niagara Falls, Van Halen had risen to the top. Now they were headlining their own gigs and when we got backstage, oh fuck did it show. We arrived to find David Lee Roth appraising the local Toronto chicks as if they were prize cattle at a rodeo.

'You're not bad.' Dave twirled the index finger of one hand to indicate to the girl that she should turn around. Then he ran his other hand and eyes over her body. 'Not bad at all . . .' He picked up an ice cube and shot it down the girl's top. 'Next please.'

We moved on into the bar. Bess sat down for a drink with Les Martin, a Black Sabbath roadie that he knew, and I pulled up a stool nearby. I was hanging out, sipping a beer, when Michael Anthony, Van Halen's bassist, walked by.

'Hey, man.' I extended a hand. 'Congratulations on your success. Great show. Fantastic.'

'Yeah, man.' Michael stopped walking and pointed at the ground. 'See these boots?'

'Yeah.' They were awesome cowboy boots. 'Cool.'

'Fifteen grand, man. Wouldn't you like to be in them?'

'Oh . . . OK.'

'Listen, can you do me a favour? Can you stand right here?' Taking me by the shoulders, Michael directed me to a position to the side of him. 'Now turn around.'

Bewildered at Michael's instructions, I faced away from him.

'That's perfect.' Michael patted me on my back. 'There's somebody over there I don't want to see me.'

I wasn't sure whether Michael genuinely wanted to use me as a human shield to prevent someone across the room from seeing him or whether he wanted just to humiliate me. Probably both, I thought as he walked away. Maybe he was joking but he'd left me feeling totally deflated, wondering what was wrong with Michael Anthony that he had to do that? What had made him so arrogant and disdainful of other people's feelings? I went over to where Les and Bess were sitting. I told Les that we were in the middle of recording our first album, that we'd become a pretty serious band and that we were about to make the breakthrough into bigger clubs. Compared with Van Halen, our achievements were very small, but to us it felt like we were taking the first steps to where they were.

As I said it I noticed Eddie Van Halen sitting at the other side of the bar, looking nervous and smoking a cigarette while a girl was talking to him. I heard Eddie mumble, 'Yeah, whatever,' a few times but he didn't look happy, just uncomfortable, withdrawn and un-approachable. It was a massive contrast to the atmosphere in the Van Halen dressing room when we'd seen them support Black Sabbath at Niagara Falls only a year earlier. Twelve months earlier, Van Halen were up and coming and an intense excitement surrounded them. Now they'd arrived at the top, yet it felt like they'd lost something on the way.

Robb and I wanted success more than almost any-thing. It wasn't just about financial reward and a better class of groupie. Success would mean recognition for our music. It would mean freedom to pursue that pact we'd made – to rock together for ever – without having to worry about where the next dollar would come from or where we'd be sleeping that night. Right then, achieving success was everything to me, the reason I got up in the morning, the reason I was alive. But as I walked away from the gig that night, a tiny doubt was entering my mind. Judging by what I'd just seen back-stage at Van Halen and a year earlier in the Black Sabbath dressing room, success carried a heavy burden. Maybe success wasn't such a great thing after all.

6 GERBILS, GIGS AND GROUPIES

ROBB: Within a few weeks of seeing Van Halen we had a finished album in our hands. We pressed a thousand copies and started selling them off the stage at clubs for five dollars apiece. We were back on the road again and with it a return to everything that went with being on the road.

As well as building a buzz for our music, we were gaining a rep for being real partiers. Bands that arrived in rooms after we'd been there would know just from the state of the place that we'd passed through town. Like the time that Desperate Debbie turned up at a particularly wild gig.

Desperate Debbie picked up her nickname for her eagerness to sleep with any musician who wanted it. With few sexual scruples, she revelled in her reputation and it wasn't unusual to find her backstage with a cock in each hand, living fully up to her name.

It was our last night at that club. After the gig, a party started in our changing room and Desperate Debbie became very intoxicated, so much so that we couldn't wake her when the time came to leave for home. As I walked out of the room, I looked back at the carnage we'd created. I didn't know exactly who'd done it, but this is what I saw. In the middle of everything was Desperate Debbie, lying naked on a bed, her head hanging over the edge above a garbage can in which she had vomited. For Debbie's convenience, the garbage had been emptied from the can. A considerate touch, I thought, even if it had been emptied all over her. The vibrator Lips had used in his stage act, well, let's just say it was still buzzing and that he was going to have to buy a new one if he didn't want to liberate it from where it had ended up. There was blood on the sheets and empty beer bottles everywhere. Desperate Debbie was the last survivor and we were out of there.

A few weeks later Lips and I bumped into Gary Greenblatt. His covers band Izod had been playing the club the day after we left. They'd showed up at the club and Gary had led them to the changing room. He'd opened the door to be greeted by a vision of Desperate Debbie still lying asleep on the bed, still surrounded by the detritus of our partying. It was no wonder we were gaining a hard partying rep.

Partying with groupies and chicks never got us into

trouble with owners or managements of venues. I guess bands were expected to get up to that kind of mischief, but other types of misbehaviour weren't so easily tolerated, like what happened one of the many times we were playing at the Electric Circle, a club in Quebec City. The club management had rented us an apartment for the duration of our week of gigs at their venue. Belonging to a Madame Tourelle, the apartment was old-style Quebec with high ceilings and very pretty. Trouble was we got bored hanging around the apartment for a week, waiting to play every night. And what does a band do when it gets bored? It goes to the pet store. You've got to have pets, man. Especially when you're a band on the road.

I got some gerbils, Squirrely got a hamster and Bess got a hamster and a tarantula, which he named Precious. One of Squirrely's hamsters was called Gonzo. I'm sure the other pets all had names, but you know how it is with too much dope and memory loss.

Our little menagerie was existing very happily, keeping us amused, until Bess's hamster spoiled things by escaping out of its cage. With us running behind it, trying to capture it, the little critter dived behind a sofa in Madame Tourelle's apartment and couldn't be found.

Over the next few days, we tried enticing the hamster out of its hiding place with baits of peanut butter and hamburger meat, but it never reappeared. Sadly we had to leave the apartment without one of the newest members of our entourage.

A few days later, the agent that booked us into the Electric Circle called us into his office.

'What the fuck is this?' The agent was holding up a letter and freaking out.

'What's the matter, man?'

The agent read out a list of accusations from Madame Tourelle. It said peanut butter had been smeared all over the walls and the sheets were encrusted with hamburger. In fairness, it was true. We'd all lost it a bit when we hadn't been able to find Bess's hamster. Lips had flung peanut butter straight out of the jar over the walls. And yes, somebody had stuffed hamburger between the sheets. We'd gone a bit crazy and wrecked the place. No wonder the shit had now hit the fan.

The agent said he'd never had such a terrible letter of complaint about a band. 'You guys are the absolute fucking pits. It says here you beseeched a mouse.'

'We what?'

'You beseeched a mouse.'

We weren't sure what Madame Tourelle meant by 'beseeched' in her letter, but at least it proved the little critter had turned up after all. That was the last time we were allowed to stay in Madame Tourelle's apartment.

As for the pets, we kept them for quite some time. Our other roadies added to the collection and they all lived in our tour truck. Eventually we took our little zoo out west, introducing its members to other bands we met on tour across Canada. And the other bands loved it. How often did they get to see pets away from home?

'You guys have got pets?' other bands would say. 'That's pretty wild. That's different.'

And the pets were a perfect antidote to the boredom of touring. We tried all kinds of experiments on them, like feeding a mouse to Precious. But Precious just ignored it, so we figured tarantulas are probably vegetarians.

We took great care of our pets, particularly of Precious because she was a girl spider, although we stopped short of dedicating songs to her. Bess would take her out of her cage, let her run into the palm of his hand and put her on visitors to our dressing room. The paranoia surrounding tarantula bites is huge but it's a myth that they're deadly. They're no worse than a bee sting and although Precious occasionally tried to bite Bess, none of us was ever hurt.

One by one the hamsters passed away, but the gerbils and Precious were made of stronger stuff. They were proper rock 'n' roll gerbils fully capable of withstanding the rigours of touring with a band like Lips. And the only distress we ever saw from Precious was when she would shed a leg or moult her old exoskeleton, something that was quite natural for a tarantula. But

Precious eventually retired from the road with Bess. She'd seen too much debauchery for a little spider. And when the time came to give my gerbils a rest from almost constant travelling, I transferred them to a cage at home, where I'd have fun feeding them dollar bills. It was pure entertainment watching other people freak out as the gerbils chewed through hundred-dollar bills. And I wasn't rich. Just nuts.

LIPS: We were still battling away with the Gas Works, trying to move up to a class-A club, but whatever we did, the guy who owned the Gas Works insisted we wouldn't last and wouldn't cave in to our pleas. So we accepted a booking for a string of gigs in Northern Ontario, one of which was a place on a logging road near Sault Ste Marie.

Although we'd hired a newer, more reliable truck for the long journey north, we were running late. Robbo and the rest of the band and roadies were in a car, but I was following in the truck with Bess. As soon as we followed the car on to a gravel road, I felt we'd made a mistake.

'Bess, man. What the fuck are we doing on this road?' I quickly pulled on my seatbelt. 'Let's turn back.'

'Quit your fuckin' whining. We're late and we've only got forty-five minutes to get there. Now shut the fuck up.'

On the map the gravel road looked like it would cut out a significant part of the journey, but I could see it was a treacherous road, OK for a car but not ideally suited to a truck fully laden with gear.

Bess was driving like a maniac. The gravel road cut through very steep hills, and then started to climb. On one side of the truck, a steep cliff rose vertically above us. On the other side, the cliff dropped for hundreds of feet. There was no fence or barrier. If we drove off the road we'd be dead. No doubt about it. I was scared shitless.

We were making good time, but I wasn't convinced we were going to survive the journey. About one hundred yards from the end of the road, we descended a hill to some railroad tracks. As we hit the railroad tracks, the truck started to rock. Bess tried to bring the truck under control before the curve, but as we went round the curve, the whole rig lifted and flipped right into a ditch.

Bess blew out of his seat. Twisting in the air, his ass had hit the windshield, sending the glass flying forwards out of the cab instead of inwards, thank God. He was now lying on the ceiling of the cab. Beside him, I was hanging upside down in the goddamn truck with my seatbelt on, looking at Bess.

'Shut the fucking truck off, right now.' I yelled. 'Shut the fucking truck off.'

The engine was still running, the wheels were spinning and maybe I should have been freaking out, but I was just relieved to be alive. My survival instinct kicked in. As the car with Robbo and the others returned to find out what had happened to us, we crawled out of the cab to greet them. A bank of scrubby bushes had cushioned the fall and some cast-iron poles from the lighting rig had shot through the roof, suspending the truck above the ground so that it didn't fall over and crush us. We were very lucky to be alive and unharmed. If the accident had happened anywhere else along the gravel road, we'd have been dead. It was a big warning for us not to take chances like that again.

A cop turned up and took me aside.

'I want you to answer me honestly.' The cop pointed at Bess. 'In your opinion was he driving recklessly?'

'No.' I wanted no more trouble than we'd already got.

'OK. I'll take your word. I'm not going to charge him.'

We brought in tow trucks to get our truck upright and taken to an accident compound. At the compound, we discovered that almost nothing was damaged inside the truck. Only one skin of Robbo's snare was snapped.

We spent the night sweating it in a motel room because we'd lied to the motel owner about how many guys we'd squeezed into the room. When he discovered we had six guys in a two-bed room, he flipped out, parked his car across the door and called the police. Fortunately the cop that turned up was the same one that had helped us out of the ditch and he told the motel owner to give us a break.

That week we stayed in rooms above a disco club at a hotel and we had a hell of a time. It was party night every night. Maybe it was the exhilaration of escaping serious injury, but there seemed to be something in the air that week.

Bess was black and blue with bruises, but that didn't stop him carrying on with a girl he'd picked up in the bar downstairs. I woke up at dawn one morning to find the guys having an orgy with this girl. It's not often anyone is greeted by the words 'Oh Megan, you've got such nice hairy legs' as they wake up.

A big girl called Debbie Morrison took an interest in me, in part because I wore very tight pants and she liked my outline, which inspired her to nickname me Horse Dick. She really had the hots for me, but I wasn't interested. The shock of what had happened in the truck with Bess had started to hit me and I felt very shaky. I also had other things on my mind, which came to a head towards the end of the week.

While the guys were playing in a penny arcade, I went for a walk down on the shore of St Marys River, which separated Sault Ste Marie from Sault Michigan in America. It was late summer and leaves were starting to fall from a tree that I sat beneath, gazing across the river and trying to make sense of how and why I had survived the accident without a mark on me. Although the accident left no lasting physical effect, it had a profound spiritual effect on me. I was convinced I'd survived for a reason. It was a sign that my life had a purpose. A sign that I was meant to have some kind of future. Maybe it was to have offspring or maybe it was to make it in rock 'n' roll. Whatever the reason, it convinced me that my existence was important to this world.

The revelation that afternoon was a life-changing event for me. If I'd had any doubts about my future purpose, I was now convinced that a very important destiny awaited me. I'd cheated death. That was for proof enough for me.

ROBB: Suddenly everything fell into place. The Gas Works booked us, record company execs came to see us and we got a recording contract. An 'overnight success' – only three years after we formed Lips. Maybe that's what it looked like. The truth was slightly different.

After our fourth sold-out appearance at the Yonge Station, the owner of the Gas Works had to face reality: when we were in town, every other bar was empty, including his. He had no choice but to book us. At last we'd got through the door of Toronto's Mecca of all

Meccas. From one day to the next our fee nearly doubled. Good money at last.

A few days before we were due to play our first date at the Gas Works, we got a call from Tom Williams, head of A&R at Attic Records, at that time the biggest independent Canadian label. We'd sent our album to every record company in Canada and it had now landed on Tom's desk. Although Attic wasn't a heavy metal label, Tom liked the record. 'Let's see how good you guys are,' he said. 'Your dates at the Gas Works? Let's treat them as a showcase.'

We decided to put on a totally awesome show for our simultaneous Gas Works debut and Attic showcase. Tom was bringing Al Mair, president of Attic, with him. If we smoked both of them, we might get ourselves a deal.

We had it all planned. After playing a super-tight set, the show would climax with our flash bombs exploding as Lips played his solo. Other bands had flash bombs, but they were professionally made lame-ass bombs compared to our homemade bombs stuffed with tea leaves for extra sparkles. Of one thing we could be sure: Tom and Al would never have seen anything like our bombs.

The set went very well. Then the crucial moment arrived. Lips was about to launch into his solo on 'Ooh Baby'. At this point he would usually jump down from the stage into the audience as behind him the pyrotechnics exploded in a flash of sparkles.

The seconds counted down to Lips's big moment. Then, perfectly on cue, Lips leaped forward at exactly the same moment as the bombs exploded. Perhaps it was because it was our first time in a new and larger venue, but one of the bombs had been positioned in the wrong place. Instead of leaping through the gap between the two bombs, Lips stepped directly over one of the bombs as it detonated.

When the smoke cleared, Lips found himself standing directly in front of Al Mair, an acrid burning smell surrounding them and only one thought in his mind: Like . . . oh fuck.

Lips concentrated on his solo, and then as his guitar wailed he stole a glance at his arm. All the hairs had burned off. That explained the smell of burning hair. Then he realized it wasn't just his arm hairs that had been fried. His head hair had also gone up in flames. In more ways than one, Lips was on fire that night.

When we came off stage, we assessed the damage. Fortunately only Lips's hair was burned. His skin was unharmed. Nearby Tom was waiting with Al.

'Lips, that was fucking awesome,' said Al. 'A fucking great show.'

Tom turned to Bruce Wilson, our booking agent at that time. 'If you haven't got fifty grand invested in this band, you are out of your fucking mind. They are gonna be fucking *huge*.'

Clearly we'd blown Al and Tom away. We'd smoked the guys.

Tom was already pumped up about us from our record, but he couldn't sign anything without the big guy's approval, so it was a great help that Al had seen us perform. Tom, a down-to-earth guy who championed bands, was in the business because he loved music and musicians. By contrast, Al was motivated by only one thing. He was a shrewd and cold-hearted businessman interested only in the bottom line. We had to respect him for that but it meant that without Al's approval, Tom's enthusiasm was worthless.

'I like you guys.' Al looked us up and down, and then extended a hand. 'You guys have got yourselves a record deal.'

'Like . . . fuck, man.' The smile on Lips's face said it all. We'd arrived. We'd got signed. 'Like . . . fucking wow.'

'Come into the office next week,' said Al. 'We'll get some words together for the contract.'

The meeting the next week was short, but not that sweet. Instead of meeting with Al Mair, we sat down with a lawyer who was handling the deal. His opening words laid out the conditions.

'We're not going to negotiate.'

'What, man?' As far as I was aware, we'd not even seen a contract, so there was nothing for us to negotiate over. 'What do you mean?'

'There is going to be no negotiation.'

'Right . . .' Lips was just as bewildered as me. 'What does that mean?'

'You sign it or you forget about a deal.'

'So what are the terms?'

'You become their property. And whatever you give them belongs to them.'

'For how long?'

'For ever.'

It wasn't all bad. Attic was going to repackage our first Lips album and distribute it. For that we'd get an advance of ten thousand dollars. Given that we'd already recouped all our production and printing costs by selling the record at our gigs, that ten thousand was pure profit. Well, not exactly profit as it was an advance against our royalty earnings, so we'd have to repay it through our sales, but it was like an interest-free ten-thousand-dollar loan, only in our naivety we didn't see it that way at that time. The deal was a typical old-school recording contract, designed in such a way that unless a miracle occurred the artist could never repay the advance. But we were young guys and we didn't realize the full implications of what we were about to sign. We didn't realize that we could be in debt to the record company for ever. At that moment, only one thing was apparent to us: We've got a record deal, they've given us ten grand, so let's fucking party.

'This is great,' said Squirrely. 'Ten big ones – that's fucking great.'

'It's a goddam record deal,' said Dix. 'What more do we want?'

And it did feel that way. We were going to make a few more albums with Attic, so this was just the beginning. It felt like the future was ours. Things were really happening. Everything we'd dreamed about had come true. We'd been only a club band, but the buzz had got loud enough and the following had got big enough to attract a label. And now these guys were going to distribute our Lips album right across Canada. It seemed like a beautiful thing. And we'd done it all on our own.

We used the ten-grand advance to pay off the loan on our sound and lighting equipment and to buy some new musical equipment. After those expenses, very little was left.

With the contract signed, we went to meet the Attic execs in their offices. Tom Williams led the discussions.

'Awesome to have you guys on board.' Tom smiled. 'Now, it's all good and everything, but the name of your band. Lips . . . I don't know. It doesn't really describe your music. Lips could be anything. It's just not heavy metal . . .'

There were several other bands with Lips in their name, said Tom. Like Horslips and Lips Inc. 'There's too much confusion here. You guys better go home and think of a really good name. Try to come up with something that represents what you are.'

A few nights later we were in Cobourg, playing a gig in a hotel and trying to think of new names.

'Ramrod?'

No response.

'Jackhammer?'

'*No!*' I really hated that one.

I wrote a list of words on a pad, hoping to stumble upon a cool name, and then I got it.

'How about Anvil?'

'Hmm.'

'You know what?' I quite liked it. 'It sounds . . . it's got the right shape. I mean, it's a big bit of heavy metal.'

Squirrely interjected. 'Think about it. Our first album: Lips, *Hard'N'Heavy*. OK? Now: Anvil, *Hard and Heavy . . .*'

'Fuck, that really works.' It sounded right to me. 'That really works.'

'It makes like total sense . . . Anvil.' Lips was very enthusiastic. 'This is heavy metal, man. This is a heavy thing. And you smash metal . . . you hammer it. Anvil? It rocks.'

I wasn't particularly fond of it at first because I

wondered if the average person knew what an anvil was. Then I realized that didn't matter. For those people it would be mysterious. And when they found out what an anvil was then they'd immediately associate it with heavy metal. That was ideal.

We asked for a meeting with the label to discuss the name. Tom was waiting for us.

'Hey, guys.' Tom looked excited as he stuck out his hand. 'I've been thinking of a name.'

'Oh, OK.'

'Boil the Haggis.'

Silence. 'Er . . .' Then we cracked up.

'You guys . . .' Tom looked awkward. 'Boil the Haggis . . . just think about it.'

'Haggis?' Lips's eyes were big. 'What the fuck . . .'

'You don't like Boil the Haggis? I thought it was awesome. OK. Whaddya got?'

'We're gonna call the band Anvil.'

Tom immediately got it. 'That's great.' He loved it. 'That's an inanimate object. That's gonna work. Amazing.'

Like us, Tom had instantly fallen in love with the name. It *meant* heavy metal. It was fucking genius.

LIPS: Things moved fast after we signed with Attic. The label put out a press release saying we'd signed with them and mentioning that we were about to tour

Canada with Girlschool and our menagerie of gerbils, hamsters and a tarantula. But the first and most awesomely cool thing of all was that we were asked to open for Motörhead in Toronto.

Motörhead had just released *Ace Of Spades* and were at an absolute creative peak. We were big fans and in total awe of them. Before the show I went in search of Lemmy, but knowing him only by his hard partying reputation, I had no idea what to expect.

'Hey, Lemmy, man.' It was a home show, so I was with my family. 'This is my girlfriend Lee.'

Lemmy smiled, leaned forward and took Lee's hand. 'Hello, madam,' he said. Then he lifted Lee's hand to his lips and kissed it.

Lee didn't say anything, but I knew what she was thinking. She was totally like: Oh my God. As for me, I just freaked out. Lemmy was such a gentleman. Like: oh fuck, that was quite the opposite of what I had expected.

The gig was amazing, a home crowd that knew us well and gave us massive support. It went great. And everyone from Motörhead, the crew and the band, were really good people who couldn't do enough to help us. They let us use their backline – their drum kit and speaker stacks – and their monitors. We could hear what we were playing loud and clear, which much smaller, less significant bands had often denied us.

After the gig, Lindsay Gillespie, one of the execs from Attic, was waiting for us.

'Hey, guys!' Lindsay waved at us. 'Come and have a look at this. Here's what your record is going to look like.'

Lindsay held up a record sleeve. It looked very different from the Lips cover, which been a simple red lipstick imprint of a pair of lips on a white background with the band's name imposed in typewriter script.

I stood back and took it all in. The front cover had a black anvil on a black chain-bedecked plinth being struck by a hammer that sent orange sparks flying over the red background. With Anvil in red letters embossed on the front of the anvil, it looked much stronger than our old cover. On the back were four pictures of us live on stage at the Gas Works. I thought the lettering was a bit corny, but otherwise it was a totally cool cover.

Two weeks later, the album came out and because of Attic's backing, it received much more attention than the Lips edition of *Hard'N'Heavy*. It was very well received. Reviews came in from America, Europe and Japan saying that the music was fresh and innovative and the playing was awesome. We got on the cover of *Arrdshok*, a Dutch metal magazine. When I saw that and realized that people in Holland and England, the birthplace of heavy metal, liked *Hard'N'Heavy*, to me it was like wow.

At last we felt like we were making it, that we were getting discovered and that all our work was paying off. After years of small-minded people saying the band sucked or the songs weren't any good, now we had proof that other people recognized the energy and power of our music. Things were moving forward.

Possibly the biggest indication that we were doing something right came from some of the other bands in Toronto, who didn't hide their envy and jealousy of our success or our approach of not compromising our sound and approach to get a deal. We got a lot of snobbery from other bands, who thought their progressive rock was more sophisticated than our music, which they called primitive dinosaur rock. It was the same as the arguments that Robb and I had endured on school buses over whether Emerson, Lake & Palmer were better than Black Sabbath. Now that I had released an album through Canada's largest independent label, I didn't give a fuck. What the hell did they know? I listened to Black Sabbath and heaviness and I knew it was cool. I didn't care.

A short while after playing with Motörhead, Attic sent us out on the road with Girlschool. The tour took us right across Canada and we did it all by road. Girlschool's album *Hit And Run* had gone gold in Canada and there was a feeling that they were at their peak with some good relevant songs, the feel of which had an influence on the tracks we had already begun writing for the next album. As for the girls, they were totally cool. We became very good friends and are still friends to this day. Robbo and I recognized that Denise Dufort and Kim McAuliffe were our female counterparts. Like us, they were drummer and lead guitarist-vocalist. And like us, they'd vowed to rock together for ever. Nothing would ever make them stop.

It was our first tour of larger venues, mainly theatres with capacities up to two thousand people. By our standards, it was a sedate and tame tour backstage, maybe because we were touring with an all-female band. We spent a lot of time hanging out with Girlschool in their dressing room, just getting to know each other. As for the audience, we could tell most of them were not really there for us. Robbo remembers the gigs going down pretty good, but I was never able to get over the fact that as a support act we didn't get encores. That made the audience feel unresponsive towards us, but it was good exposure for us and the label was backing it fully.

After the tour we continued playing one-off gigs wherever they would have us. At every one of them we could sense the album was having an impact. Tickets sold out quickly and we were greeted on stage with a roar in every venue. Then, at a high school in Hamilton, some kids presented us with an anvil that they'd painted

Right: Born to rock. At sixteen Robb knew drumming was his destiny.

Below left: Robb with his parents, already itching to get out of his bow tie.

Below right: Robb as a dad with his son Tyler.

Bottom: Robb's wife Jane with their beloved terrier Sacha – named after their long-lost friend Teabag.

Above: Lips – such an angelic-looking baby.

Right: By 1976 Steve was becoming the Lips we know and love.

Left: A well-behaved young Jewish boy called Steve. Where did it all go wrong?

Right: Lips (middle) with the rest of the Kudlow family.

Below: Lips aged fifteen.

Above: Starting out with Gravestone – Lips' and Robb's first band.

Below: The Anvil of the eighties discovered that travelling with a drum kit wasn't always easy. From the left: Squirrely, Robb, Lips and Dix.

Right: Before they became Anvil and got hard and heavy, there were the Lips years. Dix (left), Squirrely (middle), Robb (far right), Lips (sitting).

Above and left: Babe magnet Dave Allison aka Squirrely illustrates how he earnt his nickname by showing off his nuts.

Right: Dix – a smiling and dependable rock legend.

Left: A tube photo of Sacha taken the day he met Anvil at the Marquee.

Below: Sacha with his gorgeous French girlfriend Alexandra.

Hanging out with the band.

Left: Robb and Sacha at Yorkdale Shopping Centre in Toronto.

Below: Lips and Sacha on a tour of Canadian hockey arenas in summer 1985.

Left: David Krebs, metal manager extraordinaire (middle) with Dee Snider of Twisted Sister (left) and Robb (right).

Below left: Phil Harvey with Dix (right).

Below right: Dix surrounded by adoring fans.

Bottom: Robb doing what he does best.

with the band's logo as it appeared on the cover of *Hard'N'Heavy*.

'We ripped this off from the school metal shop,' the kids said proudly. 'It's an honour to meet you guys.'

From that day, that anvil joined the menagerie of pets and travelled everywhere with us. It was always put on the drum riser at gigs and appeared on the cover of several albums. The roadies would sometimes get tired of hauling it around – it weighed 95 lbs – and once, after a gig in Montreal, they threw it off the top of our tour truck, but it made such a huge hole in the pavement that they couldn't leave it there. Any cop would have worked it out immediately. A hole about a foot deep with an anvil painted with the word Anvil at its centre: guess who did it?

One of the sweetest moments following the release of the first album came when we were asked back to the Gas Works and we were able to dictate the terms. First, we would play only original music. No covers. Second, we would play only one set and we would have an opening band. Anvil was the first metal band in Canada to impose those kinds of conditions and after that we insisted on the same conditions at every club and bar venue. Some venues baulked at our method, so we told them they'd still be getting the three forty-five-minute sets that they'd been used to for years, but now the first set would be played by a support band, and the second and third sets would be rolled into one long set played by Anvil. The clubs soon embraced our direction and the audiences thought it was totally cool. So when we returned to the Gas Works with Kraken as support, we totally rode the place.

Other bands before us had tried similar tactics, such as insisting on only playing original material, but the system had crushed them. We'd stuck to our guns, fought the system and we'd won. We'd changed things for all the bands that followed in our wake. That's the truth, and it's something of which we could always be proud.

7 METAL ON METAL

ROBB: While touring venues in Ontario, we started writing the songs for our so-called 'difficult second album', the one we were convinced would be our big breakthrough – the moment when the whole world would wake up to the majesty of Anvil.

Whenever there was a gap of a few days between dates on the road, we'd rent a rehearsal space to try out new tracks. We played some at gigs in Quebec and they all went down well even though the audiences had never heard them before. Reassured by the audience response, we gradually put together a demo tape with ten tracks for the next album and sent it to Tom Williams, who called us into the Attic offices.

'I really like your demos, man.' Tom was super enthusiastic. 'I really like that song "Sex Sex Sex".'

'No,' said Lips. 'It's "Six Six Six".'

'I don't care what *you* call it. *"Sex Sex Sex"* – do you like that one?'

'Yeah . . . erm . . .'

'I got a really good idea. There's this English producer that I'm looking at. He produced Tygers of Pan Tang, he's just finished Thin Lizzy . . .'

'We know . . .' This sounded exciting. 'We know who he is.'

'. . . Judas Priest . . .'

'We know him. We know him.'

'What do you think?' Tom handed over some records. 'Listen to these. This guy could be right for you.'

This guy was Chris 'CT' Tsangarides. We'd already heard of him as he was building up an awesome reputation as a producer of the new wave of British heavy metal bands. We auditioned the records and all got hooked.

'Fuck, Lips,' I said. 'These records sound pretty fucking good.'

Lips agreed, so we went back to Tom and told him our thoughts.

'Whaddya think, Robb?'

'Yeah.' I nodded. 'Fucking right.'

'And you, Lips?'

'Fucking right. We're getting him, man.'

'Sure.' Tom was all smiles. 'We want to connect you with him for your next project. We're completely up for it.'

This was awesome. Before the contract we'd had to do everything ourselves. We'd hired the studio, produced the record, mixed it and put it out. Now producers were vying to work with us. CT flew over and we met him at Attic Records. We chatted about the excitement of making a record and that he was English and English producers were the hottest around at the time. And that he wanted to work with Anvil. I was in total awe.

CT was a totally cool guy, really pleasant and likeable. We were all about the same age and we hit it off right away. We were into the same music, musicians, songs and production values. And it was a big thing for CT too. He'd produced plenty of British bands, but we were his first North American gig. He was totally up for it. I left the meeting buzzing with positive energy, feeling gung-ho like crazy.

'Lips, this is just fucking awesome.'

'Totally, Gaze. We are going to get produced by an English producer! We've always kind of sounded English, so thank fuck we are going to get to do it with the real guy.'

Then we started making the album and it went very quickly. No trouble, no bullshit, twenty-one days from start to finish. *Metal On Metal*. Bang. Done.

It was a total learning experience. CT taught us everything about how to produce music and what it was like to work with a creative producer. He got amazing performances out of Lips in particular. It couldn't have gone better. It was like magic.

We'd gone into the studio with fourteen songs, all of which we recorded before narrowing down the selection to ten for the record. Lips and I knew what kind of sound we wanted – 'We gotta go harder,' we kept saying – and CT saw it in exactly the same way. He was really big on cranking up the bass drums to blow the speakers out. It was a big deal to him.

'Look at those twenty-eights.' CT was pointing at my 28-inch bass drums. 'Man, those twenty-eights are smoking.'

Meanwhile the fuses were blowing in the speakers.

CT also brought in things that were totally new to us, like a vocoder and a technique for building guitar vortexes. He had a huge imagination for sound and would devise ways to create new effects. For the *Metal On Metal* title track he found a manhole cover in the bay at the back of the studio and had us bang it with a hammer. Initially I was doubtful, but CT got me to go for it.

'Hey, look, give it a whack.' CT showed me how he wanted me to hit it. 'Robb, man, it's going to work. Fucking go for it.'

And the next thing I knew, I was doing it. And it worked. What was really awesome was that despite all these new production techniques, CT brought the record in super fast. In part that was because we'd been playing the songs at gigs before going into the studio and the material was pretty honed. Lips had the lyrics well memorized, so he recorded his contribution to a lot of the tracks in one take. The drums took us a few days, Lips sang everything in a couple more days, and we took a few days to play all the overdubs. Then CT put on all the special effects, creating lots of cool sounds, mixed the record and we delivered it. All in three weeks.

When we were finished we held a listening party at the studio with the record company. They all came and appraised the record. I was totally into this gig and thought we had an awesome record, but we still had to convince the execs from Attic.

As the first few tracks played, I watched the guys for their reactions. There were a lot of happy faces, but the one who was most blown away was Tom Williams. He looked so happy. He always thought he had signed a fucking good band, that we had something special. Now he knew it for sure.

I could see they were loving it. By 'Stop Me', the third song on the album, they were blown away. And the good stuff kept on coming, right through to the last track, Tom's favourite, '666'. At the end, everyone applauded.

'This is fucking awesome, guys.' Al Mair was on his feet, standing beside the mixing desk. 'We are going to reach out with this.' Then he gave some details of how they would market it. He was totally hyped.

Two months later the record came out to universally good reviews.

LIPS: The title track of *Metal On Metal* became our first minor hit, much to my surprise as it's in discord and was never meant to be a commercial song. Instead I always saw it as the song that set out my musical philosophy – one of no compromise for commerciality – so my jaw dropped when I first heard it on the radio.

I was driving in my car with the radio tuned to an AM station that usually played sickly commercial pop. Out of nowhere I heard what sounded like Robb hammering the manhole cover at the start of 'Metal On Metal'. A few seconds later my riff jumped in and then the lyrics.

Metal on metal
It's what I crave
The louder the better
I'll turn in my grave
Metal on metal
Ears start to bleed
Cranking it up
Fulfilling my need

I flipped out. I couldn't believe what I was hearing. On an AM station of all places. I stopped the car to phone Robbo.

'Gaze, man. You won't fucking believe it. I just heard "Metal On Metal" on fucking 890 Hamilton. I thought I was dreaming, man. But the car only had AM radio in it.'

It was completely shocking. There'd been no orchestrated marketing campaign. We just made music and now it was on the radio. Maybe it was a sign that heavy rock was starting to creep into the mainstream. Whatever the reason, it felt strange to have a song that was so personal to me blaring out of a car radio.

With its dirty and nasty sound and its uncompromising lyrics, 'Metal On Metal' represented my inner philosophy. It laid out my manifesto: heavy metal will never go away; I am its messenger and I will preach it for ever. It says to the listener that I really have no choice but to follow the heavy metal creed and that I can't turn my back on what I've started.

I was serious about the message in 'Metal On Metal'. My belief was that we should only accept success on our own terms. If that meant Anvil had to remain underground for fifteen albums before we finally made it, then that was fine with me. We had to stay hardcore. Commercialization too soon would ruin everything. I could see no sense in achieving success on our third or fourth album because everything would be downhill from there.

This attitude meant that I would at times write crazy explicit lyrics for a song that was musically strong with a catchy riff. I reasoned that if it worked for bands like Poison, it ought to work for Anvil too, especially if we combined sexual innuendo with really heavy music. Songs like 'Show Me Your Tits' or 'Mad Dog' were prime examples. And it meant that if we achieved success, it would be on my terms. I would be loved for what I really did, not for what I was prepared to do.

I believed success should happen by accident as that was the only way to avoid compromising our sound. Making it big meant the beginning of the end. So when I heard 'Metal On Metal' on the radio, I was worried. Radio play represented success. The question was had we achieved it by compromise or by accident?

The best songs always come quick and simple. It might be a cliché because every artist says it, but that's because it's the truth. So I'm going to say it too. Those first moments of inspiration when you pick up your instrument are the moments of pure artistic creation.

The sound of the 'Metal On Metal' riff only came about because the tone on my Flying V was shut off when I picked it up. Call it a moment of inspiration or call it the product of the subconscious, but it's when the artist is not aware of their actions that they create their greatest works.

The first thing I did was play an F chord, the lowest bar chord that you can play on the guitar. And then, for whatever reason, I just slid the chord up the fretboard and put my finger down. Immediately it sounded awesome. Wow, that's really cool, I thought. Then I went and repeated it. Holy Christ, what is that? I wondered. I liked it. It sounded like a buzz saw. And immediately I could hear the song in my head: 'Metal On Metal'. It just sounded that way, so I played it again for the rest of the band.

'That sounds like metal on metal. Listen to it, guys. We gotta write something called "Metal On Metal". We can make it an anthem about heavy metal and how much we love it.'

So that's what we did.

Robb had a suggestion. 'We should start every verse with *"metal on metal"*.'

'Yeah OK . . . I guess we could do that.' So we started thinking. I went: ' *"It's the only way – to hell with tomorrow. Let's live for today."* OK. That will be the model. OK?'

And everyone was like: Hey, we got something going here. The song got written in ten minutes. Fifteen minutes max. Fully realized in pure innocence. We just felt good and we went with it. The four of us guys, standing around, throwing ideas around, suggesting stuff and saying different things.

To this day I think we hit on a fundamental truth in 'Metal On Metal' about the heavy metal fight. Metal has always been trying to fight its way into the mainstream, but it never really wins. If it does win, the victory doesn't last long. And we captured the essence of that heavy metal fight on *Metal On Metal*. It's tough. It's mean. And you've always got shit going against you. Nothing could make more sense than a song by Anvil called 'Metal On Metal'. What *could* make more sense than that? Nothing.

As for the other tracks on the album, 'Mothra' was written at Black Lake in Quebec. We were in a rundown hotel and Dix was partying with a girl we called the rock 'n' roll nurse. I wanted to give him privacy so I went over to Robbo's room. Squirrely was already sleeping, but Bess and Robb were awake. We grabbed guitars and the three of us wrote the song. Robb came up with the riff, but, being a drummer, his approach was like nothing anyone had ever seen. That's why the chord progression was so complicated. It also had the unique distinction of being played by me with a vibrator instead of a plectrum. As for the lyrics, we liked the idea of something really heavy like a destructive monster such as Godzilla.

'Stop Me' was classic Squirrely. The lyrics made that obvious.

You come backstage to talk a while
I wanna party 'cause that's my style
Young and tight you're what I need
Your fantasies I wanna feed
So come with me, back to my place
You know you've got such a pretty face
I'll show you how it is to be
Hanging around with a rocker like me

I could never write those kinds of lyrics. It came from the same place as Squirrely's comment that he sold to the pussy and we sold to the guys. On the other hand, the instrumental 'March Of The Crabs' was completely my idea. I wasn't really sure what to call it until I noticed the way my fingers crept along the fretboard like a crab.

'Jackhammer' was devised when we were playing a club in Arvida, Quebec. I was sitting on the edge of the stage when I came up with a riff that could go in a complete cycle. The following gig was in Ottawa and Ian was in the next bed to me with a girl he'd picked up. On the way back from the club to the hotel she'd been in the back seat of the car rubbing everybody. Cocks in both hands. And when Ian had got her back to our shared bedroom, she'd kept me awake all night going at it. When I woke up in the morning, the chick still had a mouthful. Realizing I was awake, she looked up at me.

'Too bad you missed us fucking.'

It was nine in the morning and we'd come off stage at three, so I was really pissed off.

'Not only do you fuckin' keep me up all night, but when I finally fall asleep, you fuckin' wake me up again only to tell me that? Fuck you.'

I got up, went next door to Robb and Squirrely's room and let rip.

'She fuckin' kept me awake all fuckin' night, squealin' like a fuckin' pig.'

Squirrely sat up in his bed. 'Hey, let's start writing this shit down.'

'What the fuck you doin', man?' I was raging and I couldn't believe Squirrely wanted to take notes. 'What the fuck you doin'?'

I left the room. Twenty minutes later I returned to find Robb and Squirrely had all the lyrics to 'Jackhammer'. Squirrely said the lyrics fitted the holes in the song perfectly.

'Oh really?' I was surprised. 'OK. Let me see.'

I burst out laughing. It was almost everything I'd said, but it was very funny. We rehearsed the song over the next couple of days and then, when we were on stage, I announced it as the first song.

'This is about Joan. Jackhammer Joan.'

As the set went on, I noticed Jackhammer Joan was in the audience. And she looked pissed off. Really fucking pissed off. She went next door, bought a dozen eggs from the variety store, returned to the club and started throwing them at me while I was playing. Given the lyrics, it's not that surprising.

In the car you're ready to move
In the back seat you start to groove
Right turn, left turn, got the boys in both hands
Playin' in stereo like you do with most bands
Unlocking the door
I can tell you can't wait
Seekin' power rockin'
Girl you love to vibrate
Can't get to sleep 'cause I hear you squealin'
Like a stuck little pig you love the feelin'

The next track, 'Heat Sink', was an attempt to write a song like 'Highway Star' by Deep Purple. Having taken electronics at school, I knew a heat sink was something that drew away heat from transistors, but I thought it might also sound sexual. The lyrics were a collaborative effort. 'Tag Team' was about some of the crazy shit that happened on the road. I thought I could write about gang bangs and orgies as if they were like tag wrestling, with each man taking their turn with the chick.

The lyrics to 'Scenery' were inspired by two groupies we met when we went across Canada with Girlschool. These groupies were full of attitude. They boasted, 'I could fuck better guys than you guys,' and I was pretty disgusted by it.

> *You were standing in your favourite light*
> *You thought you were hot, thought that you*
>   *were tight*
> *I've seen you and I know your type*
> *I know you'll be at the party tonight*
> *Scenery, that's all you are to me*

The music for the next track, 'Tease Me Please Me', was a joint collaboration from the entire band, but Robb came up with the lyrics having heard me say it to Lee when he was living at our apartment. And '666' was an attempt to be dark and heavy.

When it was released, *Metal On Metal* changed everything for us. Everyone wanted a piece of Anvil and everyone wanted to tell us how awesome they thought the record was. Other musicians and bands were inspired by it. The press came banging on our door, wanting interviews and pictures. We ended up on the front cover of *Sounds* and Robbo was voted the best drummer in the world by *Drum* magazine. The whole world opened up to us. *Metal On Metal* established us as a band.

But although our music was reviewed with respect, some of the comments suggested that we wouldn't be able to keep it up and that *Metal On Metal* would be a one-off. They thought it was too good to be sustained. But Robbo and I knew that *Metal On Metal* was just the beginning. We knew we could turn it up to eleven. To twelve. For fuck's sake, we knew we could turn it up to twenty.

Metal On Metal turned us into an international act and got us on to the books of the Agency Group, a proper agency for bands. Everything changed. We played more gigs, better gigs and higher paying gigs. We didn't have to fight for them. They were just handed to us. In a couple of years we'd gone from class-B clubs with a capacity of maybe 150 to class-A clubs that held five hundred when full. Now we were playing concert halls and arenas with audiences of ten thousand. People wanted to see Anvil. The word was out that we were a great band and an awesome live act.

We were asked to support Iron Maiden on a tour of Canada. We arrived in Ottawa for the first of five gigs. Looking out at the auditorium at the Ottawa Pacific Center, an ice-hockey rink, was a pretty nerve-racking experience. While Robbo and I were gazing at the rows of empty seats, talking to a couple from America that followed Iron Maiden around, I spotted Steve Harris, the founder, bassist and songwriter of Iron Maiden, ambling around the other side of the rink. Then I realized he's walking towards me. My first thought was: Oh my fucking God, he's coming to talk to me, does he know who I am?

'Are you the guy from the support band? From Anvil?'

'Er, yes.'

'I just wanted to ask you something. You guys got a song called "Six Six Six"?'

'Yeah. It's on our new album.'

'That's amazing. You know the name of our next album is *Number Of The Beast*?'

'What?' I was open-mouthed. What a coincidence. 'That is really weird.'

We immediately hit it off. Steve was a really down-to-earth kind of guy. 'Fuck, man,' I said. 'I'm a big fan of your band.' It was quite shocking to meet someone so similar to me from another band. 'You know why it's called "Six Six Six"?'

'No, mate.'

I explained that the title came from the musical arrangement. In the middle of the song the beat changes from four beats to the bar to six beats to the bar for three bars. When we'd been in the studio, I'd explained it to the band as: 'The first one is four and then it's six, six, six.' As soon as I said it, we knew what to call the song. What we didn't know then was that the musical style of '666' would become the blueprint for speed metal. At the time it was unique, but within a year, we'd hear dozens of tracks like it.

ROBB: Touring with Iron Maiden was a major break-through for us, not because we'd not supported a band as big as Maiden before, but because we blew them off stage in Toronto. We were on our home ground and just as many people in the audience were there to see us as Iron Maiden, but it was still a difficult thing for them to take. *Anvil Smashes British Headliners* said the banners in the press.

It was particularly satisfying as we weren't a typically Canadian band and had always associated ourselves more with British music, particularly the new wave of British heavy metal. This association with the élite of British heavy metal did us a lot of favours and led to us being invited to play some dates in New Jersey.

We'd never played outside Canada – hell, we hadn't played that much outside Quebec and Ontario – so the invitation to travel down to New Jersey was an awesome shot from the dark.

John Zazula, known to everyone on the heavy metal scene as Jonny Z, was a heavy rock überfan who ran an independent metal record store called Rock'n'Roll Heaven at a flea market in East Brunswick near the New Jersey turnpike. Like many of the records that Jonny Z stocked, *Metal On Metal* was sold as an import. After a while, Jonny noticed that he kept selling out of it and ordering more, so out of the blue he called us up.

'Hey, boys, I want to put a concert on here at the flea market. I'm selling fucking mega records here and you got fans here. I want to bring you down.'

With an offer like that, how could we refuse? The stage was set up in a massive open area at the centre of the flea market. We were expecting maybe one hundred people to drop by. That night more than 1,500 people turned up, a complete fucking freak-out beyond anything we had ever seen for an underground gig on that level.

Playing on stage that night was a total what-the-fuck-holy-Christ experience. We didn't know we had so many fans in the States, but it was obvious the crowd was there primarily for us and that they loved us. They had the record and they knew all the songs.

After the show, Jonny was full on about the electricity, the fire and the eye of the tiger, as he put it, of our performance. He took Lips and me aside.

'Do you realize what you're on the verge of, what you're bringing to the market?'

I knew something awesome was happening that

night, but not quite what Jonny Z was freaked out about.

'You're bringing metal to the United States. This is a legendary moment. We're living in a really serious time and place. And you guys are at the front of it.'

After that night, Jonny would say that what he'd seen when we were on stage, the way the crowd had reacted to our type of music, had persuaded him of 'what I had to do in my journey'. The next year the route of that journey became clearer when Jonny signed Metallica and Anthrax to his label, a major step in the emergence of the big four of speed metal.

A few months after our first visit, things on the New Jersey metal scene began to escalate and we returned to do a bunch of dates with Raven, from England, and Riot, a New York band. In the crowd that night was an eighteen-year-old Scott Ian, the founder and rhythm guitarist of Anthrax.

But on that night in East Brunswick, we had no idea that we were in the midst of a pivotal change. It might have been ground-breaking shit, but we were just stoked to be playing in the States for the first time and meeting Jonny's friends Jethro, Rockin' Ray and Metal Joe when we stayed at his house to save dough. They were totally dedicated metal fans from Oldbridge, New Jersey, part of a movement of enthusiasts called the Oldbridge Metal Militia. They helped out by providing sleeping places to visiting musicians and ended up becoming friends to many of the bands at that time. Metal Joe was a really big, loud guy full of enthusiasm. Ray was much slimmer and quieter. Jethro was larger than life in both physique and personality. We had some totally awesome times with these three guys.

Jonny Z was extremely active in getting the new wave of heavy metal rolling, bringing in lots of groups. It was soon totally massive in the New York and New Jersey area and we were getting invitations to play clubs, other concerts and the Headbangers Hallowe'en gig.

Now, whenever we visited, we'd stay with Rockin' Ray or Metal Joe and it would be a total party from start to finish. That whole Metal Militia scene was really over the top, everyone banging hot chicks and doing New Jersey crank, a coarse homemade drug. Rumours had it that crank was derived from arsenic or rat poison, but really it was a form of speed made in bathtubs. As for the American groupies, they made their Canadian sisters look like nuns. Everything was far more plentiful, far more open, far wilder. It was fucking crazy. We'd go to a gig and there'd be tons of girls all dressed up. It was pretty cool.

After playing a gig with Raven, we were back at Rockin' Ray's house. Dix had brought back some chick who he said would faint when she reached orgasm. We couldn't fucking believe it, but the next day we were down in Rockin' Ray's basement, working out and doing shit. Lips was playing with the treadmill and talking to Rob 'Wacko' Hunter, the drummer with Raven, when Dix started up with the chick on one of the workout mats. The cry soon went round.

'Dix is on the mat.' This was something we all wanted to see. 'He's got her on the mat!'

The other guys in Raven had just come down the stairs and, by the looks on their faces, they were struggling to believe what they were seeing. A couple of guys were lifting weights, Lips was running on the treadmill, another couple of guys were doing stretching exercises, and right beside them this guy was fucking a chick. Eventually the chick passed out and Dix got off.

'See?' Dix was walking around, pointing at the chick on the floor. She was totally out cold. 'See? Look, guys. What did I tell you?'

We're all looking at her, awed and going like: What the fuck? After a couple of minutes, the chick came round. It was totally freaky and awesome. None of us had ever seen anything like it. You fuck a chick and she blacks out when she comes? How totally fucking rock 'n' roll is that?

LIPS: Between the first and second trips to New Jersey, our record company sent us to England on a trip that would prove life-changing.

Metal On Metal had made such a big splash in the music press that Attic agreed to finance a trip to the Monsters of Rock festival at Castle Donnington in the north of England, followed ten days later by two dates at the legendary Marquee Club in London. It was an awesome honour to be asked to play at Donnington. Only in its third year, the festival had already played host to several of our heroes, including Judas Priest, AC/DC and Whitesnake. This year we were bottom of a bill headed by Status Quo, a privilege that cost us thirty thousand dollars. It seemed like a lot of money, but we were already on the red line with Attic for life, so another thirty grand wasn't going to make a whole heap of shit difference.

The plane to England landed at about six o'clock in the morning, but I didn't care. I was totally wide awake, walking around, trying to come to terms with the cool fact that I was in England. It was difficult to take it all in: our record was doing well; we'd just played a gig in the States for the first time; and now we were in fucking England. I was starting to feel like we were actually getting somewhere, the four of us rising as a brotherhood.

It was quite a shock to find ourselves going to a big English metal festival, kind of like: Fuck me, check this out, what are we doing here? But it was only when we arrived at Castle Donnington that the missile of awareness penetrated my consciousness. Seventy thousand people were in attendance. It was huge.

We went to our dressing room, a Portakabin, and checked in. Then Robbo and I went up to the stage to check out the size of the festival. It was a big fucking space in front of an immense fucking crowd – a total sea of people – and we were the first band who had to face them: the opening band, due on stage at one o'clock; an obscure band from Canada, not widely known; and no one before us to warm up the crowd. Oh shit. But what was really wild were the clumps of grass and mud all over the stage.

'Holy fucking shit, Lips.' Robbo and I were festival virgins. We'd never seen anything like it. 'What a mess.'

'Brother, I don't think it's been thrown up there. I think people have dragged it up on the bottoms of their shoes.'

It was everywhere, even on the drum rise. Plastic bottles, shit and muck. Robbo went to position his bass drum pedals and adjust his kit. Out of nowhere, hundreds of lumps of mud rained down on him as he crouched beside the drum riser. Now it was obvious the mud hadn't arrived on the stage on people's feet.

Robb ran back to the side of the stage. 'Those fucking bastards. I can't fucking believe it. I mean, what the fuck's the matter?'

We'd never experienced anything like it and Robb was totally distressed. 'You wouldn't fucking believe what's going on out there, Lips. They were fucking throwing shit at me as I was trying to set up my drums. People are throwing *shit* at me!'

But from the backstage vibe, we got the impression that flying mud and shit was nothing unusual. It always happened. We were just unaware of this whole new art form. And when we started to play, it became even more intense. Kicking off into the first song of our set, we were ducking the projectiles. Robb's cymbals got hit with bottles full of fuck knows what. Shit was just flying everywhere as we were playing, making us feel like why the fuck are we fucking doing this?

After the third song, the mud and shit slowed down. By the fifth song it stopped altogether. It had nothing to do with people not liking the band. It was a cultural thing and the more shit we had thrown us, the better it was supposed to be – at least that's what everyone back-stage told us afterwards.

A week later we went to the Reading festival, like the Monsters of Rock at Donnington, another shrine to heavy metal. We weren't playing but we went along to hang out and to watch the bands, which were being headlined by Iron Maiden and the Michael Schenker Group. The backstage area was full of rock stars: people like Gary Moore and Ian Paice. I was talking to Steve Harris and his wife, Lorraine, when I noticed this really hot chick in fishnet stockings.

'Don't go near those boilers.' Lorraine had noticed that the chick had caught my eye. 'Take my advice, Lips. Don't go near those boilers.'

I guess I should have taken Lorraine's warning, but I didn't. Instead I went over to the blonde and got talking. She was kind of attractive, her name was Dawn Crosbie and she was an aspiring singer from a band. And – what can I say? – some stuff happened but nothing that lasted or had any real significance. As far as I was concerned, it amounted to nothing – although like some things that appear insignificant and meaningless at the time, my dalliance with Dawn ended up stinging me in the ass big time. What seemed like harmless fun had long-lasting repercussions.

From Reading we moved on to London, where we were booked to play two nights at the Marquee Club in Wardour Street. This dark, sweaty venue in Soho in the heart of London was a legend in heavy metal circles. Every cool British band had played here. When Robbo and I had first formed Lips, one of my goals had been to play in London in the same places that the Who and the Beatles had played. Now I was there, playing my music in a foreign country. And judging by the fact that both nights were sold out and there were line-ups of headbangers snaking down the street, people liked us.

The gig was awesome. We blew the people away. It was fucking hot and everyone was sweating like pigs.

The energy in the room was totally intense. That night I felt I'd really made it. I felt I was a real rock star. The dream I'd carried since my dad bought me my first guitar had come true. Everything that I wished for had happened.

As I came off stage I was crying. I knew I would never have this moment again. I knew I would spend the rest of my life looking for what had happened that night. I'd made it, but now what? My all-time dream had come true, so what now?

There wasn't much time for reflection or wallowing in my emotions. Backstage was freaking out. People were hassling for our autographs and asking to have their pictures taken with us. The first person I recognized was this totally eccentric English dude we'd met backstage at Donnington when he introduced himself as the Lord of Metal. This dude had just arrived in his Land-Rover from Africa, where he'd gone on safari in a Judas Priest T-shirt. He was seriously aristocratic but appeared to know all the big British rock stars. The Lord of Metal had been with Jimi Hendrix the night before Jimi died, having invited him back to his London pad with three girls to drink tea and smoke hash. Dressed in what he called 'some serious denims' and with long hair around a bald dome, this dude was kind of odd-looking but also totally charming. We didn't know what a lord was or what a lord did, but it didn't matter because we liked him. Actually we didn't know if he was like a real lord at all – the dude might have been like messing with us or 'pulling our leg' as he called it – but he mentioned that his father was a Conservative member of the British Parliament and he talked about going to the House of Lords for a drink. And we later noticed that he was sometimes described as the Honourable Philip Harvey and someone told us that meant he was the son of a viscount or baron. But all this didn't matter because Lord Phil was just a great guy.

I told Lord Phil about my strange mixed feelings about playing the Marquee and how I felt that I was mentally in a completely different place to everyone else, a place of perfect clarity. As I was speaking, a journalist came over and started asking questions.

'Hey, Lips, so how did it go for you?'

'It feels like a dream has come true . . .'

'Right, man. What was that dream?'

'. . . but it also feels like a profound sense of loss.'

'Blimey. Maybe you should explain.'

The interview went on for quite some time. I guess I was so overwhelmed by the profundity of playing the Marquee that I couldn't stop talking about it, but eventually I became aware there was a party going on in the dressing room and I excused myself.

Walking into our changing room, I saw Robb talking

to this puppyish kid with long curly black hair. And this kid could really talk. He was yapping on and on with an amazing sense of humour and no fear of speaking to us rock stars.

'You know that part in "Jackhammer" when you do the two tom-tom rolls and then you do that . . . ah . . . what is that?'

This kid knew his stuff. It was obvious he was a drummer and that he was standing in front of his idol, talking passionately and deeply about our music.

'. . . and then, you know, you do like a . . . what's happening with those bass drums? It sounds like you're doing like four pedals . . .'

Dressed in a denim jacket covered with heavy metal patches, this kid looked like a metal kid but he didn't talk like the other metal kids I'd met at home. He was wearing pants with a studded black belt and pointy boots. He was kind of cool, but he wasn't one of those guys that goes completely quiet when they're standing in front of their idol. He just yakked and yakked with a massive smile and full of enthusiasm.

He told us how he spent all his spare time hanging out with musicians at the Marquee. He knew Gary Barden, lead singer of the Michael Schenker Group, and he'd met Tommy Lee and Vince Neil from Mötley Crüe and the guys from Marillion. He was on first name terms with Ronnie James Dio and the guys from Iron Maiden.

'There's loads more clubs where metal's going on, man. It's all happening at the Bandwagon and the Heavy Metal Disco, and everyone over here knows you guys. *Metal On Metal* just blew up this summer in the UK. I mean, your album is amazing.'

Clearly this kid was totally well connected. Then he told us he knew Lord Phil, as if it would be a surprise that these two highly extrovert London metal fans wouldn't know each other. He had a French girlfriend called Alexandra, whom he'd take to a lot of metal gigs and she knew Lord Phil too. And then the kid changed the subject. He was always doing that, speaking totally fast and leaping around all the time.

'So what are you guys doing in London? Do you know where to go?'

'Hey, man, you wanna show us around?' said Robb. 'Me and Lips wanna get some English clothes. Do you know where we can get some bullet belts? Maybe you could show us some cool English shops?'

'Yeah, sure.' The kid nodded. 'Let's get together. We'll go to Carnaby Street. I'll show you guys round, man.'

'Cool, dude.' Robb had totally clicked with this kid. 'Do you wanna hang out with us? Do you wanna come to our hotel and party with some chicks?'

'Yeah, sure.'

'So how old are you?'

'I'm like fifteen, man.'

'And what's your name, kid?'

'Sacha.' The kid stuck out his hand. 'Sacha Gervasi. Cool to meet you, Robb.'

8 SACHA

ROBB: We never made it back to the hotel with Sacha. The Lord Phil dude put paid to that.

'I'm going to have a party for you guys,' he announced. 'Come back to my place.'

It was some huge fucking place. And some wild fucking party. The house was a mansion in a part of central London called Marylebone. It was full of hippy stuff like all kinds of concoctions and psychedelic mushrooms in jars. When we arrived, the Lord of Metal had changed from his 'serious denims' into silk pyjamas and a fancy dressing gown. Sashaying around the place like a heavy metal Hugh Hefner, he had a small silver box in his hand.

'Have a look in here, Robb.' Lord Phil opened the box carefully. It folded open to reveal hash and grass in one side and a huge pile of coke in the other side.

'Help yourself.'

Like . . . oh fuck.

It seemed that Lord Phil's entire purpose was to hang out with rockers, provide a party space and make sure the vibe was right for the stars of the metal scene. Looking around, I spotted the guys from Motörhead, CT, and Brian Downey and Brian Robertson from Thin Lizzy. While a chick was being introduced to me as Hendrix's last girlfriend, I watched as Phil 'Philthy Animal' Taylor, the drummer with Motörhead, darted in and out from behind a velvet curtain under the stairs. There was a small bed in the little nook and a whole bunch of shit was happening in there. And when Phil came out, Lips disappeared in there with Dawn Crosbie.

And in the middle of it, looking totally at home in spite of his young age, was Sacha. Like Lord Phil, Sacha appeared to know everyone in the room.

Sacha told us about his family. After his parents' divorce his father had left Oxford and moved back to New York, where he was now working as a diplomat for the United Nations. Sacha was still living in the family's gigantic gothic house on Abbey Road with his mother, a Canadian concert pianist from our city, Toronto, but he saw a lot of his dad too. He also told us how he'd got to know Phil Harvey. It seemed Sacha and his girlfriend Alexandra spent a lot of time with Phil. Often they'd turn up, find the door was open, walk in and wait for an hour downstairs in Phil's living room while Phil was upstairs with a couple of girls doing coke. For a kid of fifteen it was paradise. There'd be booze and drugs and rock videos playing. And sometimes Sacha would sit waiting for a while, thinking he and Alexandra were on their own, and then some rock star would stumble out from the nook under the stairs, where he'd been shagging a chick or sleeping off the previous night's excesses.

I was discovering Sacha was a great one for telling stories. He took me into Phil's kitchen, where we sat down at the kind of plastic picnic table that you'd normally take camping.

'The last time I was sitting here' – Sacha pointed at the table – 'it was a Sunday afternoon and Phil and I were smoking weed when a VW camper van pulled up right outside the kitchen window. So Phil goes to the van and opens the door and this guy comes in. He's got big bushy hair covering his face and he's like clearly stoned. He's got baseball sneakers with holes in them, holes in his jeans and he kind of smells.

'So this guy sits down and I say hello and we're just rolling this big joint and we're getting high. I'm like as high as a fucking kite, just reaching the apogee of my highness, when the guy from the camper van pulls back his hair and I realize it's Jimmy fucking Page.'

'No way.'

'Believe it, dude. Of Led fucking Zeppelin!'

'Like . . . wow.'

'It was the most insane moment. There I was sitting at this very table with Jimmy Page getting fucking blasted out of my mind.'

'Insane, man.'

Sacha smiled. 'Like totally. I tell you, Phil knows everyone.'

In the summer, Lord Phil would have barbecues on his roof terrace. Sacha told us about a time when he met Monika Dannemann, Jimi Hendrix's last girlfriend, at one of Phil's barbecues. Monika had just returned from Hawaii with some Hawaiian pressed hash-weed combination.

'We were all smoking this stuff, having a barbecue and then like Joey Kramer from Aerosmith dropped by. It's like totally bizarre who turns up here.'

We smoked some hash. Then we split. The next day, Sacha turned up at our hotel and took us down Carnaby Street to buy some English clothes, like bullet belts and cool leather jackets. We signed some autographs for two Swedish fans who had seen Anvil at Monsters of Rock and the Marquee Club, and then, wanting to meet us, had called every hotel in town asking for Mr Robb Reiner. One of the hotels said they did have a Mr Reiner staying, so they went to the guy's room and knocked at the door. This old guy came to the door – whoops, wrong Robb Reiner – so they gave up searching and went to Carnaby Street, where they ran into us by accident. We posed for a picture with them, and then moved on.

Back at the hotel later on, the phone rang. I picked it up but before I could get it to my ear I could hear the screaming of a woman with a North American accent totally losing it.

'I think it's for you,' I said, passing the phone to Sacha.

Even a few feet away from the phone, we could hear the woman on the other end of the line. It was Sacha's mother.

'What are you doing? Who are you with? Where exactly have you been all day?' She was totally flipping out.

'How did you find me?'

As if he needed to ask. There are few things more formidable and resourceful than an irate Jewish mother whose fifteen-year-old son is holed up in a Paddington hotel room with a bunch of long-haired Canadian heavy rockers.

Through the squawk of the phone, we heard something about tracing the hotel through the cab company and then cross-questioning the concierge about whether a band was staying at the hotel. Then Sacha put the phone down.

'Guys, I gotta go. That was my mother. She's pretty pissed with me.'

'OK, kid.' Thinking we'd never see him again, we said goodbye, but Sacha had news for us.

'Listen, guys. I have relatives in Toronto. I promise you haven't heard the last of me.'

LIPS: The gigging and partying continued when we got back to Canada, but our minds were really only on one thing: making the next album. We'd gone to England with a number of the songs written and we'd returned with a few more. Attic suggested we should call in CT again. 'This metal thing worked really well with CT,' said Al Mair, 'why don't you go and do it again?' It made total sense.

Within a month or two of being home from England and starting work on *Forged In Fire*, the phone rang.

'It's Sacha. I'm in Toronto.'

I was astounded. This kid was persistent. He wasn't one for making throwaway promises or giving up.

Robb picked up Sacha from his uncle Marty's apartment in downtown Toronto and for the next few weeks we hung out together, smoking pot in Robb's parents' basement, going to Yorkdale shopping mall, goofing around, going to McDonald's, just being kids. Nothing significant, just hanging out and having a good time. We nicknamed Sacha Teabag, simply because he was a little English kid, and he immediately embraced it, realizing that having a nickname was a sign he'd been adopted into the Anvil family. And that seemed right because there was something about Sacha that reminded me of Ashley.

It was all fine while we were in Toronto. Sacha could stay with his relatives or with us. But when we had to leave town for a while to play some gigs, Sacha couldn't come if he was going to take up a bed in a hotel room for nothing, so Robb made a suggestion.

'Hey, man, if maybe you wanna come out and roll with us, maybe on a trip, then if you helped out, just from a friend perspective, not like as a job with us paying you money, then you could come along and hang with us. Maybe as an experience, just so we can still be together and be buddies.'

Listening to Robb, I sometimes wondered if it had become more a case of Robb needing Sacha along for the ride. Part of Robb's character was that he loved adulation. And Sacha had become his greatest cheer-leader. They'd formed a very close bond – they were both drummers – so Sacha became like Robb's personal drum roadie. He'd help set up Robb's kit every night. The other roadies – Jethro, Brick, Vegas and Dog Boy – would rag on Sacha at times because he'd only carry Robb's drums and wouldn't help with anything else, but in fairness he wasn't getting paid and he was only doing it as a favour.

During the shows Sacha would stand at the side of the stage, watching Robb intently. And when Robb did something awesome, he'd shoot a glance at Sacha to let him know it. They were both really into it.

We played a string of small ice-hockey rinks in Quebec and Northern Ontario, then some big club gigs. While he was with us, Sacha told his father he was visiting his mum in Toronto and he told his mum he was visiting his dad in New York. Both of them were in the dark, which was a good thing, considering some of the backstage partying that Sacha saw.

Even then Sacha was living a fast life. He travelled with us for a few weeks, and then he disappeared to visit some friends in New York. He might have been only fifteen, but Teabag got round the place more than we did. Way more. He also had way more money than us. Although our albums were selling well and we were gigging all the time, we had less money than ever. When we visited New Jersey for the second time, Rockin' Ray refused to believe we weren't doing well because our profile was already high and climbing higher all the time.

'Hey, you guys are styling now.'

'Fuck no, Ray,' said Robbo. 'We got less money now than ever.'

'Oh c'mon, man.' From the look on Ray's face, he thought we were either lying or stupid. 'You guys are doing good financials, man.'

'No. We're not. Really.'

The trouble was that most of our support tours were buy-ons. We paid the headline band for the honour of touring with them so that we could get the exposure. We'd get a small daily allowance for personal expenses, but that was it. And even that was booked against our royalties. With every date we played we went further into debt with Attic. Club gigs would still earn us two thousand dollars a night but now our egos were making demands that our incomes couldn't honour. Anvil was a band with a profile and a following, and a band of our stature had standards.

'We can't use that piece of shit no more.' Squirrely was pointing at the little sound system we'd bought with the loan backed by Robb's and my dads. 'Anvil deserves something bigger.'

None of us argued because we all thought the same way. So we brought in a huge, extravagant system and burned through some more of the money we didn't have. By now, we were realizing that we'd signed our names to a deal that would never earn us any dough, so we never questioned what difference another few tens of thousands of dollars' debt would make.

Slowly our eyes were opening to the reality of our

situation: everyone else, including our pal Al Mair and the other dudes at Attic, were doing very well out of Anvil. Our records were selling, but we weren't getting any money.

We discovered that thousands of copies of *Hard'N'Heavy* and *Metal On Metal* that we didn't know about were circulating. They'd been made into picture discs, which appeared to have been licensed in France, and they were being distributed all over the world for a fraction of the price our official records were sold for in the stores. We confronted the label, but the execs said they knew nothing about it. We asked them to investigate, but they never got to the bottom of the mystery of whom outside Attic had counterfeited our albums. Meanwhile, we existed on packet foods as we plunged further into debt.

When I stopped to think about it, very little had changed since Robb's days on the road with Whalebone. In those days he lived off the generosity of chicks and the financial support of strippers. Now we were living off our girlfriends. Our mantra had become: If she ain't got some shopping, she's not coming in the house. Chicks were an almighty one-way support system. But it was taking a toll on our relationships. It was like what happens to a pair of tyres on a car that's been driven too hard: living off Lee was wearing down our relationship.

* * *

ROBB: Whining about our total lack of dough was going to get us nowhere. That much we all knew. We needed to focus on the future. That meant getting a decent manager and, more importantly, recording our third album.

We started work on *Forged In Fire* with CT towards the end of 1982 just as Lips was approached by Motörhead to fill in for Eddie Clarke, who'd had a hissy fit and was threatening to quit the band. But Lips always knew where his loyalties lay – with his Anvil brothers – and turned down the offer. CT began the sessions by going through the songs we'd written and had been playing on the road for a few months.

Four days into the recording, the call came from David Krebs that I believed would totally transform our lives. Here at last was a big-time manager that was interested in us. He hadn't seen Anvil perform, he hadn't heard our records, but still he was hot for us because of the buzz on the street. After the initial conversation, everything went quiet for a week. We recorded five bed tracks – mainly the bass and drums – before we got another call telling us to leave the next day for a support tour with Aerosmith for a week. By the end of the short support tour, David Krebs was convinced that we were the next big thing.

'Sign with me,' he said to Lips, 'and your band will go all the way to the top.'

It was the break we'd been hoping for since the day Lips and I put the advert in the Toronto paper calling for musicians to join our supergroup. At last we'd got a manager, the one thing I was convinced would totally change our fortunes.

But Krebs wasn't the only guy interested in representing Anvil. Jonny Z had called me too.

'I want to manage your band.'

'Jonny, you know we've got David Krebs interested in us. He says we're the next big thing.'

'I'm serious, man. I want to get involved. I've seen the kind of audiences you draw when you come down to Jersey. We could build on that.'

'I don't know, Jonny . . .'

'You're the beginning of a new movement. You've got the sound that everyone wants. You need to stick to that sound and work at it.'

It was a difficult choice. Jonny Z was a true fan and appreciated our music for what it was, but he was a small independent compared to Krebs. Jonny had a lot of vision and energy and he talked a good game, but he also ran a shop at a flea market and didn't seem to have a lot of money. By contrast, everyone knew the name and reputation of David Krebs. To me, the choice was a no-brainer. With a powerful, established manager – and Krebs was the biggest of the biggest – we'd be able to dictate the terms. The days of being ripped off by record companies and living in poverty would end. Someone like Krebs would take our music and our careers on to a new level. Of that I was convinced. I called Jonny Z.

'Jonny, we're good friends and maybe it's best to leave it that way. We're gonna go with Krebs. I'm sorry.'

At the time, Jonny was cut up about it, but very soon after that he signed Metallica and founded a record label, Megaforce, to release their debut album, *Kill 'Em All*. After that he signed Anthrax and released their debut album. Two bands out of the big four of speed metal: not a bad hit rate, in retrospect.

However, our future, we had decided, would be better in Krebs's experienced hands. And all we needed to do now was persuade Attic to license our music to Krebs so that he could find us a global deal. But first we needed to finish recording *Forged In Fire*.

Finishing our third album proved to be a whole deal more problematic than any of us had anticipated. When we returned to the studio immediately after the Aerosmith tour, we discovered that we had to tear down all the recordings we'd already made as we couldn't match them up to our new recordings. Our new sound system, which we'd taken on the road with us, sounded different when we brought it back into the studio, so we had to start again from scratch.

Our biggest problem, however, wasn't so easy to fix. Weird things were going on at home for CT. He was calling his wife desperately and we could see that something was bothering him. He needed help, so Robbo tried to come to the rescue.

'Hey, CT. What the fuck's up? You're always calling home.'

'I need to go on a diet.'

CT wasn't being forthcoming, but gradually we pieced the story together. Before coming out to Toronto, CT had been producing Thin Lizzy in London. In that time he'd brought in John Sykes, a guitarist who was previously with Tygers of Pan Tang and later played with Whitesnake, as Thin Lizzy had recently lost their guitarist, Snowy White. One night, CT brought Sykes home and introduced him to his wife. Sykes needed somewhere to live and moved in. CT was worried that now he was with us in Toronto, John may have moved in permanently.

In some ways, it was no surprise to us. We'd all visited CT's house when we were in England. John Sykes had been there and, not having met CT's wife before, Lips put his foot in it.

'So is this your girlfriend, John?' Lips pointed at the woman John was sitting beside.

'No. She's CT's wife.'

They looked as if they were an item already. It had been pretty weird back then, and now it was a real mess. A real fucking mess. It was painful enough to watch it happening to the poor guy, let alone to live through it as CT was having to do. And as the sessions went on, he seemed a bit preoccupied to say the least. As well as putting himself on a diet, he also started to dye his hair. He was in pain.

I felt CT's angst meant he rushed the mixing of the album. It felt as though he wanted to get away to sort out his life, so he mixed *Forged In Fire* very quickly. When we heard the mixes, we felt the guitars were not powerful enough. I wondered whether CT's pain had become our problem.

LIPS: In my eyes, CT's problems were only a small part of our troubles. A far bigger problem was that years of 24/7 partying had started to take its toll on Anvil. Squirrely, in particular, was having difficulty laying down his vocals. He was wasted. Smoking like a chimney had started to affect his ability to sing without coughing after every third word. It was on the edge of being a complete fucking joke. I was frustrated and embarrassed, while CT was tearing out his newly dyed hair.

'Fuck, man. We're recording this great album and you should have a good guitarist who can play the same thing twice and give us good backing vocals.'

What was I to say? I knew CT was right, but Squirrely was a member of the Anvil brotherhood.

CT had a solution. 'Let's get Charlie in.'

Charlie Huhn, who had played with Gary Moore and for Ted Nugent, flew in from Detroit to meet us. We talked it over. Nothing came of Charlie helping us out, but he had interesting things to say about the difficulties of finding and dealing with success.

'It takes a man to make it,' Charlie said. 'But it takes a real man to not make it and still stand.'

I understood what he meant. Charlie had played the big stages with Ted Nugent and Gary Moore, but now those days appeared to be over for him. He was still standing and he still had his pride. I respected that. I thought it was very cool and from then on I tried to live by that motto.

Through meeting other rock stars, I was realizing that a part of finding my own identity was seeing it in somebody else. And Charlie's wise words were telling me something I think I knew already, but hadn't totally accepted yet. It was very easy to go: Should have, would have, could have. But it wouldn't change a thing. Not a damn thing, man.

There were dozens of things I knew we 'shoulda, woulda and coulda' changed about the recording of *Forged In Fire*. For one, I knew that it was really too bad that Robbo didn't use the drum heads that CT told him he should have used to get a cleaner, better sound.

'You shouldn't be using twenty-eight-inch bass

drums, Robb.' CT was adamant. 'You shouldn't be using clear plastic heads.'

'Fuck you. I'm the drummer and I know better.'

'Man, you're doing this for a record. That means you're doing it for *ever*. You should do it right.'

But it took another album before Robb conceded that white heads on his drums would let everyone really hear what he was playing instead of the muffled rumble produced by clear heads.

And to be honest there were times when Robbo didn't think my performance was good enough and that I could have done better. We were trying a take on 'Future Wars' that we'd played so fast that it had become almost impossible for me to sing the lyrics. We had to slow down the tape so that I could sing it at all. At the end of the song, when we'd finished recording, Robb came striding across the studio towards me. He was already flipping out.

'You didn't sing the end of that song like Rob Halford would.'

I went nuts. 'Maybe you haven't noticed it yet, but I am Lips, front man of Anvil, not the lead vocalist of Judas Priest.'

'What the fuck difference does it make anyway, Lips? You coulda done better but you and CT settle for crap takes every time.'

Same shit, different year, I thought. My vocal was

good. I'd worked hard, CT had put me through it for several hours and that was the best I could do. Excessive partying wasn't blunting my blade, thanks. I wasn't underperforming in the way that other members of the band were. So when Robbo said it was crap, I was fucking enraged.

'Tell me why I should sing like the guy in Judas Priest? I'm Lips, I sing like me. And while I'm working my ass off, you guys sit around doing nothing for weeks. And then you come in and chop on me? Like fuck off!'

Robb hit me. I hit him back and we went at it full tilt, brawling all round the studio kitchen. It was the first physical fight I'd ever had with Robb, but that wasn't making either of us hold our punches. Robb gave me a fucking big shove and I fell against the dishwasher.

'Fucking aaaagggh!'

I was impaled on a piece of metal that protruded from the front of the dishwasher. It had cut through my jeans and punctured my leg. Squirrely and CT jumped in and pulled me and Robb apart. I assessed the damage. I'd been cut deep. The *Forged In Fire* wound I called it after that.

That was the way that men like us solved their problems: with their fists. We 'coulda and shoulda' talked about it, but at least we got it out in the open.

I also knew it was really too bad that Squirrely wasn't a better guitarist who could have taken more care of his voice. And I knew that Dix should have practised more so that he would have been a faster bass player. On songs like 'Motormount', 'Winged Assassins' and 'Butter-Bust Jerky', Robbo and I played all the base tracks because Squirrely and Dix couldn't keep up with us. Sitting behind his kit, trying to put down the drum base track against the rhythm guitar and bass base tracks, Robb often lost his temper.

'Fuck! Take this thing outta here!' Robb pointed at his headphones. 'Shut 'em out of my fucking head-phones so I don't have to hear it. They're fucking up all over the place and it's fucking me up. Shut 'em up.'

CT was sympathetic. 'You know, Robb, just dis-connect it. Just let Lips do it afterwards. No bother. Don't worry.'

So that's what we did. We felt that Squirrely and Dix were at the edge of their talent and not capable of play-ing songs like 'Butter-Bust Jerky' to the standard required for a recording. The songs were just too fast and difficult for them to play.

All of these shortcomings meant there were things we 'woulda, shoulda and coulda' done to make sure Anvil got the record it deserved. But we didn't. And because of that we didn't get the quality that we wanted on *Forged In Fire*.

In fairness to CT, although he was upset he had to finish the mix because he was contracted to move on to another production job in San Francisco. It was our fault we ran out of time; CT went as far as he could with what we gave him. He couldn't turn Squirrely's guitar up any louder in the mix when it wasn't a clear, present vibe. It meant we had to use reverb to mask the inadequacies of Squirrely's playing when the track would have been much better without it.

CT might have had his problems at home, but it's not fair to blame him for things that we weren't happy about on *Forged In Fire*. He put up with a hell of a lot with Anvil. He really fucking did.

And although I hadn't partied as hard or as long as the other guys in the band, I had my own troubles. Like them, I was in pain from self-inflicted damage, although mine was damage to the heart. Shortly before we went into the studio, Lee discovered about my infidelity in England with Dawn Crosbie. Philip Harvey had innocently sent a couple of photographs in a letter to Squirrely. Someone who shared Squirrely's apartment had passed them on to Lee. To make matters worse, a photograph had also appeared in the *Canadian New Music Express* newspaper. Taken by someone backstage, the snap-shot was of me hanging out with Dawn. Beneath it was a caption: *Anvil's Conquest of Britain*. That didn't go over well at home.

Lee suspected everything and she wasn't far wrong. Not much was said. After all, what was there to say? Things between me and Lee never felt the same again.

Although I'd been on the road for more than four years, until then I'd never given Lee anything to worry about – nothing she knew about, anyway – but now I'd been caught with my pants around my ankles and it changed everything.

My response was to write songs like 'Make It Up To You' but I discovered that it was really hard for two people to recover from infidelity. It left an impression and you can't bang that dent out.

The combination of my personal problems, CT's suspicions that his wife was having an affair and the effects of excessive partying on the band made the recording of *Forged In Fire* extraordinarily difficult. By the time we'd finished in the studio I'd come to a realization that boiled down to one thing: I was not going to make it with Squirrely and Dix. I knew it, I felt it, I sensed it and I regretted it, but they were just not there any more. They'd become ornamentation on stage, the pussy magnets for the band, but beyond that they weren't adding anything. In particular, Squirrely seemed burned out. After *Forged In Fire* it was as if there was nothing left in him. He was just gone. The edge, the rebelliousness, the excitement, enthusiasm and innocence, the teenage part of him was spent. He was jaded and took things for granted. Too many people in the band were acting like rock stars before we'd got close to making it.

With the album mixed, we called in the execs from Attic for a listening party. They'd loved *Metal On Metal* and were hyped to hear it. Robb was convinced we had a future metal masterpiece in *Forged In Fire*. I thought our decision to make it harder and faster than *Metal On Metal* was the right one, but I didn't know how well we'd accomplished it.

The listening party was held at Attic's office with record company staff and a few press people. Drinks had been poured and everyone was seated. Anticipation was high. Everybody was very excited. The big moment had arrived. After the first song, 'Forged In Fire', I looked around the room. The execs looked kind of shocked, but they were going with it. Next up was 'Shadow Zone'; for many of the people present this was the first time they'd ever heard speed metal. 'Free As The Wind' and 'Butter-Bust Jerky' followed next and the execs' expressions went from confused to like: What the fuck? Between tracks, the room was silent. They didn't know what to make of it.

Robbo, Squirrely, Dix and I knew what it was. It was the new Anvil, harder and faster than anything they'd ever heard before. But the execs weren't just indifferent to it. Oh no. They didn't get it at all. Nobody had said it was horrible, but it was a big change from the listening party for *Metal On Metal*. I thought back to how that ended:

'Wow.' Al Mair had been on his feet, a big smile on his face as he punched the air.

'Great work, guys. Great work.' Tom had looked really proud.

But now the room was silent. Nobody said a thing, but I could tell what was going through their minds: I don't know if I like it.

In spite of their lukewarm response, the record company geared up like crazy to launch the record. They sent the finished album to Malcolm Dome, a specialist reviewer of new wave heavy metal for *Kerrang!* and other publications. Malcolm wrote that he didn't know if it was a fault on his tape, but the sound was quite bad. He said it sounded better to him when he was not in the same room as his stereo. He was very enthusiastic about Anvil, but didn't rate the album at all.

ROBB: It was time to go on the road with *Forged In Fire*. We went down to the States to play a bunch of clubs in New Jersey and New York. Rockin' Ray had invited us to stay at his house, but at the last moment he called to say he couldn't put us up. A band from San Francisco called Metallica were staying. We'd have to stay with Metal Joe instead. We met the guys from Metallica – their founding lead guitarist Dave Mustaine had just been replaced by Kirk Hammett – and listened to their first album *Kill 'Em All* at Ray's place. Musically it had similarities to our material and it felt good to hear another band charting the same course as us.

Sacha was in New York at the time, visiting his dad, who was still working for the United Nations. As if on cue, Sacha turned up, and there was only one thing that needed to be said.

'Hey, man, wanna come on the road?'

'Fucking right.'

We had a great time. Sacha got to see the band every night. And he actually contributed. He sold some T-shirts and helped set up the drums. Sacha was a proper part of our little crew on a short tour around Ontario and Quebec. In Albany, we stopped in a cheap hotel. Me and Squirrely shared a room. With our third album under our belts, we were now full-on rock stars, but not so much that we couldn't make space for Sacha to sleep on the floor at the foot of our beds.

I felt less concerned about Sacha now that he was sixteen. He saw a lot of partying, a lot of drugs and a lot of chicks, but that's what bands did on the road. I was cool with it. Sacha wasn't fazed by the chick activities – he was still with Alexandra – and from what he told me of his life in London, he wasn't exactly a stranger to drugs. Our relationship was also changing. To start with, it had been all about the drumming and Sacha had felt like a male groupie, but now it was more a people thing. Sacha had become a genuine friend. He had a good heart and a good soul. Beneath the big hair, the red leather jacket and the attitude, there was a beautiful little kid.

LIPS: While we were on the road, news came that Attic had got us geared up with Malcolm Dome for an interview with a British magazine. We were in Detroit at the time and Lee had come along as it was only a couple of hundred miles from Toronto, hitching a lift in the back of a Triumph TR2, all crunched up and getting claustrophobic. By the time she got to our motel, she was feeling totally fucked up.

To accompany the interview, a photo shoot was arranged with Ross Halfin, legendary rock and metal photographer. Ross was a real kook, always trying to push the boundaries by getting musicians to do outrageous things. He wanted a picture of me, because I was the Anvil front man, and after taking a few shots in my motel room, Ross made a suggestion.

'Let's do a Peter Sellers.'

'Like . . . what?'

'You in the shower with the guitar.'

'Naked?'

'Oh yeah.'

I was totally into it. 'That's great, man. This is going

to look fucking awesome. Let's do something outrageous. I'm into that.'

We took a few pictures in the shower, and then Ross pointed at Lee, who was lying in the bed.

'OK, now I wanna get a picture of your girlfriend sucking your toes. Let's do that.'

'No, no, no.' Me naked was totally OK. Lee sucking my toes was totally not. 'I think you ought to leave her alone. She's not feeling great. She had a tough time getting here. Let's leave her alone.'

'OK, then let's get a picture of you opening the door and you're naked, just holding your guitar.'

'Fuck man, you can't just go outside naked!'

Ross grinned. 'No . . . just stand in the doorway. Don't worry about it.'

The motel was one of those roadside joints with all the rooms laid out in a horseshoe shape around a central parking lot. If I opened the door, everybody would be able to see me.

'Come on, Ross. We're going to get in shit, man.'

'No, come on, Lips, do it!'

Having already refused to do the picture of Lee sucking my toes, I felt my options were running out. 'OK. Fuck. OK.'

'It'll just be for my private collection. Don't worry. I've got pictures of Richie Blackmore in fishnet stockings. It's just a laugh for me to get these crazy shots.'

Although I had misgivings, I was like: OK, Ross, whatever you say, man.

'Just make it quick, OK?'

I stood in the doorway, buck naked and brandishing my Flying V while Ross clicked away. Then the phone rang. Lee picked it up.

'Yeah . . . OK . . . I'll tell them right now.' She put down the receiver. 'Get in here! They're going to call the police. Fuck, Lips, you can't stand out there naked.'

So what happened to that picture of me naked, taken for Ross's private collection? *Kerrang!* published it in its next issue with a sign over my dick that said *Please Don't Disturb*.

ROBB: After Lips's naked photo shoot, Ross followed us to our gig at Harpos in Detroit, one of the oldest concert theatres in America. Before the show, he came up with another of his weird requests.

'OK, guys. I want to get a picture of you throwing the anvil around the stage.'

That sounded OK. Lips would be the one who had to do it and he was fine with it. 'OK. Beautiful. I'll do it. No problem.'

A couple of hours later, we were on stage and had finished 'Bondage', the last song in the set. From behind my drums I watched as Lips grabbed the anvil from the front of the drum riser, staggered a few paces forwards, and then with all his might, threw the anvil towards Ross, who was in the photographers' pit at the front of the stage. As the huge lump of metal bounced forwards, then disappeared over the edge of the stage, I saw Lips mouth two words.

'Oh no!'

The headbangers in front of the stage saw the anvil coming directly towards them and split apart. No one got hurt, but as soon as the anvil had dented the floor, one of the headbangers picked it up and started running out of the hall with it.

'Where the fuck do you think you're going with that?'

Brick, our sound man, was standing in the way of the anvil-toting headbanger.

'How could you think that you're going to run out of this building with that ninety-five-pound thing?'

The guy was running down the aisle with the anvil between his legs.

'Er . . .'

'You're stealing our anvil. You're going nowhere with it, buddy. Give it the fuck back.'

The headbanger dropped the anvil and disappeared out the door. And Ross? He missed the fucking picture.

After the short tour, we were called in to Attic to discuss finances. One of our roadies had returned from the tour and then used the record company's credit card to rent a truck for a couple of weeks. As he listened to one of the execs relate the story, Al Mair's eye was twitching, a characteristic we'd seen before when we returned to the Attic office after touring *Metal On Metal*.

Attic had given us a box of *Metal On Metal* albums to give away after gigs. The price of the albums was built into the ticket price and the records were all stamped with the words *Promotional Copy – Not For Sale*. It was a way for the record company to sell more copies of the record without having to pass on royalties to us.

We'd driven down to Brooklyn for the first of a string of gigs involving this promotion. After the gig we'd handed out a bunch of albums at the door, just like we'd been told to do. But when we'd returned to our tour truck, we'd discovered that our entire supply of promotional albums was gone. One thousand five hundred promo albums stolen. At the first fucking gig.

When we'd got back to Toronto, we'd gone into the Attic offices.

'Sorry to tell you this, Al. We lost them in New York.'

Al's eye had immediately started to twitch then. Now it was doing it again. In both instances, Al was hearing bad financial news and didn't like it, even if we were the ones who ultimately got billed for these mishaps. Both of them went on our red line, but we were now in so deep we were never going to pay it back.

Having long ago adopted a what's-the-difference attitude, the reality of our situation had sunk in. We now knew what was going on. The facts were staring us in the face: we had a record deal; we were in demand; we were selling records; big sums of money were being made; and almost none of it was filtering down to us guys in the group. The worst thing about it was that our story was such a fucking rock 'n' roll cliché.

That afternoon in the Attic offices, our totally fucked-up existence really shifted gear for the worse. Attic told us they were going to stop paying any royalties at all.

'We're imposing a cross-collateralization on your albums,' said one of the Attic execs.

Cross-collateralization was a technical term that meant they were spreading our debts across all our records. In non-technical terms its meaning was simple: We've pulled the plug. We don't have to give you anything and we're not going to.

Tom and Al couched the message in softer terms, telling us they'd been nice, they'd helped us out and they'd given us support. Although they didn't say it directly, the implication was clear: We've been doing all these things, but you know what? Now we're going to stop.

Suddenly everything fell into place. I saw the big picture. I saw how the deal that we had and the band that we were would never lead to financial success. A heavy metal band creating cutting-edge innovative music like us could never sell enough records to pay back the record company's investment. And if I was feeling cynical, I'd suspect that the record company knew that even when they signed us.

From that moment on, as far as Attic was concerned, it was all a big wind-down. As Lips put it: 'From *Forged In Fire* everything went for a big shit.'

It left us with two choices: either scale back our ambitions or somehow achieve global mega-success to pay off our debts. The former meant continuing to survive on macaroni cheese and fifty dollars a week on tour and living off our girlfriends or parents when at home. Lee paid Lips's rent and worked while he went out and rock and rolled. As for me, at the age of twenty-five, I was still living with my folks. They didn't give me hundreds of dollars, but they fed me and put up with the inconvenience of having a rock star living in their basement. For a few years, they also gave a home to Dix.

Worse than the lack of money was the mental adjustment of coming back from touring with Aerosmith or Motörhead to living at home, just like it was weird to be playing an arena in front of thousands one night and then a shithole for one hundred people the next night. I'd always tell my parents the best parts of life on the road, not the stories of banging broads or getting cranked up on drugs. My parents knew that I was into that stuff and I didn't have to talk about it.

But the hardest thing was that when I was on the road I actually felt like a rock star. I knew what it felt like to be adored by an audience for my music and my playing. I loved it and it was a big part of who I was. I felt really alive when we were on the road and when we were performing. That was who I was supposed to be and it felt better than anything, even banging chicks. But when I came off tour, the reality struck. I suffered then. I got it bad. When I was at home I felt dead. Back to the coffin, I used to say.

As far as I was concerned, scaling back our ambitions simply wasn't an option. I wasn't going to give up so easily. We had to go for global success or bust. And, fortunately, we'd found the man who could take us there. It was time to put all our money on one horse: David Krebs.

9 BIG TIME

LIPS: Signing with David Krebs immediately changed our fortunes. Within a short time of putting our names on the dotted line, we were off to Britain for a tour with Motörhead. A week before that we played the Heavy Sounds festival in Bruges, where the overwhelming response of the crowd convinced me I'd found an audience that would stick with us for ever.

The *Forged In Fire* album had just been released and as soon as we joined Motörhead at Chippenham in the west of England, we wanted to know what Lemmy thought of it.

'You're great players but you put too many hard parts in your songs.'

It was a fair assessment that reflected the difficulties Squirrely and Dix had in the studio playing some of the faster tracks, but during the UK tour with them, in June and July 1983, we blew the crowd away.

But if we were holding our own with Motörhead on the stage, things were quite different backstage, where we were very much also-rans at partying. In North America, Anvil had a reputation as one of the hardest partying bands on the circuit, but by Motörhead standards we were pussycats.

On 26 June we played a gig in Birmingham. After the show we had a rare day off before we had to travel to Cardiff for the next show on 28 June, so Lemmy cornered me in the corridor of our hotel.

'Come on, we'll have a drink in my room.'

An invitation from Lemmy was not to be refused. And anyway, I wanted to see for myself if he lived up to his hard-living reputation.

'Sure.'

Lemmy pulled out a 40-oz bottle of vodka and divided it between two very large glasses, filling to about two-thirds full. A few glugs of orange juice raised the mixture in the glasses to the brim. Drinks fixed, Lemmy pulled out a little leather pouch from his pocket and with a blade chopped out two huge white lines of white powder.

'Here, have some of this.'

'OK.' Like . . . fuck. I didn't know what I was doing, but I was with Lemmy and Lemmy was someone to whom you didn't say no. When in Rome . . . I supposed. So I decided to have fun and live it up. It was the biggest thing I'd ever done, being on the Motörhead tour, and I was partying with the man himself. How could I say no?

Bing! The lights went on full blast in my head. Sitting in Lemmy's hotel room, my teeth were gritted and my head itched all over. I was completely fucked, so I started drinking, but nothing happened. I wasn't getting drunk, even though I was so thirsty I was drinking vodka like water.

A couple of hours later, there was a knock at the door. One of the road crew stuck his head around the door.

'OK, guys, get ready. Let's go.'

'Whaaat?' I couldn't understand why we were being told to leave. I thought we had a day off before the next gig.

'Let's go.'

'Where are we going?'

'To Cardiff. For the gig.'

'What the fuck!'

It seemed like just a couple of hours had passed, but everything had speeded up and twenty-four hours had disappeared in a drug-fuelled haze.

By the time we reached the venue a couple of hours later, I was totally fucked. Lemmy spotted me struggling to engage with reality. Walking over, he pulled out a small plastic bag containing little black capsules.

'These are called Black Bombers. Have a couple of 'em.'

'No, I'm OK. Thanks, man.'

'Listen to me, Lips. Take them. You'll need 'em.'

'OK, I'll do one.'

'Take two. They'll make you feel a whole lot better.'

I swallowed the pills and washed them down with several large gulps of vodka. Ten minutes later, full service was restored. Let's go, guys. Party time. My headlights were on full beam. I was ready to rock.

Although I didn't repeat that experience with Lemmy, the Motörhead tour marked a turning point in Anvil's drug consumption. Before that tour, it had been nothing harder than weed, hash and New Jersey crank. In interviews, Lemmy even poked fun at us because of our relatively lame drug consumption, saying we were small-town kids. But after Motörhead, cocaine, other forms of speed and various pills joined the cocktail menu as we tried to keep up with Lemmy – an impossible feat.

We were getting tuned up all the time, rarely having to buy it because other people were always turning us on to it. Other band members, friends, hard-rocking locals when we were gigging in other cities, all of them gave freely of their gear. 'Here's some crankers . . . Want some blow? . . . Do a line . . . Here's a bag . . .' Whoever it was, everybody had shit.

Robb even drummed on cocaine for a short time, which he'd always dissed previously. It made him edgy and the music less relaxed, although he insisted it had no effect on him. 'I played amazing. Second to none. Completely fucking awesome,' he'd say, but I knew he didn't enjoy it and eventually he gave up playing on coke, relying only on weed and hash to get him in the performance vibe.

It didn't help that one of our crew was carrying some severe addiction problems. And being on the road with Motörhead was just about the worst place for someone with drug issues. He soon discovered that some of the guys in the Motörhead operation had an almost endless supply of hard drugs and he blew all the money we were making on tour on cocaine. By the time the thirty-date tour culminated with three nights at the Marquee Club in London, we were thousands of dollars in debt. When we returned to North America, we were asked to square up our finances with David, but the kitty was empty and Krebs had to swallow the bill.

ROBB: The way we blew Motörhead off the stage night after night convinced me that *Forged In Fire* was the real fucking deal and that anyone who was negative about it just didn't realize that the music was ahead of its time. It was like nothing anybody had ever heard before. The backbone was innovative techno speed metal and the arrangements were slightly un-conventional – often the chorus would only come in at the end of the song – and that was too much for some people.

We'd innovated innocently, not knowing that we were creating a metal masterpiece in the process. *Forged In Fire* came from Robbo's heart. It was like my internal motivation motor kicked in. I was convinced we had invented something that would change the world. Lips's riffs were the heaviest and fastest he could play. He was on fire. And I created faster, more technical and awesomely cool time changes. Nobody was doing anything like it and I really believed in my heart it was the right thing for us. And it was.

Whereas the *Metal On Metal* title track was a theme song for all metal, the *Forged In Fire* title track was the song for our band.

> *Altered shape, affected matter*
> *Giving form, an ominous factor*
> *Never break it, it will never bend*
> *The Anvil was Forged In Fire*

Pretty profound lyrics, we thought all would agree. Similarly, 'Free As The Wind', to this day the most requested song at our gigs, was about the total awesomeness of being a heavy metal rocker. The next track, 'Shadowzone', was about the end of the world, while 'Never Deceive Me' was a Squirrely composition about a girl who broke his heart in the days before he joined the band. 'Butter-Bust Jerky' was a play on words that referred to a party activity that involved putting butter on a chick's boobs and then tit-fucking her. It had a really fast, crazy riff so we figured it needed a crazy lyric, but none of us could get it right in the studio. Lips arrived back in the studio the next day with the chorus written. He'd played the riff to Lee and explained what we meant by a Butter-Bust Jerky. She'd despaired at us – 'You guys are so fucking nuts,' she said – and then she came up with the lyrics:

Dip your fingers in the butter
Spread it all across your chest
In between one another
You know what I like best
Push 'em close together
The tighter the better
Doin' the Butter-Bust Jerky
We're gonna get down and dirty
Doin' the Butter-Bust Jerky
And makin' me feel so good

Inspired by some sci-fi books he was reading, Squirrely wrote the lyrics to the next track 'Future Wars', and 'Hard Times, Fast Ladies' was about the Kissettes, an all-female band we met in England.

The hard times in the song title was a simple sexual innuendo. Lips wrote 'Make It Up To You' for Lee, asking for forgiveness for his affair with Dawn Crosbie, 'Motormount' put the sexual thing in an automotive context, and 'Winged Assassins' was a look at mutual nuclear annihilation, but from a hippy point of view as Lips was a pacifist.

After a couple of months at home – back in the coffin in my case – Attic fixed us up with a few dates in Europe, followed by a headline tour of Japan. The climax of our European itinerary was a support slot on the final date of Whitesnake's 1983 tour at the Brussels Forest National in Belgium. Years later, Dee Snider, the front man of Twisted Sister, who were second on the bill, conceded that we blew them off the stage that night.

After that, as I thought befitted our status by this time, I insisted that I wasn't going to play on a hired back line in Japan. When we arrived at Paris airport to take a flight to Tokyo, I phoned Paul O'Neill, an assistant appointed by David Krebs to handle us, to tell him in no uncertain terms what I expected.

'I want my drums in Japan. No fucking argument about it.'

Initially O'Neill refused because it would cost twenty thousand dollars to ship my drums to Japan and then home to Canada. But Robbo wasn't going to give way.

Robbo had just been named the best drummer in the world by *Drum* magazine.

'I don't fucking care, man. I'm not playing on anything but my kit. I don't care who fucking pays for it – Attic or Krebs – but I'm telling you one thing: no drums, no me.'

'I'll see what I can do.'

O'Neill called off. In the New York office, he'd gone to speak to Krebs. About fifteen minutes later, he called back.

'OK, Robb, we will send the drums.'

Krebs had agreed to pay the costs and my drums flew with us to Japan. I'd asked for a reasonable thing and I'd got it. As I saw it, we'd already brought the drums over to Europe from North America and Krebs had the money. He was now our manager and he could afford to pay for it. If I didn't ask for something, I wasn't going to get it. It was money well spent, I thought.

Since we'd signed with Krebs, things had started at last to move for us. Having played some more gigs in the New York and New Jersey area, we were building up a substantial following in an area where there was a large potential fandom. Krebs wanted us to move to the States, so that we were more available to American record companies and audiences, but Lips was reluctant to leave Lee and his family in Toronto, so we postponed any relocation plans.

Now we were on our way to Japan, where Al Mair had licensed our three albums to Polydor. They'd sold well and the local Polydor exec had organized a tour to promote Anvil. As soon as we arrived, we felt like rock stars. Japan seemed like another planet and there was a kind of Beatlemania thing at the airport with loads of screaming chicks. We had a record signing. The place was packed and camera flashes were going nuts. And wherever we went, an entourage of fifty to a hundred young girls would follow us, all freaking out over Anvil. I was kind of like: Oh fuck, we have conquered Japan.

Tokyo looked like a very compressed New York with neon lights everywhere and millions of people, but culturally it was very different. It was overwhelming, but we embraced it. Things were much more advanced in a number of different ways, from the electronics on sale and the way that you entered stores to the way that pop and cigarettes were sold on the streets. There was an air of wealth. We didn't see a single rusty or dented car in the entire time of our visit. Nobody was sleeping on the streets and there was a sense of complete trust between people compared to the dog-eat-dog society of North America. And as far as the band was concerned, it was a successful tour for us. Every gig was sold out, although to our surprise more than 90 per cent of the audience was female. At home, we were down 'n' dirty sleazy metal guys. In Japan, our long hair and leathers made us metal pretty boys.

The Japanese chicks couldn't get enough of white skinny guys, particularly if they were blond, so Squirrely was a rock superstar in Japan. And, holy shit, did he take advantage of it. We had to take the phone off the hook in our hotel rooms because girls were calling it twenty-four hours a day. None of us could sleep.

Outside our room, the girls were lining up in the corridor to meet us. And if we'd thought North American groupies were like dogs on heat, it was nothing compared to the Japanese chicks, who would stop at nothing to carve up on each other to get one of us in the sack. Maybe it was because they saw far fewer white rock stars, but these chicks were ruthless and way younger than any we'd come across before.

We returned from Japan, tired and sore from partying, to discover that my drums had been impounded in America because Krebs refused to pay the shipping bill. For the next six months we couldn't play or rehearse. The reputation of the band was rising, but we couldn't do fucking anything. All we could do was sit around and get frustrated while we waited for Krebs to pay the bill so that I could get my drums back. I was going crazy. Without music, we just existed, but nothing more.

* * *

LIPS: Robb's drums being stuck in a container somewhere in America wasn't just a huge inconvenience. To me, it was the moment when our chances of success and a long-term career slipped through our fingers. From the moment that Robb refused to back down to Paul O'Neill about transporting our drums to Japan, our management days with Krebs were numbered.

We'd arrived at Paris airport and Robb's drums were in a container ready for shipping. But when our tour manager went to get the container transferred to the flight to Japan, his credit card was refused. He called Paul O'Neill who said they had decided not to go ahead with the shipment because Robb had been offered an endorsement by Pearl drums, who had made a customized kit for Robb to use in Japan.

Not only was Pearl providing a kit, but it was going to pay to ship Robb's drum set from France back to Canada and ship his new kit from Japan to home. On Robb's insistence, Pearl was also building 28-inch bass drums especially for him as they didn't usually make them.

We were being paid fifty thousand dollars to play six gigs in Japan, a fee that was way out of our league and which we desperately needed. Everything appeared fine and wonderful until we arrived at Paris and our tour manager discovered it was going to cost twenty thousand to ship Robb's drums, an operation that had now become superfluous because of Pearl's endorsement offer. I tried to make Robb see sense.

'Why are we doing this, Gaze? Pearl is going to give you a brand-new kit when you get there.'

'No, man. I want my drums there. My fucking drums.'

Robb was insistent so I contacted Paul O'Neill in the hope that he could talk down a very heated, angry Robb. But when push came to shove, Robb pulled the most almighty ultimatum.

'I'm not going. I'm going to go buy a ticket right now and I'm going to get myself home. I have money and I'll see you guys later.'

The tour manager had a freak-out. He was like: What do I do now? The band can't go to Japan without the drummer. This guy's threatening to go AWOL and he sounds like he means it.

In the end the money went through and the drums got shipped to Japan. We were experiencing real success and maybe some of that was going to our heads. It felt like Robb was having difficulties dealing with it at times. The only downside was that after what we had put Krebs through, I wasn't at all surprised that he did not rush to pay the shipping fee on Robb's drums and left them waiting in storage for several months. For that, I was absolutely furious with Robb.

Three albums and several tours of North America,

Europe and Japan didn't detract from the fact that we were still a relatively small-time band. All the admiration of hardcore headbangers and the kudos from other musicians would amount to nothing if we didn't have the support of a good manager. But Krebs was getting wise to us. We were throwing our weight around and making demands before we'd earned that kind of clout. The drums fiasco and the impact of our heavy-partying tour manager had cost Krebs a lot of money before we'd earned him a cent.

In our defence, Krebs had seen that we'd worked extremely hard since we signed with him. We'd played a lot of gigs and we'd been writing like crazy, but we were sending tapes to Krebs and rarely hearing anything back. When he did acknowledge our new songs, we felt it wasn't in a positive way. He'd say things that gave us the impression that he didn't believe in what we were doing. And he'd say that he had to believe in what we were doing before he could go out to bat for us. We were getting into a tailspin with Krebs and I was concerned we wouldn't be able to pull ourselves out of it.

To make matters worse, the money that was spent on the drums was supposed to have set up an apartment for us in the New York area. Instead of paying for hotels, we would have had a base. If we were going to get a major deal, a base in the States was essential, but we'd just blown that option.

We needed to be careful. Krebs was a very influential and powerful guy. And you don't fuck around with influential and powerful people. Period.

ROBB: It was time to start thinking about our next album. Under pressure from Attic and David Krebs, we were considering loosening up our heavy sound.

'Don't play "Six Six Six",' Krebs had said one of the times he came to see us play. 'It's not accessible. It's too fucking fast.'

Although we knew *Forged In Fire* was an awesome, innovative metal masterpiece, it hadn't sold in the volumes we'd expected and some of the critics had a negative vibe about it. Squirrely suggested we needed to look at successful North American heavy rock bands for inspiration. Bands like Aerosmith or Van Halen. Lips thought these bands were lame and that we should stick to the Anvil sound, but Squirrely, Dix and I disagreed. I looked at these bands and I felt inspired. They'd started just like us and they were now global rock stars. If we really wanted success, maybe we needed to change our influences.

To stand any chance of making the next album more successful than *Forged In Fire*, we needed to get proper distribution in America and Europe. Krebs had tried licensing our work to labels in America. He'd even set up a showcase for us at the Palladium in New York City to which he'd invited along the guys from all the major labels in town. But the likes of Elektra passed on us. We were too heavy. They didn't get us, although a couple of years later they were fighting to sign bands like Metallica who followed in our wake. They didn't realize that with Anvil they were getting an early preview of the future of metal.

Licensing wasn't the answer, said Krebs. We needed a global deal and that wasn't possible while our Canadian rights were still held by Attic. So Krebs called Al Mair and us down to New York for a discussion in his office, several dozen floors up in a skyscraper.

'I'm going to need at least a million-dollar commitment for a global deal, Mr Maer.'

Krebs laid down the demands thick and fast, including that funds should be made available to allow us to move down to the New York area.

'Either you can fill these stipulations, Mr Mair, or you have to let the band go.'

All of Al Mair's worst nightmares were coming true at once. He broke out in a sweat. His eye started twitching.

'No. I won't do it. I really don't want to do that.'

The irony was that Al was only now getting seriously interested in us. Tom Williams was the guy who'd hyped us up and hooked Al into us. But since Krebs got involved in us, Al's excitement for us had grown. His thought processes were obvious because anyone in his position would have had them: I've got the goods, now look at the level of the people that are wanting to get involved; the boys have been out with Aerosmith and to Japan; these guys could go a long way.

We knew that Al was nervous about losing us. Lips had sat next to him at one of the Aerosmith shows and he'd laid his cards on the table.

'I've got a feeling I'm going to lose you guys.' Al looked glum. 'It seems more than likely. I'd really like to hold on and maybe there's some more that we could do. Maybe we could find somebody with another label that I could trust and we could go in together on your next album.'

Al had known then what was coming. And now we were all in a swanky New York office and what Al had feared was now being outlined by Mr Big, David Krebs.

'Mr Maer, we've got to get this band to the next level. That requires the commitment of a lot of money. It's time for you to make a decision.

'OK . . . OK . . .' Al's eye twitched. 'Let me think about it.'

Two weeks later, we got a call to visit Al in his Toronto office.

'I'm gonna drop you guys. I'm gonna let you go. It looks like David is going to be able to help you out. Good luck.'

Our immediate reaction was: Fucking yeah. But as money-grabbing and bottom-line-focused as Al was, I had respect for him. He'd put Anvil's name on the map and we had a lot for which to be grateful, but now we'd become too big for Attic and it was time for us to go.

Krebs said we'd now get a deal with CBS Records. He had plenty of other artists with CBS and he was a big manager, so we believed it was all going to happen. Krebs wanted us to move away from heavy metal and told us we'd have more chance of being signed if we went for more of a hard rock sound. Maybe he was right, I thought. After all, one or two music journalist losers had given *Forged In Fire* shitty reviews. If changing our sound was necessary for bigger success, then I thought it was worth considering, especially if it meant we'd be signed with a major label at last.

At this time, our buddy Sacha suddenly appeared. There was a knock on the door of Lips's apartment. Lips opened the door and there was Sacha, a big smile on his face. As always, he was buzzing full of energy, his knee jittering up and down as he sat on Lips's sofa and told us his news.

'I'm in a band. It's called Conspiracy. I'm the drummer.' You could have shovelled a plate of food into Sacha's grin, it was that wide. 'We've got a major record deal, and we just shot our first video in Paris. I think this band might actually take off!'

'Oh . . . oh, OK, man.'

Here we were searching for a major record deal and Sacha had got himself one just like that. I wasn't that surprised. Sacha had a way of getting things to happen for him.

'So, Teabag, what kind of music is it?'

'Rock, well . . . more like pop music, man.'

'Like . . . really? *Pop* music?

'Yes, but with a rock edge. We're playing some big festival in Italy. Totally sick!'

Everything seemed to be happening for Sacha. He had recently turned seventeen and Philip Harvey had thrown a birthday party for him at a private club in Mayfair called The Studio Valbonne. At the party were Angus Young of AC/DC, Lemmy from Motörhead, Kelly Johnson and Kim McAuliffe from Girlschool, Vicki Blue from the Runaways and assorted other people. To us in Toronto, it seemed unreal. I mean, Motörhead, AC/DC and Girlschool at a kid's seventeenth birthday party. Awesome.

Sacha hung out with us for a few weeks, doing the usual partying. One night, after smoking some hash and doing some shit, we noticed Sacha was missing. One minute he'd been his usual buzzy self, yapping away. Then he was gone. We looked all round the apartment. No Sacha. He wasn't outside the door, so we went down to the street.

Walking towards my car parked by the side of the road, I thought I could see something inside it. I peered through the window and there was Teabag, laid out on the back seat, comatose.

'Like . . . wow,' said Lips. We didn't know what had happened to him. Maybe he got a little bit overwhelmed.

We called Sacha's uncle to collect him. The next day we ripped into Sacha, teasing him relentlessly.

'You little punk. You just can't take it, you little wimp.'

Teabag was growing up, but he still had a lot to learn before he could party like Anvil.

10 LOSING FOCUS

LIPS: In early 1984 Robb finally got his drums back and we could get our shit together again, rehearsing and writing songs. But by then it was obvious that Krebs didn't like anything about the tracks we'd been writing and was never going to come through on the global record deal. It just wasn't going to happen for us and him. Maybe his business style alienated some labels. Maybe we were too ahead of our time. Maybe Krebs simply lost interest in us because we were too much trouble. Who knows?

I reckoned Krebs went cool on us because the huge expense of shipping Robb's drums to Japan made him think we could be costly and troublesome, but Robb didn't agree at all. He thought the drums incident was irrelevant and that Krebs lost interest because he couldn't secure us a deal with his record company buddies. And Robb insisted that Krebs kept our drums impounded because he was pissed that a member of the tour team had blown a large portion of the tour budget up his nose. I disagreed, but the truth was no one knew for sure because nobody gave us reasons; we just knew that Krebs didn't have the same fire for us. Then Paul O'Neill called.

'Guys, we got something for you.' I could hear the awkwardness in Paul's voice. 'We've got a tour of Japan for you with a bunch of other bands. We're calling it Super Rock '84. It's gonna be huge. And maybe . . . hey . . . one of the labels in Japan'll pick you up.'

I could read between the lines. I knew Paul well enough to realize what he was probably thinking but couldn't say. I guessed that there was a sense of guilt toward us, of a debt owing, because Krebs had pulled us out of a record deal and had then lost his taste for us before he'd secured a replacement deal. And that as Krebs's assistant, Paul had the clout to make it up to us by putting us on the bill for this Super Rock festival. But before agreeing to anything, Paul wanted assurances from me.

'I can make this happen for you, but you've got to promise me that you keep this under control. I don't want Robb taking drums. He can certainly take his cymbal and stands but he's not to take any of his drums.'

I had absolutely no problem with that. No problem at all.

The deal was that the gig would be the first outdoor baseball-stadium festival tour in Japan. Five bands – Scorpions, Michael Schenker, Whitesnake, Bon Jovi and Anvil – would play Osaka, Tokyo, Nagoya, Fukuoka and Sapporo. We were first on the bill. Bon Jovi, who were still on their first album and almost unknown, would be second. Scorpions were in the middle all the time, while Whitesnake and Michael Schenker rotated as headliners in different cities. As it turned out, Scorpions stole the show each night and everything after that went downhill.

It didn't compare to getting the global record deal that Krebs had promised, but as a consolation prize at least it allowed us to spread the majesty of Anvil to places it had not yet reached. And to share the bill with some serious fucking rock stars was seriously awesome.

From the moment we landed at Narita airport outside Tokyo and Bon Jovi followed us into the hospitality room, the partying was full on. Squirrely was drinking as soon as we landed, while David Bryan, the Bon Jovi keyboardist, collapsed on the couch with a groan.

'I am so fucking baked.'

It had taken twenty hours to fly to Tokyo, but we were ready to rock straight away. Bon Jovi were just an upcoming band, but they had a totally awesome manager in Doc McGhee and their destiny seemed clear as daylight. Jon Bon Jovi was a pretty boy on fire who totally wanted what he ended up getting. Like Richie Sambora, his guitarist, he knew he was going to be a rock star. They had only one album to our three, but from the first moment I met him Jon totally acted like he was a global superstar. He was frigging fucked up that his first single hadn't been a hit in the States, but he was a cool guy and I liked him.

ROBB: With five bands on the tour, backstage was like a heavy metal musicians' convention. Meeting Cozy Powell, the Whitesnake drummer, was one of the most profound and memorable moments in my whole life. To me, Cozy was an idol, a mentor, a drum god and a legend. I'd got a picture of his white drumming boots when we supported Whitesnake in Belgium and that was like a total orgasm to me. So when I first spotted him talking with John Sykes, I was like: Totally awesomely fuck, man.

I knew John through CT, so I went up, shook Cozy's hand and introduced myself. It felt like a whole new status had been logged in my being. Cozy was very cool while I busted his balls over the opening to 'Stargazer'.

'Just play for me, man.' I wouldn't shut up about 'Stargazer' to this world-famous drummer, but Cozy just danced around, avoiding my pleas. 'Just do it. Just do it. Do it, do it, do it.'

Finally he did. And it was just like I'd imagined. I'd

figured out most of Cozy's drum patterns by ear from records, but there was nothing like seeing the real guy play it. The only difference was that he hit two of the toms back and forth when I would have done the same with the high toms. The whole thing just blew me away. I was like: Fucking yeah! I made him feel like I was a fan, like a kid just getting off on his totally godlike drumming. And I think he enjoyed it, giving me a thrill.

We posed for a picture that became one of my most treasured possessions. Anyone who has met me and seen that picture is very jealous and respectful of the fact that I was so fortunate to meet Cozy. And of course it is totally profound because Cozy is not around any more.

That was probably the most intense and overwhelming moment of the tour, just ahead of the moment when I was in the bathroom and some chick gave me a piece of hash that she got from an American soldier on a US Army base.

Although Japanese chicks had been plentiful and just as mind-blowingly party-friendly as on the previous year's Anvil tour of Japan, drugs had been in very short supply. The chick's gift was pretty fucking cool. Knowing Japan had no tolerance for any drug consumption, Lips and I went in search of a place to hide and smoke a joint. We located an empty changing room with an empty bathroom and then locked ourselves into one of the men's toilet cubicles. With Lips sitting on the cistern and only my legs showing beneath the cubicle door, we thought it would look totally innocent to any passerby. The only problem was the smell. And the danger that we were about to start giggling.

'Fuck, this is great.' Lips coughed. If you don't cough, you don't get off, we always said. 'We are doing it, man.'

We'd just started sorting ourselves out when the door to the bathroom flew open. Someone walked in just as I exhaled a large cloud of smoke. Oh fucking shit.

We heard footsteps march up and down the room. By the sound of the swish of a costume, either it was Michael Schenker in the samurai outfit he wore on stage or it was a cop. The footsteps came closer to our cubicle.

'You guys are up to no good.' It was a German accent, so we knew it must be Michael. 'I used to be a bad boy too.'

We came out of the cubicle. Lips was just as awed to meet Michael as I had been about Cozy.

'Oh, Michael, man. I love you so much. I love your fucking guitar-playing.'

Lips continued in the same vein, giving Michael Schenker the full kudos treatment. Michael was such a cool guy. He just stood listening to Lips with an amused smile on his face.

'You know, I should take you on the road with me as a cheerleader.'

LIPS: I was totally blown away after meeting Michael Schenker. Michael was a very friendly, professional gentleman. We hung out with the Scorpions too, later in the tour. They were cool guys; they posed for pictures and talked to us, but that's as far as it went. We knew all the time that they were on a different level to us. They had no time for anybody when it came down to it because they were the Scorpions and we were just Anvil.

I also got to meet David Coverdale, the front man of Whitesnake. He was totally cool and I was like an excited kid wanting to hear everything from one of my all-time heroes.

'What was it like to play at California Jam?' I said.

California Jam was a huge festival in front of a crowd of two hundred thousand in 1974. It was one of Coverdale's first performances with Deep Purple. At the end of the show Ritchie Blackmore attacked a television camera with his guitar, then doused his amplifiers with petrol and set them alight. The explosion blew off Ian Paice's glasses. David smiled as he told his story.

'I tell you right now, it was quite the moment of my life. I went on that stage with a cheque for a million dollars in my back pocket. I was on top of the world.'

Playing the same baseball stadiums full of thirty thousand people as David Coverdale was an awesome turn-on, but the experience was tinged with a sadness because we knew that it might be the last time we played in front of such a large audience. As the tour came to an end, neither Robbo nor I were expecting Krebs to find us a recording contract or many gigs when we got back to Canada. We could tell his love affair with Anvil was cooling. He had other things on his mind. Marriages were fucking up and Steven Tyler of Aerosmith was on hard drugs. With shit like that, who needed to spend time finding a record contract for a band like Anvil?

Throughout the last twelve months, I'd faced demands from Squirrely, Dix and Robbo to change direction. Squirrely had already written several songs, all of them lame limp-wristed numbers with titles like 'Worlds Apart', 'Dream Of It Tonight' and 'Good Love Gone Bad'. Robbo and Dix were keen to incorporate them into our set. I was totally opposed to it. Anvil was about hard, fast, foot-to-the-floor metal. We needed to get heavier, I thought. But while we were walking down a street in Tokyo, Robbo made it clear that he wasn't with me on that.

'I'm going to make a band with Squirrely.'

'What, Gaze? Fucking . . . I don't believe I'm hearing this. Why?'

'He's more happening than you are. He's got a better attitude than you do.'

What was I to say? I didn't know if he was maybe just testing me. Or perhaps it was just his cruel streak, I didn't know. But as I listened to Robb tell me that he believed in Squirrely's vision for the band, I realized at last how the critical response to *Forged In Fire* had destroyed Robb. He was a broken man. The two things that made one metal band different to another were the vocals and the drums. But having been lauded as the best drummer of his generation after *Metal On Metal*, Robb couldn't deal with the lukewarm reaction to *Forged In Fire*.

'*Forged In Fire* was our chance, Lips. And we blew it, man.'

When I heard that from Robb, I knew his spirit was crushed. He wanted someone else to take the wheel. And he wanted someone to right what he felt was wrong. He wanted that person to be me, but having lost trust in his own judgement he'd now turned to Squirrely. And Squirrely's favourite bands had always been more like Foreigner and Bon Jovi than Black Sabbath and Deep Purple. So when Robbo said he wanted to change direction, Robbo meant it. He was telling me I had no choice but to do what the rest of the band wanted. For eight years, Anvil had been my band. Robbo and I had formed it and we'd been united in our vision of the kind of music we wanted to make. Now I was being told in the bluntest terms that I had to follow Squirrely's and Robb's vision or leave.

I couldn't believe it. Outside influences had ruined what we had going. Robbo and I had always agreed on everything. Robbo was always pushing me to be heavier and we'd worked off each other. It had always been real. But now it seemed those days were over. For months, Robbo had been agreeing with everything that Squirrely said. Now he was fully signed up to Squirrely's vision. I knew exactly what was going through my best friend's mind: It hasn't worked Lips's way, so Squirrely's way must be right. Follow Squirrely.

I'd always suspected that Squirrely and Robbo, who were both first-born, did not like it that I was the centre of attention. They had huge egos that made them want to be the focus.

Robbo and I discussed it with the other guys and Squirrely said what he'd often said before, but I'd always ignored.

'We just make you believe that you're the most happening guy. We say it because we want you to believe it.'

'Well, fuck. Am I not the main singer? Am I not the lead guitarist? Didn't I write most of the songs? Am I missing something here?'

I knew then where this was all coming from.

Squirrely, I suspected, knew after the farce of his performance in the *Forged In Fire* recording sessions that he could be replaced in a blink and no one would notice the difference. Only the chicks would be disappointed. His insecurity was driving this, I thought. And after the critical reaction to *Forged In Fire*, Robbo was just as insecure as Squirrely.

ROBB: When we got back to Toronto the after-tour depression – back to the coffin – was back as bad as ever. After a few days, we started playing again, like we'd always done; only now Squirrely was taking the lead.

Lips continued to handle the business side of the band and was forever calling Krebs's office, trying to get in touch. There was only one thing we really needed to say to Krebs: You say you don't believe in the songs we've been writing, so release us from our contract. But Krebs wouldn't take our calls. We had the feeling that he was keeping us in his top drawer, ready to be pulled out if he felt the time was right, but just as likely to be left neglected and forgotten. Lips struggled to contain his frustration.

'Krebs is doing nothing for us now. What the fuck do we need to do to get out of this contract? I keep phoning, but how the hell are we gonna get us a release if Krebs doesn't respond?'

Day in, day out, Lips called Krebs, telling him we needed a clean slate before we could go looking for a new recording contract. I no longer had the spirit for it. I felt broken and unable to make sense of what I saw happening around me. Metallica was starting to become popular in the underground scene and Megadeth was making a dent too. Bands just like us were starting to surface all around us. But then we were also around bands like Whitesnake, Bon Jovi and Scorpions, all of which were highly successful. Every fucking one of them. And I thought: Wouldn't it be nice to be as successful as the bands we shared a stage with in Japan? Their success inspired me. I thought their sound was the kind of sound we should be pursuing. I knew we had the ability and the musical talent necessary to make our music more palatable to the mass market. We needed to sweeten it, make the arrangements more simple, squeeze ourselves into the mainstream box.

Me, Squirrely and Dix tried to persuade Lips, but he wouldn't see it our way.

'Fuck no! Gaze, that man Krebs is a loser, a goof. He doesn't understand us.'

'Come on, Lips. We *can* be more commercial. We've got it in us.'

I tried to persuade Lips to play some of the songs that Squirrely had written and arranged. He didn't like it.

'The bands that are mega-successful are not bands like

Anvil,' I said. 'We've got the ability to change, Lips. Let's use it.'

'No way, man. It feels like I'm putting on the wrong trousers. We've gotta be heavy. We're Anvil. Heavy, heavy, heavy.'

Fortunately we knew of one way to get things happening. We were a band that made friends along our journey, not enemies. We thought back to the guy with whom we recorded our first album, Paul Lachapelle, who had become a dear friend. Whenever we could, we'd always insisted to Attic that we recorded demos with Paul. However, Paul had only a 16-track recording set-up, so after recording demos with him, we'd lay down the actual album recordings in a more sophisticated studio. Now we didn't have the luxury of a record company budget to demo and record the next album, so we contacted Paul to see if he could help.

LIPS: I thought it was the biggest fucking cheek that my brother Robbo had threatened to start a new band with Squirrely, in effect sacking me if I didn't agree to a change in direction. I'd always shown Robbo total loyalty. I'd turned down the offer to join Motörhead and I'd rejected Attic's entreaties to form a new Anvil without Robbo and Squirrely, who had pissed off Attic so much with their demands and ingratitude that they'd told me to recruit a new drummer and guitarist before they'd consider financing the recording of *Forged In Fire*. They'd also asked me to join Lee Aaron, the Canadian 'Metal Queen', an Attic artist who was really hot and sold gold in Canada, but who could have used the services of an additional good writer and guitarist.

I rejected all offers and pleas. I stuck by Gaze because I'd vowed more than a decade earlier to rock with him for ever. I knew that when Robbo and I rocked together, nothing and nobody was better. I also knew that we had to acknowledge that Attic had spent a quarter of a million dollars on getting Anvil to where we now resided in the consciousness of metal fans. They'd helped us to make our name. And to our fans, the name of Anvil stood for *heavy* metal. *Really heavy metal.* We'd be total fools if we chucked away that legacy and reputation. My only regret about Attic was that when Krebs told Al Mair to drop us, Al should have ended the conversation with two words: 'Fuck you.'

In my eyes, David Krebs was the worst thing that happened to Anvil. It felt as if he promised so much, but delivered so little. I found his influence was overwhelmingly negative, causing Robb and Squirrely to act like arrogant rock stars with Attic and eventually to threaten what Anvil was all about. I wasn't going to let anyone destroy my band or my friendship with Robbo, and at that moment in time, the only way I could ensure that both survived was to go along with what Squirrely and Robbo wanted. And before things got better, they needed to get a whole lot worse.

We went down to New York to play a showcase gig at L'Amour, a club in Brooklyn near where *Saturday Night Fever* was filmed. It was our first gig as the new and supposedly improved Anvil. Overkill opened for us and all the leading record executives were there, including Jonny Z, who now had an independent metal label, Megaforce. The show had also attracted all the Oldbridge Metal Militia, including our buddies Jethro, Rockin' Ray and Metal Joe.

We were premiering new material, all of it written by Squirrely. Now he was the front man, not me, and he was singing lead vocals. Within minutes of Squirrely walking up to the microphone and starting the gig, the audience was walking out. Halfway into the second song, I looked over at the exits and there were queues filing through them. Squirrely's singing simply wasn't good enough and I could see the look on people's faces as the song progressed. Their expressions had been excited and full of anticipation as we walked on stage. A few of them had appeared confused when Squirrely had taken position centre stage at the lead microphone. And then I'd seen surprise and amazement on their faces when they heard Anvil's new Squirrely-originated material. Having always been the singer, I'd never had the chance to watch the audience so closely. But now

Squirrely was singing and I was watching the audience collectively go: Oh fuck.

When we came off stage, things were just as strange for us. Where for years there had been crowds of people wanting our attention, not a single person was asking for an autograph. Instead, dozens of strangers and loyal fans alike were coming up to me and flipping out. It was terrible. A fucking nightmare.

That night, we shot a rocket into Anvil. At best, we'd put the band in extreme need of intensive care. At worst, we'd committed suicide. It could not have been worse. Our biggest diehard fans had been in the crowd and Squirrely had gone out and sung 'Good Love Gone Bad' and 'Worlds Apart', songs that told our audience to get the fuck out of there. It was as if we'd spent years telling our audiences that we were hard men in leathers and now we'd walked on stage to declare we were pussies in tutus. It was like: Get the fuck out.

'We thought you guys were fast and heavy,' said one of the fans. 'But you're commercial fuckers like Ratt, Poison and all the other shit. You guys . . . you guys . . . we thought you were better than what we heard tonight. Much fucking better.'

I put up with some shit that night. People came up, looking at me as if I'd stabbed their mothers. As they poked me right in the chest, I heard the same refrain again and again.

'From the heart, motherfucker. From the heart. *That* was not from the heart. You're the metal god and you're fucking playing lame.'

For years I'd been the focal point of the band, so now I was being blamed for all of it. Everybody thought it was me leading the mutiny. I got it from both sides – the band and the audience – and I became the fall guy. It was brutal. I don't know why I didn't head for the door and tell everyone: That's it, I'm outta here. But I didn't go down easy. I was a fighter. And I suppose I'd asked for it. I hadn't fought hard enough against the Squirrely and Robbo vision. I'd let it happen, so I took responsibility when I should not have done.

That night I was very despondent, hostile and moody. I was totally disenchanted with Anvil and I knew that nothing could be rectified without a lot of conflict. I felt powerless, but that didn't stop me telling Squirrely and Robbo what I thought of what had happened on stage that night.

'You guys lost your fucking hard-ons, man. I feel like I wanted to go and get laid, but you guys lost your hard-ons. C'mon, guys. We should be saying: Let's go and fuck. We should be playing speed intense metal but you're trying to play commercial shit. Let's get the fuck out of it, man.'

As soon as I got home from the gig, the phone rang. It was Jonny Z.

'You motherfucker. You fuckin' stuck a knife in my heart, you fuckin' motherfucker.'

There was nothing I could say in my defence and Jonny didn't pull his punches.

'I would have fuckin' signed you. I would have done anything. I would have gone to the end of the world with you, but you fuckin' killed me tonight, man.'

So now it was all my fault. And I suppose Jonny Z was correct. I shouldn't have allowed it to happen. That night the end of chapter one of Anvil was written. Had we stayed heavy, we could have signed then with Jonny Z, no doubt about that, and that would have been the springboard to a major deal, even without Krebs. We could have got everything we wanted. That night, I realized what we'd thrown away.

It couldn't have happened in a worse place. New York was the epicentre of our fanbase in the States. It was a disaster, almost entirely of Squirrely's making, so the next night, I told him what I thought.

'Squirrely, you're a fuckin' troublemaker. You listened to the fuckin' influence of fuckin' Krebs, but we're not Whitesnake or fuckin' Aerosmith. We never were. And I told you we weren't.'

Squirrely didn't put up a defence, so I continued.

'What the fuck were you doing? What the fuck? You derailed our fuckin' trip.'

That's the way I saw it and I still do. That night

wrecked a lotta shit for Anvil. It truly did. However, it was a two-night gig, so after having said 'Fuck this, fuck this, fuck this' to anybody who spoke to me backstage, I went on stage, admitted all the crap of the previous night, and then blasted full steam ahead into heaviness. It was a complete reversal of the night before, but it was too late. We had less than a third of the crowd of the previous night. Word had got around and the crowd had dropped from 1,500 to 300 people. Overnight our rep had gone from 'These guys are cool' to 'These guys are the animal that went lame'.

Outside the gig, I heard the crowds dissing us. 'Their next album is going to be shit. They went fuckin' lame. They let Allison sing.'

It was too late. The damage had been done. And now it would be really hard to rectify. We really fucked up.

ROBB: Squirrely never again sang lead vocals on an Anvil song. However, I was still not convinced that we should abandon our search for a more commercial sound if that might be the recipe for success. I recognized that the response to the material we premiered at the Brooklyn gig had not been good, but thought at the time that maybe it was more a reaction against our image change than the music. Before Brooklyn, our image had always been black denim, leather and studs, but at that gig we went for a less hardcore appearance.

With red leather and fancier hair, we looked more slick, like Bon Jovi, Scorpions or Mötley Crüe. Maybe that was a mistake.

The Brooklyn gig was in late 1984. In early 1985, Attic released *Backwaxed*, an album of rejected tracks and demos. After the effect of the Brooklyn gig on our fans, we totally didn't need our former record company to release a record that had below-par performances of songs that we'd rejected. But having sold our souls and all rights to our songs to Attic, we had no control over the release. Recoupment, the Attic execs called it.

The first track, 'Backwaxed', had been recorded for *Forged In Fire*, but rejected. The remaining four tracks on side one were from a demo, none of which we regarded as suitable for release. Our only input was to argue which four demo tracks we objected least to being used. Side two was a compilation of five tracks from the three Anvil albums released by Attic. It was packaged with the Anvil logo, but for the first and only time there was no picture of an anvil on the front cover. On the back, Attic used some outtake pictures that we'd rejected from the *Forged In Fire* photo sessions.

Lips took a totally negative vibe to the album, telling people they shouldn't buy it because it was the record company trying to make money with songs that he said were sub-quality crap. Lips didn't want to be judged on songs that the record company had picked up from the studio floor. But at the time I totally supported *Backwaxed*. I wanted to achieve success and I believed that I was going to achieve it simply because I was great enough. It didn't matter to me if the record company did its usual shit, I thought, because it didn't do the band any harm.

As for the songs on the album, only four were demos. The title track, 'Backwaxed', was a pearl. Musically, it was totally top notch with a great melody and arrangement, but Lips had pulled his usual trick of torpedoing a great song with lyrics that were too outrageous and over the top to make it commercial. You could regard 'Backwaxed' as being about the responsibilities of birth control.

Don't you worry, don't you fret
I've got a method that ain't thought of yet
Put it in and pull it out
Slap it on your back and watch it spout

I didn't care that Lips didn't like his lyrics. I thought it didn't hurt the band one bit to release a record that showed fans the songs we'd got in our vault. And to this day, our fans beg us to play 'Backwaxed', but Lips always refuses.

LIPS: In the summer of 1985 we went out on tour through the north-east states of America and Canada.

Again Sacha came along for the ride and as before it was good having him help us out. This time, however, his mother found out he wasn't staying with his father in New York but touring with a bunch of Canadian rockers. She freaked out and sent Sacha's dad to rescue him from our influence.

We'd just finished playing a set at a club in New York State when we noticed an extremely aristocratic-looking man walking towards us. This dude was Teabag's dad. Wearing a three-piece suit, expensive cologne and gold cufflinks, you could tell this was the kind of guy who taught economics at Oxford and worked for John F. Kennedy on his White House staff. He looked well out of place in a dirty rock club. He wanted to take Sacha home immediately, but in typical fashion, Teabag had persuaded his father to allow him to stay.

'You've just got to meet the guys,' Teabag had pleaded. 'I promise that once you get to know them, you'll see they're not so bad. Please don't judge a book by its cover, Dad.'

So Teabag's father, Sean Gervasi, interviewed Robb and me for about ten minutes. At the end he stood up.

'OK, I'm going to trust you with him. Please don't let me down.'

To Sacha he said that we seemed OK. 'As long as you stay away from drugs, I'll see you in three weeks.'

As well as Sacha, Jethro from the Heavy Metal Militia

in New Jersey was with us as a roadie on this tour. Remembering the story that Bess had told us about the prank pulled on him when he was a Black Sabbath roadie, we persuaded Jethro that he needed a passport at the border between English-speaking Ontario and French-speaking Quebec. When Jethro, who had never been to Canada before, said he didn't have a passport, we said we'd have to smuggle him across the border. Weighing 220 lbs and more than six feet four inches tall, this big, hefty dude proceeded to crawl into a tiny space behind the back seat of our van. With all our luggage piled on top of Jethro, we drove on, and then pulled into a rest stop. Brick, our sound manager, walked around the van, banging the sides near Jethro and talking gibberish loudly in a French accent. After a short while, we drove on for about ten miles and then pulled over. Jethro emerged from his hiding hole looking totally freaked out, but not as freaked out as he was when we told him that he did it all for nothing.

For the first time since we changed the band name from Lips to Anvil, we were touring without record company or management support. It meant we were grateful for every scrap of promotional support we could get, no matter where it came from. So when a radio station in upstate New York near Woodstock said it had arranged a record signing at a local record store, we seized the chance to meet our fans. Having driven for hours, we arrived at the back door of the store. Jethro leaped out of the door of the van, opened the record store door for us and rushed us inside, making sure that no one could get to us before we met our fans. Full of anticipation and excited to be the centre of attention, Squirrely, Dix, Robb and I ran into the record store.

No one was there. Not a single person. A bit of a comedown, especially when it occurred again at an in-store signing at Oakville in Ontario, when we travelled for miles to sign one autograph for a diehard fan.

We could see that the only way to ensure we didn't spend the rest of our careers turning up to deserted record signings was going to be to get a record deal and proper management. But to do that, we needed to free ourselves from David Krebs and he still wasn't taking my phone calls. Then, out of the blue, I ran into Krebs at a Michael Schenker show in Toronto. Frustrated after months of trying to get in touch, I was not going to let Krebs get away without a confrontation, so I grabbed him by his suit collar.

'Why the hell aren't you calling me back? What's your fucking problem?'

Krebs looked shocked. Maybe the message hadn't ever got through to him that I had called. Nevertheless, I persisted.

'Give me my release. We want out of our contract and

we've been telling you that for more than a year. Sign a release and send it to me.'

A couple of days later, a release arrived in the post. Liberated from our contract with Krebs, we could now go ahead with recording *Strength Of Steel* and take up negotiations with Metal Blade Records, who had contacted us after we'd sent them a demo tape.

At last the mighty Anvil could rise again, but only if Robbo was prepared to see things my way. By early 1986 I realized that Anvil was never going to make it in its current form. Sitting in a car with Jonny Z, I ran through my predicament.

'It's never ever going to happen for us, man. Not with who's in our band. It's just not there for us.'

Jonny agreed, so I continued.

'The only great musician is Robb. Dave Allison is not star material and Dix is just enjoying the ride. It's holding me back.'

Since the disastrous Brooklyn gig, Squirrely had totally stopped contributing constructively and his partying had reached new levels of self-abuse. Robbo was my buddy Gaze, a great, innovative and ambitious musician who would always be my brother even if there were periods in which his head would be turned by outside influences. And Ian was dependable Dix, who contributed relatively little that was original but who was otherwise as steady as a metronome. Jonny and I figured that Anvil's only chance of making it was to take the fall now, get rid of the ballast that was weighing it down, and then maybe many years later the band would rise again to achieve success at last.

But I didn't have the confidence to do anything about it, so I would have to let Squirrely continue to exert his influence over Robb while partying as hard as ever. I summed up my predicament to Jonny Z.

'We're fucked, man. It's going nowhere.'

Jonny told me to look at things with cold detachment. 'Get these people out of your life if they're causing you problems, Lips. Surround yourself with better people.'

To an outsider like Jonny Z or Al Mair, changing personnel was an easy option, but that ignored all the personal ties. At that time, Squirrely was seeing Robb's sister, Andrea, which didn't make breaking ties any easier. As I looked at it, if Squirrely was going to stay, retaining influence over Robb and taking Anvil commercial, between them they'd wreck the band. Believing the band to be going nowhere, I gave up. I decided I'd take the consolation prize.

I'd get married.

Maybe it was a response to my affair with Dawn Crosbie. Perhaps it was because I'd seen too much mess on the road. More likely is the explanation that with the band going in a direction that deeply concerned me, I wanted to show my commitment to at least one relationship in my life. Ultimately, however, I don't really know why I did it. Something in me said it was time to nail my sail to just one mast.

Getting married reflected the fact that I like responsibility. It feels like a safe place to be. I'm the boss. I can deal with the good and bad. If somebody says I suck, then at least I can say: I did my best. I take responsibility.

Rabbi Paul Sheldon married me and Lee on 31 March – the day before Fools' Day – and then everyone came back to our apartment, which was above a pharmacy, for a party. We had a good time, although one guest, a roadie that we called Strange, stayed over on our couch. On my fucking wedding night! It kind of sucked, but it was strangely appropriate because my marriage was full of little things like that. Things that slowly eroded it. People just came and went in my apartment as if it was a hotel. Whoever was passing through town, whether a journalist from *Kerrang!* magazine or a musician from another band, they could always crash at my place and bring a buddy. They'd put mattresses on the floor and live in my space while my wife and I existed around them. Maybe it was bizarre, but after years on the road, I was used to pushing everything to the limit. On this occasion, however, having just got married to Lee, I wanted some privacy, so I decided to get the fuck out of my apartment. Lee and I had received a fair bit of money as gifts, so we packed up the car, took my bull-dog Beast and drove down to Myrtle Beach in South Carolina.

Sitting on the Carolina beach, watching the surf roll in, I listened to *Forged In Fire* on my Walkman and wondered about what the fuck went wrong. Why am I not a star? Why didn't we make it? I was totally baffled. In spite of all its faults, *Forged In Fire* sounded very good to me. We had done an awesome job. I couldn't understand why the critics had slagged it and why the record companies didn't want to sign us after hearing it. Like . . . why?

Then, when I listened to *Metal On Metal*, which had been recorded nearly four years earlier, I could hear how all the bands that were now successful had taken tracks from it and built entire records around our sound. 'March Of The Crabs' became Metallica; '666' became Slayer; 'Stop Me' became Bon Jovi; 'Scenery' became Mötley Crüe. And when I listened to these other bands, they weren't even as good as Anvil.

The path that our band had taken was a total mystery to me: how the cards fell; who was involved; what was around us; how Anvil was exploited or how it wasn't exploited; the way in which the investment of money was pulled at a crucial time. As soon as we finished *Forged In Fire* we should have been on a major tour with support, but instead David Krebs was pulling us out of the Attic record deal and trying to talk Al Mair out of sinking money into us.

And now Squirrely and Robb wanted to abandon all the hard work that had taken us from shitty clubs to supporting mega acts in favour of making their fucking commercial shit. It was awful. Having discovered that our ethos of being heavier than any other band hadn't immediately succeeded, Robb had blown his load. He'd lost all his spirit and blunted his edge. The driving force of the band – the engine room – had just shut off. And now we were coasting.

11 MOVING ON

ROBB: By mid-1986 we were free at last to pursue our own agenda. No Krebs. No Attic. Just Anvil. Our only problem was financing our next album. So we went to see Paul Lachapelle, our old buddy who had helped us record *Hard'N'Heavy*.

'Listen, man. We haven't got any money.'

Paul smiled. He'd heard it before.

'No money, man, but we have got all these great songs.'

We put forward our plan: he would provide enough studio time for Anvil to finish recording *Strength In Steel*. Then we'd sell the record and pay him back. It required Paul to make a big leap of faith. He was in.

'No problem, guys.'

Friendship came through. Paul believed in our band. Throughout 1984 and 1985, as we fought to free ourselves from Krebs's management, we had been writing songs. Some of them were Squirrely's new direction. Others were Lips's old style, hard and heavy full-on metal. From sixty to seventy songs, we needed to choose ten for *Strength In Steel*. By the time we'd finished, we had a great album. The production values were some of the best we'd ever had. With no time pressures and no external intervention, we focused entirely on the songs and used our limited budget to our advantage. Instead of the usual 24-track equipment, Paul's studio had only 16-track recorders. It meant less room for experimentation, but the sound quality was a lot better because the same amount of tape was being used for fewer tracks. Lips's vocals were better than ever and, to give credit where it's due, Squirrely did a great job producing the record. It sounded beautiful. The only mistake was the picture on the back of the sleeve, which showed us wearing red leather instead of black leather. We were only reflecting the way that every other band at the time was dressed, but shiny red was not the Anvil style.

With the record finished but unreleased, we went out on the road. And because it was summer vacation time, Teabag turned up again. Over the previous year, when we were still trying to get out of the deal with Krebs and Squirrely was taking the musical lead in the band, Lips and I had cranked up our use of cocaine. In part it was a way of numbing the worsening tailspin in which we felt the band was caught, but Lips remained relatively disciplined. He'd happily do coke when other people paid for it, but he'd never buy it himself. For the most part it was self-control, a way of ensuring that he kept his use within limits. Even when he was sitting in his apartment, vibrating with the shakes because he wanted more, he would not open his wallet. As for me, like Lips I usually relied on other people to get me turned on, but when they weren't around, I'd buy it, the difference being that I could stop whenever I wanted. I could party full on and then switch it off. I could go all the way, then the next day do nothing.

Teabag was an entirely different type of user. If Sacha ran out of coke, he'd immediately run over to a dealer's house and buy more. So when Lips and I looked at Sacha, we felt profound guilt. We'd dirtied this innocent kid. We'd taken him on the road where shit happened and we'd let him taste it. I felt like we'd deflowered a virgin. Now Sacha was careening fast out of control. When we went over to Sacha's mother's apartment in central Toronto, Sacha would be hanging out with his new girlfriend, who was one of the chicks from Bananarama, as well as loads of people from the Toronto music business. Many of them were there only because Sacha was able to afford the drugs they liked and because he never hesitated to help them get high. Drugs had become a big part of little Teabag's life.

It all came to a head one midsummer night in Sacha's

mother's place. The apartment was empty except for a kitchen table on which we were cooking up shit. Of course I felt guilty. Here I was in my mid-twenties teaching a kid how to cook up cocaine. Hash and weed had been OK, but freebasing led to serious problems and I didn't want to be responsible for that. On that particular evening, however, those thoughts hadn't entered my mind. Everything was totally cool until we ran out of coke. I was totally chilled, but Sacha lost his nerve.

'Come on, man. Let's get more.' Sacha was already heading out the door, but I stood still as Sacha lost his cool. 'What's up with you, man?' he said. 'C'mon, dude. Don't you want to party?'

I went ballistic. Teabag was spinning out of orbit. He no longer realized that when I said the party was over, it was totally fucking over.

I loved the kid. He was a good guy. I didn't want to see him turning to anything shit because of what was happening in the band. I knew where heavy-duty partying led. Teabag needed to be warned. And the time for that had come.

'You're a fucking rookie. You're a little fucking punk. How dare you?'

No one told Robbo how to party, especially not someone who had been an innocent kid until he met Anvil.

'You don't know what you're getting into, Teabag. You fucking learn how to party or get the fuck out.'

So Sacha got the fuck out of our lives. And that was the last we saw of him.

LIPS: Maybe if we'd never met Sacha, he wouldn't have fallen under the spell of heavy drugs. We were certainly an influence and I felt guilty about it. If nothing else, if Teabag had never met us, maybe he wouldn't have spent so much time with people like Lord Philip Harvey and all his hangers-on. Although we sometimes wondered what happened to Teabag, when he disappeared that night from his mother's apartment we didn't have time to worry about it. We needed to get on with selling the album and recouping the production money to repay Paul Lachapelle.

Strength Of Steel had some outstanding tracks. After the farce of the Brooklyn gig, I laid down the law in an extreme way.

'There'll be no full Dave Allison songs on the album.' After all the abuse I'd taken, I couldn't face being blamed for Squirrely's songs and Anvil couldn't afford to alienate our fans even further. Squirrely had to accept my terms. He'd seen what had happened with his 'Good Love Gone Bad' and 'Worlds Apart'. The only compromise on the album was 'Straight Between The Eyes', which had both of us singing. With its references to lipstick doing the trick and lyrics such as *won't you give my friend a lick* and *ring around the collar*, it was very sexual and very Anvilesque, but without Squirrely's lame-ass musical arrangements or lyrics.

Remembering the conversation with Jonny Z in his car a few years earlier, I sent a tape of *Strength Of Steel* down to New Jersey. But Jonny Z totally chopped on it.

'Sorry, Lips, but let's forget it. Unless you've got a real fuckin' company to push this, this will never fuckin' happen.'

I told Jonny that I didn't care for the big boys. I'd spent two years dancing with them and I liked the small guys, the hardcore independent enthusiasts like him.

'That's OK for some records. But this is big-time stuff. And if you want this to really go, well, this is not for anybody but for someone really big. And I'm not a big boy.'

I thought Jonny was being evasive and too modest, so I told him I'd settle for his smaller operation. It was more important to us to be represented by him than by a big corporation.

'You know what, Lips? I can't get past that night in Brooklyn when you let that second fuckin' banana fuckin' come up and sing that fuckin' shit. It stuck a knife through my heart and I really can't get past that.'

'But, Jonny, you said in the car . . .'

'Yeah, yeah, yeah. Right now, I just don't feel comfortable with it. Basically, when it comes down to it

. . . you know what, I don't like it. I'm gonna sign Overkill instead.'

I went nuts on him.

'After all the fucking promises and after all the fucking chasing you've done, I give you an album and say let's fuckin' do it. And now you're saying fuck you.'

Jonny nodded.

'Well, fuck you, man. Fuck you, Jonny fuckin' Z.'

'Fuck you too, Lips.'

It was years before we spoke again.

Whichever way I looked, doors were being slammed in Anvil's face. First Krebs, now Jonny Z. I wondered who would be next. Our options were narrowing by the day. And new problems were appearing all the time.

A short while after the bust-up with Jonny Z, Robb arrived at my apartment door. When he sat down on my couch, I noticed he was crying.

'What should I do? Jane's pregnant.'

First the band mutiny. Then Sacha, followed by Jonny Z and *Strength Of Steel*. Now Robb and Jane. In every case, friendships were being tested to breaking point. At least in this case I knew there was only one correct answer.

'You got to do what you think is right, Gaze. So what do you mean by "what should I do?"'

'She won't have an abortion. She's going to have the baby.'

'Well, of course she's going to have the baby. Get married. What's the matter with you?' Robb had been dating Jane for nearly ten years. 'Give it a rest, man. Get married.'

Robb looked like a little child, frightened and unsure of what to do next.

'Gaze, dude. Does she tolerate you?'

'Yeah.'

'Believe me, that's not going to be an easy thing to find. You'd better count your blessings.'

'Yeah. OK.'

The date for the wedding was set.

ROBB: The wedding day was a totally awesome classic rock-and-roller's wedding. On a beautiful sunny Toronto day, we split my parents' back yard down the middle. My friends were on one side and all my parents' friends were on the other. One side was freaks, rockers and cool-looking people, the other side was like regular people. I hired the same crazy rabbi who had married Lips and Lee. I thought the guy was cool and he'd made it such a wild wedding that I'd vowed that when the day came that I got married I'd have the same guy.

I was pretty sober and Lips was my best man. It was a very mellow, private, low-key ceremony followed by a party with my friends and immediate family around the house. Jane and I went to Niagara Falls for our honeymoon – for rockers it's only Niagara or Las Vegas – and had a great time hanging out, eating food, walking and fooling around for a few days.

The day we got back from honeymoon I moved out of my flat in the basement of my parents' house and in with Jane at her mother's house. My dad told me that moving in with my mother-in-law was the biggest mistake I was ever going to make and he was right. It was a disaster, but I was too stupid to see it coming.

Me and Jane's mother were never going to get along. She had no respect for me. I was a rocker and a musician and I didn't have a day job. Music was my existence, but my mother-in-law didn't see it that way. She saw Jane-o, pregnant and getting up at seven o'clock in the morning, going to work while I stayed at home. She didn't get it and I didn't have any tolerance for her views on my life. To her I was just a long-haired freak. She didn't like me and I didn't like her. But before I could do anything about it, I came home for a night off between gigs to find Jane-o in the bathroom and looking freaked out. Her waters had broken. We were having a baby.

I went to the hospital and watched Tyler being born. It was a pretty wild, energizing trip. I was all psyched up for having this kid. I wanted to have a boy, which I got, and the family started there. The next day, I split to go to New York. For the first two months of his life, I saw very little of Tyler. I had a picture of him in my pocket and at every party on the road I told everyone I now had a kid, but it wasn't until I got home that I really felt like a father. But before I could bond with my first-born, I had issues with my mother-in-law to sort out. Realizing that Jane-o's mum had no respect for my existence, I moved out of her house and returned to my parents' place. It didn't affect my relationship with my girl one bit. It was no big deal to spend the day with Jane-o and Tyler, then to go back to my place at night and see them the next day. When Tyler was six months old, I found an apartment for all of us, next door to where Lips lived.

We lived in the apartment for a year and then moved to a flat above Sunrise Foods, a supermarket on Shepherd Avenue in Bathurst Manor. All through his childhood I raised Tyler while Jane-o worked. I loved it and I was superdad. As soon as Tyler could walk and mumble a bit, I bought him a real drum kit. At night, when Tyler was sleeping, I played a power drum tape in his bedroom, with solos by all the great drummers that I idolized. I figured it might give him subconscious inspiration that he could use in later life. Although I didn't want to force anything on to Tyler, I thought it would be pretty awesome if he turned out to be a rock-star drummer and I often dreamed of Tyler achieving the kind of success that I had not yet experienced. The thought of being taken on a global rock tour by my son when I was an old dude was like totally cool to me.

An indication that my dream might come true first appeared when Tyler was about five years old. With me and Jane-o sitting in the living room, Tyler would dress up like Alice Cooper and mime to videos, using a rubber snake I had bought him in place of Alice's boa constrictor. Years later, when Tyler was about fourteen, I returned home to hear a drum beat coming out of the garage. Tyler had put parts from my various drum kits together and started banging them. I felt like: Wow man, that's really good. I left him alone with it and, even though his old man was the best drum teacher anyone could want, Tyler taught himself everything. By seventeen, he had his own band in which he drummed and sang. I was so proud. And I understood his struggle: what it meant to have no money; how hard it was to get a break; the difficulties of record contracts and simply existing as a band. I totally understood it. My son was going to be a rock star.

LIPS: *Strength Of Steel*, Anvil's fifth album (including the compilation and outtakes album *Backwaxed*), was released in the summer of 1987. Having self-financed the production and been turned down by Jonny Z for a recording contract, we tied up a distribution deal with an independent American heavy metal label. Four years after we'd started work on it, *Strength Of Steel* was released, very soon after we signed the deal with Metal Blade. It immediately got ripped apart by the critics. We thought the production was good and, although I didn't agree with the direction of all the songs, in their own way they were strong. But we were learning that public opinion of our work was shaped by a bunch of buffoons who had little idea of what was required to be a good, technically accomplished musician. Critics, they called these idiots. Our chance of long-term success was in the hands of people who could kill a record with a single dismissive joke at our expense.

The most damaging aspect of *Strength Of Steel* was the picture on the back cover. It was a total error. We looked too polished and too clean. Anvil had lost its dirt. Squirrely's hair was too puffy and he was wearing a leopard-print jacket with a red shirt that was too big and hung over his jeans, making it look like he had a pot belly. Robbo was in a red leather jacket instead of a black one. My bondage suit had gone from black to red and Dix was wearing leather trousers and a red-and-black T-shirt with a bandana tied around his arm.

The intention had been to go back to the look we'd had in the first Lips promotional picture, but it was way too much of a change for the metal audience at that time. As soon as they saw the picture, the critics looked away without even listening to the music.

In their minds, the content was tainted by the cover.

The irony was that *Strength Of Steel* became the first and only Anvil album to penetrate the charts. It only reached something like 218th place, but for us it was a milestone. And it was the first album since *Hard'N'Heavy* that made money for us. And yet it was in our – and in the critics' – opinion inferior to *Metal On Metal* and *Forged In Fire*, so that showed what we and the critics knew about public taste.

In part, the success of *Strength Of Steel* was the result of our first mainstream video. In 1987, video was a very new thing. Other groups around us were appearing on MTV, so we applied to a Canadian Government program that provided artists with loans for promotion and marketing. They gave us twenty thousand dollars to make a video for 'Mad Dog', the strongest track on the album. Having studied video production at college, I drew a storyboard that featured my dog, Beast, morphing into me when kissed on his head by a girl. It was a classic Three Stooges slapstick video interspersed with cuts of the band playing live.

When the video was completed Beast and I were invited to Much Music, the Canadian equivalent of MTV, to appear as guests. With the cameras focused on him, Beast got hold of a tin can and started chewing it, doing his usual brawling bulldog thing, but as he turned his back to the camera, all anyone could see was his ass and his balls on screen. There was a lot of shouting in the studio to change the angle of the shot, but all in all the interview went well. When we got back, Robb was waiting in the parking lot behind our apartments.

'You don't know how to conduct yourself in interviews.'

'Ah, Robb. Please don't start on me, man.'

'You don't sound positive, Lips. You don't tell them how great we are.'

That was rich. Robbo wasn't having to take responsibility for publicizing the band, but he was criticizing those who did. After more barracking from Robb, I lost my temper.

'I'm fucking fed up of you fucking insulting me, Gaze. If you don't shut up, I'll fucking kill you.'

Robb gave me a big shove. He was much larger than me and he pushed me across the parking lot. Squirrely pulled us apart before the damage got too excessive – I had a scrape on my arm; that was all. But nevertheless I was totally pissed off that we'd had the second fight in our history, especially as there was no good reason for it. It was just one of those male-on-male scraps: a few shoves and maybe a couple of punches, then it's over. But resorting to violence, however minor, was a sign that things were degenerating fast in the band.

I wasn't the only band member who was pissed off. The commercial failure of *Strength Of Steel* impacted heavily on Squirrely. He'd put everything he had into it and to him, it was the best thing we'd done. Its commercial failure was indisputable evidence that his vision should never again influence the direction of the band. When he realized that, Squirrely lost his heart for the band and started to go into meltdown.

By the time we started writing our next album, *Pound For Pound*, very soon after the release of *Strength Of Steel*, Squirrely was present only in body, not in spirit. We could tell he had opted out.

'Fuck, man, why don't you get involved?'

Squirrely shrugged. 'You go for it, guys. You know what you're doing.'

'Really, man?'

'I'm stepping back. You guys are blowing me out of the fucking deal, anyhow. I'm bored of this whole heavy metal shit. It all sounds the same.'

Squirrely always wanted to keep moving forwards. In his eyes, Robbo and I were going back to things we'd done before. But moving forward for Squirrely meant becoming more like Bon Jovi. With a band name like Anvil, taking it down the mainstream road was silly. Anvil meant heavy metal.

'I don't understand you guys,' said Squirrely. 'Why would you want to stay obscure?'

'Because that's what we have to do.'

'Why do you have to do that?'

'Because that's what we are. You're a guy. You don't put a dress on and say: "I'm a woman." You can try, but you've still got a dick. Anvil's the same.'

To me it was really simple. I knew why people liked the band. And I knew that a new paint job wouldn't change what was beneath the bonnet. I'd been made very aware of that when Jonny Z and other fans had told me to 'Play from your heart, motherfucker.'

I knew anything artistic had to be natural for it to work. If we tried something outside the box, we'd be able to do it only once because it was impossible to repeat something that wasn't true and honest. We'd been on a journey and at the end of it we'd discovered that we needed to go back to our roots.

'Don't worry about it, Squirrely. We can be the good old Anvil that we were.'

But Squirrely didn't want to be the good old Anvil because it was built around Robbo's drumming and my guitar-playing. Those building blocks were what made Anvil unique and they were quite different from the cock rock of Bon Jovi, Mötley Crüe and Poison that was taking over the music scene. Squirrely realized that after experimenting with his sound, we were gravitating back to basics and that he'd never get rich with us.

'If I can't make money from this,' Squirrely said, 'I'll find another business. I will.'

And until he found a new business, Squirrely's

response to me and Robbo going heavier with the music was to get heavier into partying. He split up with his long-term girlfriend, Andrea, and married his new girl, Stephanie, and instead of the leather and denim heavy metal uniform, he now wore dress pants and cotton shirts.

While Squirrely imploded, Ian Dickson remained, as ever, dependable Dix. Neutral, happy to be in a band with his brothers, but with little to contribute. His attitude was to let us fuck up. 'If you guys wanna fight,' Dix would say, 'go ahead. I'm above it all.'

Neither of them engaged much during the recording of *Pound For Pound*, the only exception being 'Toe Jam', a speedy song that I decided on the spur of the moment would make a totally awesome heavy metal version of a square dance.

'Let's write a square dance, man, all about sex.'

Squirrely sat up. The mention of sex was like flicking on a switch for him. He smiled. 'Oh yeah?'

'Yeah, man. Something funny but sleazy too.'

'Dude, that's my area of expertise. My forte.'

Other songs on the album were about television evangelists, corrupt politicians, ice hockey and relationships with girlfriends. One song, 'Safe Sex', reflected the changing culture at that time. Musically inspired by a Cactus groove, it had a heavy riff and awesome drumming with spaces for vocals. The lyrics put across the message that if you were going to do shit, you had to wear a condom – *If I abstain, I'll go insane. Safe sex. Give me sleaze and not disease* – and inspired us to name our next set of gigs the Rubber Glove tour.

ROBB: Metal Blade, the company that distributed *Pound For Pound*, promised tour support for the record, but pulled out at the last minute. Instead we went to the Canadian government. Through an arts promotion program, the government gave us enough money to rent a camper van and truck. The Rubber Glove tour was on.

The tour took us across the States and Canada in late 1989 and in 1990 we played a few club dates and festivals in Europe. The organization could have been better. Our first date was the Cat Club in New York, a gig in front of a couple of hundred woodworkers. From there, we drove two and a half thousand miles across the country to Los Angeles for our second date. It took us two days of non-stop driving.

The gigs were good. Although the audiences were small, they'd all turned out for us because they were long-term fans who totally appreciated our music. The response every night was awesome.

On Metal Blade's request we recorded our live album *Past And Present* at the Waters Club in San Pedro, California. We had a legendary live act and we had the feeling that we were approaching the end of the first phase of the band, so it was something worth documenting. We totally captured the honest live spirit of Anvil. The only editing after the gig was to remove the talking between songs. Otherwise, Anvil was captured in its true live essence.

For the last few years, Dix and I had killed time on the road by making Airfix models of tanks and airplanes. At the time, it seemed like a natural progression from keeping pets after the gerbils and Precious the tarantula retired from the road. Now Dix was making larger models of monsters, ghouls and aliens to order. Like Squirrely, Dix's focus seemed to be moving away from Anvil and there was a strong sense of big changes afoot. *Pound For Pound* was not a success. The response to it had been lukewarm at best. We'd sold a few thousand copies to a cult following of Anvil supporters, but nobody else knew it existed. We couldn't get it reviewed and we hadn't done one interview. The plug had been pulled on us and we were scrambling around to get any attention at all. The world had forgotten about Anvil. It didn't feel good.

I figured the support had fallen away because several bands that were of the same bloodline as us had made it big and sucked up all the hype. Metallica, Slayer and Anthrax were now filling concert halls and stadiums around the world. Five years earlier, when we were releasing *Forged In Fire*, we were all standing on the same quayside. But they had got on the boat and we had missed it.

I knew there were times when we should have thrown everything at the world to give ourselves a chance at success. In business terms, the bands that were now ruling the roost beat Anvil to the ground. They'd spent years living on chicken soup so that they could stay on the road for ever. We'd done that kind of thing in the Lips and early Anvil days, but when the rise started, maybe we'd expected to reap rewards too early and maybe that had given other bands a chance to overtake us.

We should have moved to America. That would have made a total difference. If it had been up to me, we would have left Canada, but the thing that stopped us was my love for Lips and respect for the fact that Lips didn't want to put his relationship with Lee in jeopardy by moving to New York.

Lips and I were a partnership. We were a brother-hood. And although we fought and argued, I didn't like banging heads. It always left an emptiness within me, so there were many times when I didn't fight for my beliefs or I followed Lips's lead when I thought we should do something else. And I suspect there were many times when Lips did the same.

Lips had been my brother for most of my life and

because of my love for him there was no way I could allow anything to threaten our partnership. For years I'd listened to people telling me I should get out of Anvil and play with a band in which my unique talents would be fully recognized. For me, success meant financial reward for my hard work and global recognition for my talent. I'd achieved neither of those with Anvil and yet I couldn't turn away from Lips. It hurt me to listen to those pleas to see sense and to abandon Anvil for the simple reason that Lips's friendship meant more to me than financial success and adulation. I would never abandon my brother.

Businesswise we'd made mistakes, but our music was still totally awesome. Because of that I continued to believe every minute that we were going to succeed. We would be discovered. I had to believe that because I believed passionately in what we were doing and because we were too good not to be discovered. As musicians, we were respected like gods. We'd inspired bands that were now among the biggest in the world. We would continue making great music. We'd continue to exist. If we weren't around to be discovered, we wouldn't get discovered. We were prepared to sacrifice our lives for this. Somehow we would make it.

LIPS: After the end of the Rubber Glove tour, we mixed the live album and then went back into the rehearsal studio to get things ready for the next album. As soon as we announced we were starting to write new material, Squirrely made himself scarce. In the past, Squirrely was always the first to arrive for any appointment. We were the ones who kept him waiting. But now, whenever we contacted him, he was too busy doing something else to join us. When we asked further questions, he was evasive.

Whenever Robbo spoke to Squirrely on the phone, he seemed uninterested in Anvil.

'Squirrely's trying to tell us something,' said Robbo. 'I think something big is coming.'

It was painful to watch Squirrely go into a tailspin. Years of rock 'n' roll excess had long ago taken their toll on him. We all knew what was behind it: Squirrely wanted to leave the band but he hurt over having to do it. For all his adult life, he'd been a rock and roller. Now he wanted to move on and leave his brothers behind. It was hard to say goodbye to thirteen years that had been a mega part of his existence. Although Robb had long ago mentally cut his ties with Squirrely, he still felt bad. And because I was totally sentimental, I pained too much over it.

Eventually I got hold of Squirrely and he asked Robbo, Dix and me to come over to his place. Robbo knew immediately why he'd called us over.

'He's going to quit, man. You'll see.'

'Really?' I still didn't want to believe it.

When we got to Squirrely's place, he said he wanted to make an announcement.

'I'm going to grow up. I'm married now, you know.'

The man for whom the term extreme living was coined was turning his back on his youth.

'I'm getting off this train.'

Robb spoke first. 'You mean you're leaving the band?'

'I wish you guys all the luck and success. I love you guys. I've just had enough. I'm sorry.'

'Is there anything we can say or do to change this?'

'No, Lips. I'm sorry, man. I'm done. It's over.'

Music had never been Squirrely's real love and motivation, and the fringe benefits of being in a band no longer outweighed the demands. It was no great surprise that he wanted a new life, but it still pained me deeply that someone who put all their time and effort into the cause was now leaving.

We didn't hear from Squirrely again for nearly ten years. He completely vanished out of our existence. He got divorced, moved away from the city and made a new life for himself as a lumberjack. But that was all in the future. Right then, as we walked out of Squirrely's house for the last time, I was deeply upset. I hated losing a brother.

12 DESCENT

ROBB: With Squirrely gone, things felt fresh again. I missed him as a buddy, but as a band member he'd become a liability. The first phase of Anvil was over and we could make a new start, but first we needed a new guitarist.

I wanted to recruit a guy who could really play the guitar. Squirrely had been a rhythm guitarist, but the metal sound at that time was moving towards having two lead guitarists. I thought we should do the same. It would be something new for us.

After putting out advertisements asking for a second guitarist for 'Legendary Band Anvil' we were inundated with applications. Hundreds of demo tapes arrived from guitarists all over the world, even from Japan. It was a total shock to realize how revered Anvil was among musicians. We even heard from Mark St John, who had been in KISS. A lot of these dudes were already in bands, so they weren't all desperadoes, although we weren't always impressed by their lack of camaraderie for their buddies.

We sifted quickly through the tapes, looking for a type of guitar-playing now called shredding. We wanted someone who could play very fast passages with lots of string-skipping, multi-finger-tapping and sweep-picking techniques. We checked out a lot of the guys that sounded promising, but eventually we contacted Paul Nelson, a guitarist for Liege Lord, the band that had opened for us on our Rubber Glove tour of the States. Paul wanted to form his own band, so he opted out, but he recommended the Liege Lord sound man, a guy called Sebastian Marino. Before we had a chance to contact him, Seby phoned Lips.

'Come on, man. You've got to give me a chance. I went to GIT.'

GIT was the Guitar Institute of Technology, a college in Hollywood that specialized in techniques like shredding.

'I'm a good guitarist, believe me.'

'Well . . . I know what you look like.'

Lips remembered Seby from behind the mixing desk on the Rubber Glove tour.

'I'll send you all my fucking shit, man. Then you can decide.'

Seby sent us a picture and he looked the part, so we

called him up from New York for a meeting at Lips's apartment, where we worked on 'Love Me When I'm Dead', a song we'd written for the next album, *Worth The Weight*. It was about how people who died young, such as Jimi Hendrix or James Dean, were made into icons or martyrs after their deaths.

Hearing two lead guitarists for the first time was way cool. It was amazing to watch Seby play completely by the book, while Lips played by feel. They had two completely different styles but they complemented each other perfectly.

We also hit it off as people, so we offered Seby the gig. The only downside was that Seby lived four hours away by car and long-distance relationships had a habit of not working.

At the end of 1990, just after Seby joined the band, I was at my parents' house when Dad called me down into my old bedroom in the basement. Something in the way Dad spoke told me something was wrong. I could just feel it.

'Man, what's up?' I could tell from the look on Dad's face and his watering eyes that something had changed.

'Hey, man, I've got fucking cancer. I'm going to fucking die soon.'

Dad had just come from his doctor, who had told him he had pancreatic cancer.

I broke apart. It was too much. Tears rolled down my

cheeks as we hugged. I couldn't believe what my father had just told me. I guess it was a moment of denial. A profound sadness hit me right in the centre of my chest like a physical blow.

Dad was only sixty-one and he'd been completely healthy his whole life. For years, he'd been a total hypochondriac who always thought he was sick and who would visit a bunch of doctors before he believed he was not ill. But until now there had never been anything wrong with him.

'I pulled a fucking bad card, man.'

That was some understatement. Pancreatic cancer was fatal. Dad had no more than six months left to get his affairs in order. But whereas I was struggling to come to terms with my old man's impending doom, Dad had already accepted it. I could see it from the way he was telling me.

Apart from Lips, my father was the closest human being to me. Since I was a kid, we'd been real buddies. Now he was going to be taken. I had six months to prepare myself mentally for my father's death. My response was to lose myself in heavy drugs and painting.

I'd painted landscapes since I was eight years old. Maybe it was something in my genes – my uncle and my grandfather were artists – but it had become something that I did to be creative when the band wasn't busy. I learned the basics from watching a television show.

I found it inspirational, but I soon got bored of the mountain landscapes shown on TV, so I bought some books about painting, discovered Edward Hopper and lost myself in his work. I loved his composition and his use of light and colour. I could relate to the loneliness and the quietness in his work, particularly as a contrast to the wildness of being a rocker.

I started to copy Hopper's style and it soon became a type of therapy for me. My life was chaotic and lacking the control that I wanted. My success was not entirely in my hands. But when I painted, I had total mastery over the image I was creating. I'd listen to music, smoke my dope and paint. There was no rush and no pressure. Over the years, I painted all sorts of things, including a monument of a giant anvil in a public park with people the size of dots all looking up at it. It represented the power of our band and what I thought the band deserved: a massive marble monument. And it looked so fucking cool.

I also painted a pile of hash and embedded lumps of dope in it. I liked the idea of the painting having a texture that fitted the picture. In a similar vein, on a tour of Europe we stopped at a motorway services in Germany and I took a photograph of what I saw in the toilet bowl. It had a ledge that displayed everything before it was flushed away, which I found kind of fascinating. I showed the photograph to Lips.

'Look, man. See it? That's fucking sick. It's gross, but also kinda wild.'

'Fuck, Gaze, man, you should make a painting of that. That would be so out there. Nobody has ever done it. That's sick, man.'

Like the hash painting, I added three-dimensional texture to the toilet painting, albeit in layers of paint. Everybody who saw it had some kind of profound reaction to it, to say the least.

In the months leading up to my father's death, I settled into a routine. I would drive over to a friend's house and work on a landscape of Steve's Restaurant, a well-known landmark in our north Toronto neighbourhood at which for years I'd eaten bacon and eggs. But while I was in the basement of my buddy's house, listening to my music, smoking and painting, upstairs totally different activities were going on. Although a nondescript bungalow in a decent middle-class neighbourhood, the house was a crack den. I'd chosen it on purpose, wanting to prove to myself that at my lowest ebb, when thoughts of my father's death consumed me, I could be in an environment of complete drug depravity and not succumb.

For thirty-two unbroken days I worked in the basement. On every single one of those days, someone tried to entice or coax me into smoking crack. And every day I resisted. Upstairs, the place was chaotic, filthy and depraved as a continuous stream of crack-users came, got high and crashed out. Downstairs it was clean, peaceful and ordered. When I finished the painting, I was doubly proud of creating work in such extreme surroundings and of proving to myself that I didn't need to lose myself in hard drugs to cope with my father's death. It was a way of saying to myself: Hey, I can do this shit, but I can also not do it when I don't want to.

Five and a half months after my father told me he was dying, he began to look really ill. He woke up one morning and his eyes were totally yellow and his face was drawn with lines that I swear had not been there the night before.

'Fuck, Dad, you look sick today.'

Dad didn't get a chance to reply. Instead he vomited.

We called the doctor and they checked him into the hospital. He was immediately surrounded by specialists while I, my mother and my sister looked on. It was uncanny how accurate the doctor had been about the time my father had remaining after his initial diagnosis.

For the next fourteen days, I went to the hospital every morning. And every evening I went round to my buddy's house to get totally blasted. The painting in the basement was finished and now I turned to drugs. They became my support group. A fucked-up situation, maybe, but it was as much about being with my friends as numbing the pain with narcotics.

When I wasn't at the hospital or getting wasted, I'd meet with Lips and talk it through. If we didn't meet, we'd talk on the phone every day. More than at any time in the past, I just needed to hang out with brother Lips, smoke joints and yak. Lips was the only person totally up to speed about my father because he was my buddy. Lips was the only person who could understand my pain of watching a beautiful person turn into the living dead. I was only thirty-three and it was happening so fast.

On the morning of day fourteen I walked into my father's hospital room and knew that it was time to say goodbye. I could see he was not going to last long. He was on morphine and could no longer speak or see, but he could still hear. The doctor said if it hadn't been for his very strong heart, he would have gone a long time ago.

I said goodbye to Dad, telling him that I loved him and all that kind of shit. He just responded with little sounds, but I knew that he heard me. I could feel it.

I'd done my thing. I'd said goodbye to my buddy – my dad – and so I split. That was it. Next stop the bungalow, where I obliterated my sorrows. Six hours later my mother called.

'He's gone.'

That was it.

The goodbye at the hospital had been profoundly deep, but when it came to putting his box into the

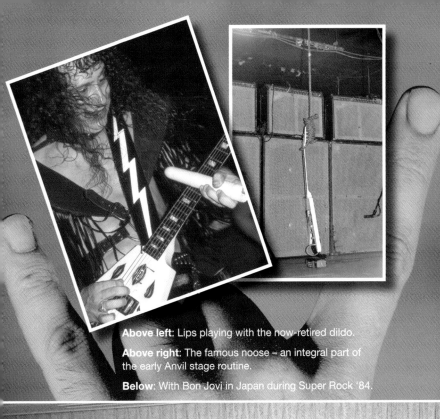

Above left: Lips playing with the now-retired dildo.

Above right: The famous noose – an integral part of the early Anvil stage routine.

Below: With Bon Jovi in Japan during Super Rock '84.

Clockwise from right: Lips still rocking in 2009; Lips back in the days of his bondage gear; Anvil, in legwarmers, blowing the crowd away; that famous naked photo, taken in Detroit in 1983.

Below: Joining the band: G5 in the early nineties.

Above: Anvil were always pushing the boundaries of style!

Above: Ivan, Lips and the Flying V.

Above: Band members came and went throughout the nineties. Seby with Dix.

Right: World-famous documentary maker Michael Moore hangs out with the Anvil boys.

Left: The *Plenty Of Power* album cover. Should it have been a tank?

Above: The Rock Salute: Lips, Robb and G5 with Sarah Brown at the London Film Festival.

Right: Sacha and Lips at the Sundance festival 2008.

Below: Fellow rocker Keanu Reeves lends his support to Anvil at the film's London premiere.

What a night! Lips, Slash, Ozzy
Osbourne and Robb at the Classic
Rock Awards, London 2008.

Above: Finally realizing a dream – Lips onstage with Slash.

Below: All together – Slash, Robb, Sacha, Scott Ian and Lips.

ground and it was really goodbye, I was totally numb.

My biggest fan was gone and although I understood that everything had to come to some kind of end, I hadn't expected it to happen when I was still so young. I was thankful that at least Dad had seen my achievements, but equally I was disappointed that he had gone before the true majesty of Anvil had been recognized by the world.

For months afterwards nothing mattered to me. The Chief was gone. Then slowly I realized that no matter what had happened to my father, for me the journey with my brother Lips had to carry on, because that's what my father would have wanted.

LIPS: It was painful to see Robb's grief after his father died, especially as I was going through troubles of my own. Things hadn't been good in my marriage with Lee for some time. If I was honest, they hadn't been good since long before our wedding, when Lee discovered I'd been unfaithful with Dawn Crosbie. The trust between us had ended that day and our relationship was never the same.

A year earlier, when we'd been out on the *Pound For Pound* tour, I'd got the feeling something was up when I returned home after three or four weeks of being on the road. Anvil had played all over the States and I'd come home for a rest because we had a couple of days off. When I got home I could tell that Lee was not very happy to see me. Not at all. It was like: What the fuck are you doing here? I could see that something wasn't right.

Not long after Robb's father died, I invited my folks over for dinner. I'd cooked a roast, but by the time my parents arrived, Lee had split. My mother shook her head.

'Where is she?'

'She said she had to go to work.'

'She's up to something, Steven. This just doesn't make sense.'

My mother was right. Lee didn't work at night. Over the next few weeks, Lee kept coming home later and later. And I became increasingly suspicious, so I started to investigate. In a drawer I found a note. Written by Lee like a diary, the note said she'd fallen in love with another man and that she was confused and didn't know what to do. Reading it, my heart pounded but I also felt vindicated. My suspicions were correct. When Lee returned home that night, I held up the note, which I was convinced she'd left on the top of a drawer so that I would find it.

'What are you doing? I've just read this.'

Lee said nothing.

'What does this mean?'

Lee said that what she'd written in the note was

exaggerated and that she was trying to sort out her thoughts. I didn't believe her but, feeling traumatized by the situation, I didn't question her any further.

A month or so later, in the early summer of 1991, Lee's car broke down. After getting it fixed, I drove it to where Lee worked. Robbo was following in his car to take me to rehearsal. As I pulled up outside Lee's workplace, I spotted her sitting on a lawn having a picnic with a co-worker. It didn't look right. They were sitting uncomfortably close for two people who were meant to be no more than colleagues. My heart sank.

Leaving Lee's car parked for her, I drove away with Rob.

'I don't know, man. I think there's shit going on.'

Rob was as cool as ever. 'Don't worry about it. Everything will be OK.'

'I don't know, man. Maybe, you know . . .'

'She's probably fucking around on you, man. You should fucking dump her.' Robb was never one for being sensitive.

But still I didn't want to face my situation, even when I came home one day after rehearsal to find Lee sitting in her car outside our apartment with her friend from work. The guy looked awkwardly at me, then got out of the car and walked off without saying anything. I knew it was over between us, but I didn't feel I could make a break with Lee because I needed her contribution to pay the rent. Our apartment wasn't much of a place – all the furniture was hand-me-downs from my parents or brother – but it was all I had. I was trapped. I couldn't afford to separate from my wife until I'd made new arrangements.

Eventually I got some money together. A Canadian government grant for artists and musicians came through and for the first time I had a small lump sum to last me a few months. As soon as I woke up the morning after the grant arrived, I knew it was time to take action.

'That's it. I want you to move out.'

Lee looked shocked. She was still half asleep.

'You've gotta go. I can't live with you like this.'

'You're a fucking bastard.'

With that, Lee climbed out of bed. As I made to follow her she pushed the ironing board at me and the metal release handle gouged into my leg. Maybe she didn't actually mean to hurt me but I was so angry that I slapped her across the face, something I'd never done before.

'Get the fuck out.' I was devastated, as much by the fact that I'd just hit Lee as by my feelings of betrayal. 'Pack your shit and get the fuck out.'

I knew there was no turning back. It was over. Really over. Lee moved into her girlfriend's apartment and I never lived with her again. Our marriage was finished.

To cover my cash shortfall following Lee's departure, I got my first job since I was a kid as a delivery boy at a florist shop, working mornings so that Anvil could still rehearse in the afternoons. Dog Boy, one of the Anvil roadies, helped me get the job and a couple of days later he moved in. It was good to have company to ease me through the low times after Lee had left, but Dog Boy was probably not the best choice.

One night, Dog Boy went down to a rundown part of Toronto that we called the Jungle and returned with some crack. I'd done cocaine before and I'd occasionally freebased if somebody else put it on the table, but I'd never bought hard drugs and I had certainly never been near crack before. But I was not in a good mental state and I needed something to obliterate the pain of my impending divorce, so when Dog Boy offered me some crack, I thought: Oh sure. Whatever.

I just about died. Within seconds of inhaling the fumes, I was going from hot to cold and shaking. I'd never felt so bad in all my life. I stumbled out of my flat and sat on a milk crate near my front door, praying to God. Let me live, I begged, and I'll never do this again. I meant it. Nothing was worth dying for; I learned my lesson that night. It was my first and last flirtation with the drug.

A few days later, Dog Boy came home with two girls.

I hooked up with one of them, who was called Sandra, and although she wasn't really my type, she soon moved in. It was more a practical thing than anything else. It meant I could go away or do whatever I wanted, yet still get my apartment half paid for. Sandra was a lot younger than me, which was flattering, but in reality she was little more than a band-aid for the wounds I was carrying from the breakdown of my marriage. I was vulnerable and a very damaged version of my usual self, so I have to admit the band-aid felt good. I needed the feeling that there was somebody to return to at home, a shoulder to cry on and a person to fill the void of what I'd lost.

It had been an eventful few weeks: Lee moving out, Dog Boy moving in, my disastrous crack experience and then getting together with Sandra. And it came to a glorious end when Dix announced his intention to quit the band. In typical reliable-old-Dix fashion, he did it in the best possible way, letting us know that he wanted to leave the band within two years, but promising to stick by us until we found a suitable replacement. It just added to the general sense that Robbo and I were going through life-changing events.

Starting work on our eighth album, *Worth The Weight*, with a brand-new guitarist and a departing bass player was not easy, but we decided to experiment with a new method of working. Instead of recording songs in complete takes, we played each instrument separately and in short sections, and then spliced together the best takes. Some of the best records had been produced that way, so we wanted to try it.

Lyrically, *Worth The Weight* was the heaviest record we ever made. Created in a period of loss – Robb's dad, my marriage, Squirrely's departure, Dix's intention to leave and reaching the end of our first three-album distribution deal with Metal Blade – the themes were very dark with titles such as 'On The Way To Hell' and 'Infanticide'. Other tracks included 'Embalmer', which was about my experiences delivering flowers to funeral homes, 'Love Me When I'm Dead' and a really cool track called 'Sadness', which Robb loved.

'Sadness' was a particularly emotional and sensitive song about Vincent Van Gogh, who, as death approached, told his brother Theo that 'the sadness will last for ever'. In an indirect way, the song was about Robbo and me. We both felt we were going to end up like Van Gogh, unrecognized for our art in our lifetimes and sticking to what we believed in when everyone else told us we were crazy. Like Vincent, we were selling nothing and making no money – our part-time jobs financed *Worth The Weight* – and I sometimes wondered if, like Van Gogh, we weren't also losing our minds.

With two lead guitars, the finished *Worth The Weight*

album was a one-off, something for the real Anvil fan. It was as hard and heavy as we ever got and many fans said it was their favourite album. Often the best work comes out of times of pain.

ROBB: After releasing *Worth The Weight*, we arranged a tour across Canada to Vancouver, taking Colin 'Mad Dog' Brown and Sony with us as roadie and sound man. Sony was an old buddy and Mad Dog was a totally good soul we'd known since the days of playing the Yonge Station, when he'd been president of the Canadian Motörhead fan club.

It was a good tour. The dates on the way out to Vancouver went so well that Lips was able to book the same clubs on the way back, effectively doubling our takings. We also sold some CDs, which helped us make enough dough to average twenty dollars each a day after paying expenses and accommodation costs.

The only trouble on the tour was Seby. He was a great guy and an awesome guitarist, but he didn't know our back catalogue sufficiently well to play it with confidence. His distance from us in Toronto meant he'd not rehearsed much with us and hadn't matched his guitar amplifier to our sound system, which meant it was either ridiculously loud or almost silent. At times it seemed like Seby spent more time with his back to the audience, fiddling with his knobs, than he did rocking out. And when he was facing the audience, he'd be watching us, not playing with us. Ultimately he never really felt like a true brother to me.

LIPS: For our entire career up to *Worth The Weight*, we released a record every twelve to eighteen months, then toured to support it. At the end of 1991, after the Canadian *Worth The Weight* tour, that routine came to a crashing halt. After the stresses of the band's collapse following Squirrely's departure, the death of Robb's father and the end of my marriage, Robbo and I ran out of steam. In 1992, we still met to rehearse and write, but we played only a few gigs and recorded nothing. It was as if the core of Anvil had gone cryogenic, put into suspended animation until the time and conditions were ready for it to be resuscitated. That time came in early 1993, when, out of the blue, a fan called from Germany. This diehard had put together a self-financed tour package of four heavy metal bands. At the last minute the headliner, called Riot, had pulled out.

'Would you guys be able to fill in for Riot?' said the fan. 'The posters are printed but we'll just stick Anvil over where it says Riot.'

We went more than willingly. It was our first chance to tour Europe since the glory years of the early 1980s. For three weeks, we played a string of clubs in Germany, Belgium, Holland, Austria and Switzerland, but now the audiences numbered in tens and hundreds, rather than the thousands we'd attracted a decade earlier. The woodworkers still turned out, many of them surprised to see us and asking what had happened to Anvil. All we could say was that we still loved playing live, but that we'd become more exclusive.

Dix came out of retirement for the tour. He had such a good time that we wondered if he'd reconsider his decision to leave Anvil, but he just wanted to get back to his new life of making plastic models of mythical creatures. Like Squirrely, he'd burned out. We were very sad to see another brother leave the band.

On returning to Toronto, Robbo and I returned to rehearsing on our own. Things were the same as before – Seby was in New York and Dix was absent – only we now knew we definitely needed a bass player.

For the next eighteen months to two years, Anvil was just Robbo and me. We'd ride our bikes to our rehearsal place and jam all day, slowly writing what would later become the *Plugged In Permanent* record. It was a dismal time, one in which I often had the feeling that we could just unplug our instruments, walk away from our shitty little rehearsal space and no one would ever know. We were so close to Anvil not existing at all, but somehow we kept going.

Having realized that there was no middle ground in heavy metal – bands were either total global superstars like AC/DC or Metallica, or total obscurities like us – the dream of making a living out of music was no longer the primary reason for Anvil continuing to exist. The only thing that kept us going was our love for each other and the vow we'd made twenty years earlier to rock together in brotherhood for ever. In these doldrum years we hung on to each other as much as we'd previously hung on to our dreams and ambitions, and through that, we kept going.

It wasn't easy. Without a bass player and with a long-distance second guitarist, we didn't have a proper band so we couldn't gig. And without gigging, I felt dead. I wasn't being who I was supposed to be. Records alone did not make Anvil. Without playing gigs, Robbo and I were just two middle-aged dudes in a room. Rehearsing kept us in touch with the feeling of manning our equipment, but that was all.

Robb was surprisingly positive through this inactive time. Like me, he missed gigging, but otherwise he maintained enthusiasm, possibly because he had more stability in his personal life than me.

At the end of 1994, we recruited a new bass player. Mike Duncan was introduced to us by a childhood friend of Robb. I was concerned that Mike wasn't a metal guy from the soul and guts, but we went with him because he played with his fingers and had the makings of a good bass player. We were bent on going a lot heavier with the new material than we'd been on *Worth The Weight*. We wanted to record something seriously crazy, but just before we were due to leave for Seby's home studio in New York, a phone call came from Mike. He'd accidentally smashed his fingers with a hammer and couldn't play, so Robbo and I were back to making demos on our own.

The next year, 1995, wasn't significantly different for the band. Hypnotic Records offered us a distribution deal with enough money to finance the recording of the next album, but just before we were going to start recording *Plugged In Permanent*, our first album for five years, Seby announced he was leaving the band to join Overkill. It was no great surprise. In the five years he'd been in the band, we'd produced only one album and toured twice. Based in New Jersey, Overkill was much closer to Seby and much more active.

About to start recording a record without a second guitarist, we hurriedly put the word about that we needed reinforcements. Through Ray 'Black Metal' Wallace, a buddy who helped us find gigs in Canada, we heard of Ivan Hurd, a Guitar Institute of Technology alumnus, and recruited him shortly before we went into Hypnotic's studio, a large facility in the centre of Toronto. Trying to integrate a new guitarist in the first days of recording an album wasn't easy and Ivan's play-ing wasn't as tight as Robbo and I would have liked, but after a lot of time and effort, we recorded satisfactory takes of his contributions. As for Mike's bass-playing, we thought the dude had put it down well. It was only when we'd torn down our equipment, left the recording studio and started to mix the album that we discovered that the engineer had not exercised any quality control over Mike's tracks. Cranking up Mike's bass so that we could hear his playing, we discovered he hadn't played in the tight innovative way that we needed. I was totally pissed.

'Flip flop, flip flop, flip flop . . . For fuck's sake, Mike, your bass is all over the place.'

'It's not my fault, Lips.'

But it was Mike's fault that his bass wasn't precisely in time with Robb's kick drums. Now we couldn't turn it up in the mix because it made everything else sound awful.

'Listen to what we've got on the tape, man. When we were in the studio and I asked you to go back in and listen to your tracks, you said everything was fine. Why the fuck did you say your playing was tight when it wasn't? Now it's too late to do anything about it. Thanks a fucking bunch.'

'Fuck you, Lips. I fucking quit.'

Packing up his gear as he yelled and cursed, Mike had a hissy fit all the way out of the studio, across the parking lot and into his car.

'You fucking buried the bass in the mix, so it don't fucking matter.'

'We buried it because it was out of time, Mike.'

'I'm not into heavy metal anyway. I never fucking liked it.'

'Yeah, yeah, yeah.' Robb was right all along. It was never going to work out with Mike.

After the experiences with Mike and Seby, Robbo insisted on keeping it local when we put the word out for a new bass player. But before we could recruit a new member, I was distracted by more pleasurable personal business.

Predictably, things hadn't worked out with Sandra, and about a year earlier, a neighbour who worked as a janitor for the local board of education fixed me up on a date with a girl with whom he worked. This girl drank me under the table – not the most attractive quality in a woman – so when he started telling me that another of his colleagues was interested in me, I ignored all his pleas to take his colleague Ginny on a date. Eventually he ran out of patience and put me on the spot.

'Listen, Lips. Just take Ginny on a date, won't you? She's nice, she's got blonde hair, she's cool, she's way intelligent and she's probably too good for you. So do me a favour and just fucking call her.'

I gave in and called Ginny. Four hours later I came off the phone. We'd hit it off immediately. Ginny was totally cool with a great attitude. She had two daughters from a marriage and she was very sorted. Intelligent and cultured, she wasn't at all like the women I knew until then, but very much the kind of woman I wanted to get to know. The next night, I called Ginny again. Another four hours later, I realized this was getting ridiculous.

'I've just spent eight hours on the phone to you in the last two days. I've gotta find out who the hell you are.'

We made arrangements to go to a comedy show and a few nights later I picked Ginny up. When she opened her door to me, I was surprised. Ginny was totally hot. Nothing wrong about that, but I'd not expected such a nice woman to be so attractive. My experience until then was that the hot chicks were high-maintenance pains in the ass. Great attitude, I found, rarely went with hot looks. Ginny changed that.

After the date, Ginny and I hooked up nearly every evening. I'd done a lot of thinking since splitting up from Sandra and Lee, and Ginny was everything I thought I needed in a partner. She was reliable and supportive; she wanted more children and a family for her daughters. She wasn't a pushover; instead she challenged me and made me act responsibly. She was the organized counterpoint to my chaotic existence. All of that was totally cool with me. Before the year was out, we'd bought a house together. As soon as the band finished recording *Plugged In Permanent*, Ginny and I were on a plane to Vegas to get married, the hassles of dealing with record companies and finding a new bass player feeling relatively insignificant to me when I was suddenly so happy and fulfilled in my personal life. After a long period of feeling lost, getting together with Ginny had turned my life around. Now all I needed to do was get the band back on track as well.

13 REBUILD

ROBB: As soon as we put out the word for a new bass player, the calls started to come in. For any free agent on the scene, the prospect of joining an established international band like Anvil was pretty fucking cool. My only demand was that the new player was local. We needed to recruit a proper brother.

The first guy turned up for his audition. I'd sent him an Anvil tape to learn some songs before coming to meet us. He carried in all his gear, set it up, tuned his bass and gave us a nod. We kicked into the first song. After a few bars, Lips stopped playing.

'OK. Stop, stop.'

I looked up from my drums. 'Lips, man. What's the matter?'

Lips nodded towards the new guy, who was standing still, looking blank. He hadn't even started playing.

'It's OK, man.' The new guy started to put his bass back in its case. 'Never mind . . .'

'Hey, dude,' I said. 'What happened?'

'It's just not for me, man. I can't play this kind of stuff, man. Can't do it.'

Walking out the door, the dude left us looking at each other open-mouthed. He hadn't lasted even ten seconds. It was like: What the fuck? So we called the next guy in for an audition. With really long hair, he seemed pretty cool.

Like the previous guy, he set up all his gear. We started to play 'Jackhammer'. At least he knew the song. We finished it, he nodded a couple of times and looked pleased with himself, and then he opened his mouth.

'Hey man, you ever think about rearranging that last verse?'

Lips looked totally horrified. 'No.'

'Maybe you should think about it.' So much for being pretty cool; this dude was a real wise guy.

'Right . . . we'll think about it. In the meantime, me and Robb were wondering, have you got any kind of criminal?'

'Yeah, I got a B and E record.' A criminal record for breaking and entering: just what we needed.

'OK, that's great,' said Lips. 'So that means you're going to have problems travelling? Very nice. OK . . . we'll be in touch.'

This dude walked out of the door and got straight into a cab, leaving his amp behind, as if he'd just stolen it. A few days later, a big guy with long hair came to audition. He had the same kind of rig as Mike Duncan, which was good news because Mike's sound had been amazing – it just hadn't been in time with my drums.

We jammed a few songs. Immediately he was locked in. He had the same finger technique as Mike and was totally awesome. He played grades with his fingers in a very aggressive style. It rubbed us all good. After the jam, I asked him if we could play with him one more time and he said sure. So we jammed again a few days later, knocking out another five of our songs that this dude had learned in the meantime. It was as good – or even better than I could remember Anvil ever sounding.

'OK, man,' I said. 'You can leave your gear here and we'll jam again tomorrow.'

He left us with a tape of some of his music. This dude definitely had all the techniques. His bass-playing was really ornate and cool, with complex structures. Lips was concerned that this dude was the lead vocalist of his band, but he told us his band hadn't played in five months and he was a reluctant lead vocalist anyway. The dude was into cool bands like Iron Maiden and Megadeath, and he respected the fact that he was joining Anvil, an established international band that had existed for twenty years and in which it was not his place to be a front man or to ask us immediately to change our arrangements.

After a third jamming session with the dude, Lips and I held a powwow. Turning to Ivan, I gestured towards the dude on bass.

'OK. This is the new line-up. This is Anvil.'

The dude had joined. His name was Glenn Gyorffy, but because he played a five-string bass, we immediately christened him G5. Integrating any new member into a band was difficult – good players were often dicks – but we hit it off right away. G5 felt totally cool.

The next day we shot a new picture for the back cover of *Plugged In Permanent* with G5 in Mike's place (although Mike was credited for all the tracks) and a week later we shot a video for one of the tracks, 'Dr Kevorkian'. At the end of it I took G5 aside.

'Listen, man. Are you a lifer?'

In his mid-twenties, G5 was at a crossroads in his musical career, not knowing whether to continue playing bass or to give it up to go to cookery school or to retrain as an architect. Music was not an easy way to make a living and it could wear out anyone's soul. With G5 now a member of the legendary band Anvil, I needed to know if he'd made a decision about his future. His reply wasn't exactly what Robbo wanted to hear, but it was totally honest.

'I won't answer that just yet. I don't have the answer.'

LIPS: *Plugged In Permanent* contained some vintage Anvil tracks, the usual Anvil mix of heaviness, social commentary and sleaze. 'Dr Kevorkian' was about a former pathologist who pioneered voluntary euthanasia. 'Killer Hills' looked at mountain biking, while 'Truth Or Consequences' reflected the O. J. Simpson case and 'Guilty' was inspired by my jury duty experiences. 'Five Knuckle Shuffle' was typical old-Anvil sleaze and the sentiment behind 'Fuck Off I'm Trying To Sleep' should have been obvious.

Musically, it was as blast your face as we could muster. At a time when everyone else was listening to grunge or unplugged acoustic music, we were giving it everything we had, trying to be as heavy as possible. No expectation of any commercial value liberated us to go for total heaviness. Tom Treumuth, who ran Hypnotic Records, had told us to be as artistic as we wanted and to give it to him 'full on'. We certainly had.

The critical response to *Plugged In Permanent* was that we'd gone too heavy. The reviewers coined the phrase 'too heavy for wimps' so we had T-shirts made with it on the chest.

But with the metal market so small in 1996, we figured we'd better listen to what the critics were saying. For our next album, *Absolutely No Alternative*, we decided to exploit the fact that we had the best bass player in Anvil's history. We wrote songs to accentuate G5's high-speed bass work.

Every day at rehearsal, Robb would bring in classic metal albums for G5 to hear. He knew Black Sabbath and Judas Priest, but bands such as Cactus, Wishbone Ash and Budgie were new to him. Giving a guy like G5, who could play super speed thrash death metal with incredible dexterity, an insight into early heavy metal history made him look at his instrument in a completely different way.

Absolutely No Alternative became the beginning of the Anvil rebuild. Slowly, and with G5's help, we raised the band's profile from total obscurity to semi-obscurity. The songs were tuned down to the key of D to give them a very low, bottomy sound and G5 was given freedom to go anywhere he wanted with his bass. In complete contrast, Ivan contributed almost nothing to the recording. Even when we recorded the base tracks in Ivan's studio, he didn't play. To us it appeared he had decided to check out of the creative process and, as long as Ivan didn't encumber the process, we ignored his lack of participation.

Having checked out spiritually, Ivan soon removed himself physically too. Deciding we needed instant air-conditioning in the studio, he started banging holes in the wall. A falling cinderblock mashed up his fingers; Ivan had to take a break. Fortunately his fingers had time to recover while we interrupted recording for Robb to deal with some long-standing legal difficulties.

ROBB: Driving back home with a buddy in the car, I pulled up in the parking lot outside the shop beneath my apartment. There was the usual bustle outside Sunshine Foods, so I guess we didn't take too much notice of two guys getting out of their car as we approached my front door. Slipping the key into the lock, I felt a hand on my shoulder. Everything froze. I knew exactly what it was because it had happened twice before. The two guys I'd seen stepping out of their car were cops and I was being busted for possession of drugs.

The first bust resulted in a caution and a fine. The second time I was sentenced to two weekends in a detention centre. This time, I knew it would be much worse. I felt sick deep inside; a total oh-fuck moment.

It took six months for the case to come to court. In that period we recruited G5 and started work on *Absolutely No Alternative*. When the time came to stand in the dock, on the advice of my lawyer I pleaded guilty to possession of marijuana. It was a done deal. Even before I got to the courtroom, the sentence was decided. I was going to get a thirty run – thirty days in jail.

The two weekends I'd served in the detention centre a couple of years earlier had been boring but uneventful. Wearing a uniform of blue overalls and shoes, I'd shared a low-security dorm room with drink-drivers and shoplifters. Lying on my bed, staring at the ceiling and yakking with my fellow inmates wasn't a great way to spend a weekend, but I'd known greater hardships on the road.

This time, from the moment I said goodbye to Jane, crying uncontrollably outside the courtroom before the sentencing, the whole experience was way worse. Being driven off from the courthouse, handcuffed to a fellow prisoner and the ceiling of the paddy wagon, peering through a little grille at the passing streets before being thrown into the Don Jail was a life-altering experience that I would never want to repeat.

Designed to house only short-term remand prisoners, the nineteenth-century jail was so overcrowded and lacking in facilities that human rights organizations and politicians had campaigned for it to be closed. Even the guards once walked out in protest and a Toronto judge regularly reduced sentences for inmates because Don Jail failed to comply with basic United Nations minimum standards for prisons.

I was thrown in on the pen range. Everybody on the range was meant to be moved on to a penitentiary, but in practice most served their sentence entirely at the Don.

Locked in my cell on the first night, I thought through

my predicament. The law had me, I figured, and I had to deal with what was coming. The jail felt like a new world, another city within the city I'd always known. It had four floors, one of which was almost entirely full of black prisoners, many of them violent gang members. If the prison staff wanted to mix things up a little, they'd throw white guys in with the black guys so that they'd be tormented, abused and beaten up. And that's what happened to me.

From the moment I was pushed in my orange convict's jumpsuit into a cell with another prisoner, I was frightened. In part that was because I didn't know anybody and I didn't fit in with the other prisoners, most of whom were career criminals. But my biggest problem was that my crime had no respect. Getting caught with a little marijuana was a loser's crime to the people inside that place. It was embarrassing when most of the other inmates had been convicted of robbery, assaulting the police, heavy drug-dealing or massive fraud, all of which were regarded as way cooler crimes than mine.

Knowing the other inmates thought I was little more than a bum, I kept to myself and didn't say much to anybody. I spent a lot of time on the phone, speaking to Jane, my friends and anyone who would accept a collect call from me. I guess I must have seemed quite an oddball; I didn't fit in and I was always yakking on the payphone.

By day twelve of my thirty run, I was going out of my mind. Time passed totally slowly when there was nothing to do and I was locked up for half the day in dead silence. Other prisoners smoked crack and did all sorts of shit, but I kept out of it. There was a lot of yelling and aggression, mainly over trivial disputes, like guys owing each other money or cigarettes.

I kept my head down, got on with serving my time and passed the locked-up hours as best I could. Imprisoned for heavy theft, my fifty-five-year-old cellmate had spent most of his life in prison and told me he preferred being inside. As soon as he was released, he'd commit another crime so that he would be imprisoned again. I couldn't understand it.

I survived until the twelfth day, when out of nowhere, the guards called for number 249, Reiner. That was me. I was transferred from the north side to the south side of the range. The guards shrugged and said they were simply moving prisoners around, but now I was in with the murderers. I felt immediately that something was wrong. Nobody had to tell me; I knew it just wasn't right.

'What's going on, man?' I said to one of the guards. 'I'm on the wrong side.'

I realized then that I had probably been profiled by the other prisoners. Having kept to myself and spent a lot of time on the phone, maybe I looked like a cop and they wanted me out of their range.

On my second day on the south range, the perpetrator of a very famous Toronto murder, a black guy with a scar on his face, sat down beside me. He looked at me with the coldest eyes I'd ever seen.

'You got to get off the range, man.'

Immediately my heart started racing like a motherfucker. 'Oh . . . OK, man.'

Standing up to move back to my cell, I could sense that something bad was about to happen and that I needed to get my shit together. Without a friend on the entire range, I was being told by a big badass guy to get the fuck out of there. And he'd told me in a way like he wasn't fucking around. As I gathered my shit together, the badass guy grabbed me.

'Come with me, motherfucker.'

Mumbling continuously, he hauled me down to the end of the range, about fifty feet away from anybody else.

'You got to get out of here, man . . . you know, you got to get off the range, you know . . . it'd be best for you if you just went, man . . .'

Again and again he said it to me. Feeling like I was being led to my death, I was gripped by panic.

My vision went totally white as I felt a tremendous force against my face. I was hit so hard that for a few seconds I didn't know where I was. When I came around, I was still standing but the badass was kneeing me repeatedly in the stomach. Hammering and kicking, he yelled at me as I cowered against the wall, frightened for my life.

'Hey, motherfucker, I'm gonna fuckin' kill ya.'

I took the blows but I didn't fall down. I slumped against the bars of a door, pushing him away and yelling.

'Cool out, man. I got your message. I'll get the fuck out of here.'

The dude cut back and I ran back to my cell, grabbed my shit and yelled, 'Guard!'

The guard arrived and I explained I'd been assaulted and that the dude wanted me dead.

'For fuck's sake get me outta here.'

Two guards dragged me to a secure side room, where I started to calm down and told them what had happened.

'Fuck, man, I got assaulted. You know these guys hate me or something.'

'They think you're an undercover cop.'

'No way, man, I'm a rock star. I'm a famous musician from a heavy metal band. I shouldn't even be fucking in here.'

They agreed I was in the wrong place and then gave me some advice.

'You have two options. You can press charges and go through that whole formality, but we recommend you don't – it would not be in your best interests to go down that road. Or you can take your belongings, do your time, get out of here and never come back.'

I didn't press any charges. I just wanted to put the whole experience behind me.

I was moved to a range with regular remand prisoners, where I spent all day on the phone to my lawyer, demanding to be released or transferred to a more suitable facility. Fearing for my life, I was freaking out like mad and phoning whoever would listen to me.

Jane-o freaked too when I told her I'd been pounded and assaulted. Lips was really upset to hear I'd got a beating. 'Gaze, man. I fuckin' feel for you,' he said. 'Is there anything I can do?'

Eventually my lawyer came good and I was transferred to the medical security ward to serve the last few days in safety. For good behaviour, my thirty run was reduced and on day twenty I was released.

Freedom never tasted so good.

LIPS: At the tail end of 1996, not long after Robbo had been released from jail, we were offered a tour of Europe with two other metal bands. We'd released *Plugged In Permanent* and started work on *Absolutely No Alternative*, so it was a good chance to play recent and new material. The deal was that Anvil would open for Overkill. The second support would be an Austrian band called Stahlhammer, which we thought was way appropriate as Stahlhammer meant steel hammer. Anvil and Stahlhammer: they belonged together.

With Seby now in Overkill's ranks, it felt like our old guitarist had come back to help us out. He'd sit at the soundboard every night during our set, mixing our sound before he went on stage with Overkill.

For Robbo, it was great to be back behind his drums after his prison experience, especially as he played a crucial part in blowing Overkill off the stage. Night after night, Overkill's lead vocalist, Bobby 'Blitz' Ellsworth, would come over to ask Robb how he played his drums with such intensity. I figured the ferocity came from Robbo's relief at being liberated from jail.

With twenty-three shows in twenty-eight days, it was a totally intense tour that brought us to a new audience and introduced G5 to the faithful woodworkers. G5's only disappointment was that the road days of sex and drugs were long gone. The only significant incident was when one of the Overkill guitarists got busted in a brothel for smashing up a room and the band had to bail him out. Other than that, the partying was very tame compared to the glory days of the 1980s. For G5, it was early nights after a few beers and long days spent learning our back catalogue. He also learned that he could go crazy if he wanted and party until he fell over, but on such a tight schedule he'd be playing the next evening like Squirrely in his heyday and regretting his previous night's exploits.

A sign of the times was that one of the guys from Stahlhammer couldn't party at all because he had a drug test due when he got home. If his piss tested positive, he'd be in trouble, which we thought was kind of funny, so we wrote 'Piss Test' about it for the next album. The intro was G5 doing a leak; there can't be many musicians who get to piss on their first album. Another song on *Absolutely No Alternative* called 'Red Light' was inspired by touring Amsterdam and Hamburg with Overkill. 'Show Us Your Tits', a long-term fan favourite, was a political song written after a Toronto student set a legal precedent when she argued in court that it was sex discrimination not to allow women to walk around topless on hot days like men. And 'Green Jesus', about money troubles, reflected our experience with record companies. Like Attic in the 1980s, our current record companies, Hypnotic and Massacre, were changing the agreed payment structure with every record we released through them. At times it felt like we were being robbed, but we had no clout – the execs told us to 'accept it or move on' – so we just let ourselves be ripped off for our art.

Not long after we'd released *Absolutely No Alternative*, we were out on the road again, touring North America on our own and then Europe as support to Flotsam and Jetsam. As in 1986, when Tyler was born and Robb left for New York the next day, G5 and I became fathers hours before heading off on the road. In both cases, our babies were ten days late and there was a danger we'd miss the births. G5's partner Crystal went into labour naturally and a few hours later Ginny was induced so that I'd be in town when she had the baby. G5's daughter Justine and my son Averey were born thirteen hours apart.

The birth was awesome, but it was pretty weird going out on tour knowing that a baby was waiting for me when I got home. In a matter of hours I'd gone from holding Averey in the hospital to the whole different mindset of being on the road. Until then, I'd always gone home to a girlfriend or wife; now I'd be going home to a family. It felt cool and extraordinarily fulfilling to be a dad, but after more than two decades of Anvil and the Lips band, I found it very easy to put my family to the back of my mind without any feelings of guilt, particularly as touring with Flotsam and Jetsam was heavy shit.

Their roadies were totally wasted, the sound was bad, the bands played for too long, the travel and venues were disorganized and the tour was plagued by chaotic behaviour. People were pissing all over the washrooms and on the floors, and the tour bus was in a disgusting state because the roadies were permanently fucked.

As the tour progressed, the conditions got me down and I felt increasingly homesick, wanting to see my son again. For G5, it was different. Only on his second tour, G5 still had a lot to learn and needed to focus totally on the music, so there was little time for reflection on what awaited him when he got home. And that lifer question that Robbo had asked him was occupying his mind. Finding the balance between the demands of home when a newborn was waiting and the lure of the road was a good way to test his dedication to Anvil.

ROBB: By the end of 1997 it was totally obvious that G5 was the best bass player that Anvil ever had. It was a total no-brainer. The only regret was that G5 hadn't been born earlier, so that he could have shared the Anvil glory years with us. On a personal level, he was an awesomely cool guy. I already felt like he was a brother, but he was still questioning whether he was a true lifer.

Since the birth of his son Averey, Lips had become much more positive about the band. But at the same time, I reached rock bottom, thinking I could be wasting the rest of my life staying dedicated to Anvil, particularly when faced by Ivan's total apathy towards the band. G5 collaborated with Lips in writing the lyrics to the next album while we were on the road with Flotsam and Jetsam, but Ivan did nothing. Often we'd start and end rehearsals without him attending. And when he did turn up, we could tell his heart wasn't in it.

The critical response to *Absolutely No Alternative* was that it was sufficiently heavy and a good album, but not fast enough, so for the next album we went: 'Oh yeah?' turned the speed up to max and called it *Speed Of Sound*. We recorded it with Pierre Rémillard, a producer recommended to us by Hypnotic Records, in an awesome RCA studio in Montreal. For the first time, Ivan didn't play any rhythm guitar at all on the album. Having not rehearsed enough, all he could do was to sit in the studio, watching us play faster and tighter than he could manage.

I wanted to fire Ivan but I couldn't because he wasn't my boy. Lips always defended Ivan. 'Maybe one day he'll be a part of it and contribute.'

I don't know why Lips defended Ivan for so long. I think it was something in his good nature that made him feel sorry for Ivan. 'Gaze, without Anvil, Ivan has got nothing. He's got potential, Gaze. Just give him a chance, Robbo. Maybe he'll come good one day.'

Midway through the recording of *Speed Of Sound*, we were invited to play the Wacken festival, by 1998 the largest and most important metal festival in Europe, if not the world. More than seventy thousand metal fans made the pilgrimage to Wacken every year. More than seventy bands played; like us none of them were mainstream or household names. Ever since we'd recruited

G5, we'd had the feeling that Anvil was on the rise again and that weekend in Wacken felt like a major turning point. It was G5's first totally big show and we had a prime spot on it. Due on stage at nine o'clock at night, we were close to headlining. Everyone was chanting and screaming for Anvil and we played an awesome set. Afterwards, many of the other bands told us they thought it was our night. It felt great. Anvil was back in the heartland of European metal, putting out the message that Anvil was well and truly back.

LIPS: We released *Speed Of Sound* in late 1998, through Hypnotic in Canada and licensed to Massacre in the US, although we'd long ago abandoned any hope of making money through our distribution deal. Early the next year, we were offered a short but intensive tour of the American Midwest with Jag Panzer, Iced Earth and the Quiet Room. With seven gigs in nine days, we covered a lot of ground in a minibus driven by Dirty, an old buddy who'd roadied for us.

The tour was uneventful until we played the Flying Machine, a club at Cleveland in Ohio. The place was packed and we were the third band out of four on the bill. After our show, I went to collect the money like I always did. The promoter and the agent pulled me into the promoter's office. They were both totally grim-faced. The promoter spoke first.

'Four people asked for their money back because you used a vibrator on stage. Why did you do something so gay?'

I was kind of shocked, especially when the agent chipped in.

'I won't book your band if you continue using this.' He pointed at my dildo. 'It's in bad taste. If you insult just one person, it's one too many.'

'Like . . .' I didn't know what to say. Anvil's reputation was built on our stage show and the dildo was a big part of it.

'You've got to start thinking about what I just said as careers advice,' said the promoter. 'You need to put some serious thought into this. One detrimental thing can work against you. That thing takes away more from your performance than it adds.'

No one had ever said anything like it to me. The dildo had never been an issue. The only problem I had with it was that it often got stolen by fans, but I could tell that to these guys, this was no light matter. They were totally offended.

Most of the time I used the dildo for totally tame stuff. I'd use it to play bottleneck guitar – we called it vibratoring – or I'd make unusual sounds by letting it buzz over my guitar pick-up. I'd bang it on the strings percussively or I'd taunt girls with it, rubbing it under their chin. They'd flip out, but it was fun and it was always done with total integrity. And sometimes I would jack it off, and as Robbo came to the climax of a drum roll, I'd spit as if it was an orgasm. That's what I'd done that night in Cleveland. For heavy metal, that was an innovation, but for the promoter and agent, it looked gay.

Robbo said that stopping me using the vibrator on stage was like asking Jimi Hendrix not to play his guitar with his teeth, an assault on my creative freedom, but I could see that maybe mores were changing. What had been fun in the early eighties, in the days before AIDS and widespread political correctness, maybe looked offensive now. The promoter certainly thought so.

'You've got to keep that thing in its box,' he said.

At least it was one less thing to worry about when I left home. And I wouldn't have to carry half a dozen around with me when we were on tour. That was always difficult to explain when all of them fell out of my bag at a customs check.

At first I resisted censorship on my stage act. But after a while, I stopped using it every night and I started to notice that no one ever complained when the dildo didn't come out. That's when I started thinking that maybe those guys in Cleveland had been right: it wasn't important enough to risk offending people. Audiences were more concerned about hearing 'Metal On Metal'. The only time we didn't play it, the promoter sent us straight back on stage with the words: 'Go out and play that fucking song. Half the people in the club are asking for their money back.'

Eventually it got to the point where I used a dildo only when a fan threw one on stage or someone bought me one as a joke. Its last appearance came at the Daniel Boone Saloon, when I used one because the owner's girlfriend gave me hers to use at a private party. When some of the guys in the audience started freaking out – yelling, 'Where's it been, man?' – I thought it was time to retire a faithful old friend that had seen enough action. Since then, Robb has always insisted that one day the dildo will return. He's convinced the fans will start screaming for it, but so far that day hasn't arrived, so it seems that maybe that Cleveland promoter was right.

After returning from the short US tour, the rest of the ycar was spent writing new material for our next album. In November we embarked on a long self-financed tour of America that marked a new nadir in the band's fortunes. For six weeks we criss-crossed the country, playing a string of shitholes in which often no one turned up to see us. We had an agent with no money whom we nicknamed the Digger, who showed some enthusiasm for old-school metal and offered us what he called 'an extensive tour'. We totally went for it. We wanted to play. It was an opportunity.

But understandably, given Anvil's obscurity, the Digger cared more about getting his booking fee up front than spending heavily on promoting Anvil. No publicity meant no one but the woodworkers knew who we were and even they were often unaware that we were passing through town. G5 did most of our marketing, calling ahead to venues, sending them our details and a photograph, but often the owners of the venues did little with them. The only good thing to be said about the Digger was that he inspired 'The Creep', a song about shyster promoters that we wrote on the road.

G5 and Ivan's first two Anvil tours had been through Europe on a tour bus with roadies, catering and a tour manager. They'd jumped a few steps up the ladder, but on this tour they paid their dues.

On a very tight budget, the only way to pull off the tour was to drive a van and trailer ourselves and sleep alternate nights on the road. Robbo drove most of the tour, usually through the night after a gig, while the rest of us slept. We'd time it so that we'd arrive at the next venue early in the morning. If we then checked into a nearby motel, we could get the whole day and the following night for the price of one night. We'd sleep all day, play the gig and then sleep the night in the motel. The following morning we'd drive to the next venue, arrive that evening, play the gig, then drive through the night to the next city, where again we'd check in early at a motel. By turning over rooms in that way, we halved our accommodation costs. It left us feeling burned out, but it was the only way to survive.

With all four of us sleeping in the van or in one motel room, sharing two double beds, inevitably tensions rose and we were frequently grumpy with one another. For G5 and Ivan, hardcore touring was a novelty and they didn't realize that all sorts of expenses needed to be paid before they saw any money. They were permanently broke, a situation that wasn't helped by Ivan blowing what little money he had on the tables in Vegas.

An even bigger cause of tension and irritation was the sheer relentlessness of the schedule. We played almost every night – thirty shows in thirty-five days – and had to travel vast distances to pull it off. A lot of the time we didn't cover our costs. We'd drive up to a venue only to discover there wasn't a gig. With a large part of our income derived from CD and merchandise sales – our gig fees covered only our accommodation and travel costs – it killed us when we trekked hundreds of miles only to find a gig was cancelled or only a handful of people had turned out. In Texas, we turned up outside a club. The place looked good and there was even a poster with our name hanging outside, but beside it was a sign saying the venue would not be open that night. No explanation, no information, nothing.

All we knew was that we were out of pocket again.

Even when a gig went well, getting paid by the promoter wasn't guaranteed. G5 spent many hours sitting in promoters' offices, while me and Robbo waited outside, urging G5 to hurry up. He was fighting to squeeze the last fifty or hundred dollars of the full fee out of the guy.

'I know I owe you three hundred, but I'll give you two hundred,' was a typical refrain.

G5 always gave the same answer – 'I'm sitting here until I get every last dollar' – except for one night in Detroit when only Mad Dog turned out to see us. Slayer was playing downtown the same night, so our tiny potential audience was busy elsewhere. Before playing in front of Mad Dog, I stood in our dressing room, feeling embarrassed in front of G5 and Ivan.

'Gee, I'm so sorry. You guys came into this band thinking that we're this happening thing and look at the gigs that I'm putting you through. We're going to have to get on stage and play in front of just Mad Dog tonight.'

'No way, man.' G5 was smiling. 'We're having the time of our lives. This is one of the greatest things we've ever been through.'

I couldn't believe it. 'My God, you poor guys. You never saw what I've seen. You're not understanding my disappointment in this.'

Permanently enthusiastic and forever trusting, G5 was someone very special. He earned his Anvil stripes on the Digger tour and after four years in the band, he felt as if he'd always been with us. A few years earlier, Robbo had asked G5 if he was a lifer. That night, he gave the answer we'd been waiting for. 'I'm a lifer now,' he said before we went on stage. G5 had become a brother, one of the boys at last. If only he'd seen the glory days of playing regularly in front of audiences of twenty thousand fans.

After the gig in front of Mad Dog, G5 went to pick up the fee. The promoter was totally cool. Having played there before, we had every reason to believe we'd get our full fee. But as the promoter walked past G5 into his office, he made it known there was a gun in the back of his pants.

'I can only give you two hundred tonight,' he said.

'That's awesome. Thanks, man.' It was Detroit, the guy had a gun and G5 wasn't about to start arguing with him.

Detroit was the only time G5 didn't get all the money and it wasn't always that bad. At Columbus in Ohio we had full support from a radio station that used 'March Of The Crabs' as the theme tune to its heavy metal show, called *Metal On Metal*. Five hundred people turned out and we played an awesome gig in a packed club. But for every Cleveland, there was a Los Angeles to balance it. We arrived at an LA club to discover that Katon DePena, the lead singer from Hirax, had hired us and was the only member of the audience. Katon pulled out a couch in front of the stage and sat by himself watching Anvil.

'I love you guys so much that I don't care if it costs me three hundred bucks to hire the club,' said Katon. 'I'm happy to sit and have my private showing of Anvil.'

We played nine songs, and then he told us to stop.

'OK, here's your money. I'm going to take you out for breakfast tomorrow. See you in the morning.'

Simple as that. No big deal.

The last date of the tour was in San Francisco. For some perverse reason, Robbo decided to fuck around with his drumming that night. The beat was haphazard and I knew it wasn't fatigue or a mistake. Robbo always boasted about never playing anything but his absolute best, so it was kind of weird to hear him purposely play like shit. He'd miss out drum rolls or play only one bass drum in parts of songs that usually had two bass drums. As the set went on, it infuriated me more and more until he fucked up an encore. I lost my temper. My adrenalin was pounding through my veins and behind me Robbo was screwing with the song. The longer it went on, the angrier I became. At the end of the song, I attacked Robbo on stage.

Yelling, 'I'm going to fucking kill you, you stupid

bastard,' I leaped over the drums. I knew exactly what I wanted to do: I wanted to wring his fucking neck. Robbo saw me coming and jumped up from his kit, so we took the fight off stage, fighting and yelling all the way up the stairs to the dressing room, where we grappled and tussled until Robbo picked me up and threw me across the room. I hit the wall with a thump. There was a tinkle of glass and a sudden drop in the lighting. My back had collided with a row of light bulbs above the top of the mirror. I had cuts all over my back.

G5 pulled us apart. We looked at each other; there wasn't much to say. We all knew why it had happened. After six weeks on the road, with only two hours' sleep in the last twenty-four and a crap crowd, we were so fed up it was no surprise we took out our frustrations on each other. It was our third fight in more than twenty years together: not a bad record considering what we went through and the amount of time we spent squeezed far too close together in each other's company.

From sunny California, we drove into the winter, heading north-east back to Toronto. It was a long drive home with some tense moments along the way. In the middle of the second night, we ran out of gas while crossing the Rocky Mountains just as Robbo warned G5 that we needed to fill up. In Nebraska the next day, the transmission dropped and we had to wait a couple of days for repairs, which wasn't ideal when G5 had a family court appointment waiting back home. As we passed through Iowa, a major ice storm came in and we couldn't drive faster than twenty miles an hour. By the end of the journey I'd given up hope of getting home on time; by then I was happy just to get home alive.

The Digger tour of November and December 1999 was the worst to date in Anvil's history. Sure, it was great to play in front of an audience almost every night, even when the members of those audiences could be counted on the fingers of one hand. But the torturous discomforts to which we had to subject ourselves made me wonder if it was all worthwhile, particularly when I realized that the experience was more than likely a glimpse into our future. When we spoke about it afterwards, Robb insisted that we'd never have to go through anything like it again. Part of me wanted Robb to admit it had been humiliating to travel six hundred miles sometimes to play to just five people.

However, an even bigger part of me wanted to believe my brother when he told me the Digger tour was an anomaly, not a totally frightening vision of the future. I didn't want to contemplate the day when we might not still be rocking together.

'We deserve better,' Robbo said. 'And one day, Lips, man, we will be discovered and the world will recognize the majesty of Anvil.'

I often said the same kind of thing to Robbo when he

was low or when he doubted Anvil. I'd told him to hang on and to never stop believing because one day it would all change. And when I said it I meant it. We were too fucking good not to receive recognition. I knew that and I felt it. But right then, after the Digger tour, I needed a lot of convincing that things would improve for Robbo and me. When Gaze told me not to lose heart and not to give up because it could only get better, I doubted him. I wanted to believe, but I couldn't see what made Robbo so sure.

14 RESCUE

ROBB: 'Your time is about to come. I'm tellin' ya, man, there's something going on and your band Anvil is at the centre of it.'

It was 2005 and we were in northern Italy, playing Ironfest, a heavy metal festival, when Mike Flyntz, the guitarist from Riot, approached me, totally hyped up.

'You've got to go down big here today, man. It's all about history now. People want bands with history and no band here's got history like Anvil.'

Mike's enthusiasm was not a surprise to me. For some time, Lips had been saying that he felt something coming on, but then my buddy Lips often got mystical about things. Like his conviction that we'd achieve success one day, but that it wasn't meant to happen for us until we'd built up a large back catalogue and an authentic underground fan base.

Similar to Anvil, Riot had a history going back thirty

years to 1975. But unlike Anvil, all the original members had departed Riot and at one stage it had disbanded altogether. Mark Reale, the founding guitarist, had reformed the band in 1986, but he was the only original member. Mike Flyntz was at least the fourth guitarist to play for Riot, so, songs apart, there was little connecting the current line-up with its roots. I could see why Mike was impressed that Lips and I were still going more than thirty years after we'd first vowed to rock together for ever.

'You guys have got the history. We toured with you many years ago and we've only done one album since then. You guys have done five.'

As ever, we'd worked solidly for the last five years, releasing albums and touring whenever we could. We still had the same problems – our audience remained fragmented and our music was exclusive – but we'd been trooping for so long now that we were gaining a special kind of respect.

We first toured with Riot in early 2000. With more than twenty gigs throughout Europe and all the travel organized in a tour bus, it was total luxury after the Digger tour across the States at the end of 1999. It was gratifying that we were the main draw. Few people were there to see Agent Steel, Riot or Domine, an Italian band that opened every night. Our third European tour in five years, it contributed to the steady rise of Anvil since G5 had joined the band. Later that year, we released *Anthology Of Anvil*, a compilation, and started on our tenth studio album, *Plenty Of Power*, the title of which came to Lips when he was driving deliveries for a Toronto sushi bar. With his foot totally to the floor of a Volkswagen van on the 401 Expressway, he muttered sarcastically that the vehicle had 'got plenty of power' and thereby stumbled upon a good title for the album. A return to old-school heavy metal, *Plenty Of Power* was the classic Anvil sound of *Metal On Metal* and *Forged In Fire*.

When we'd finished the mixes, Lips and I drove home in my car, smoking a j and rocking to a tape of *Plenty Of Power*. We looked at each other and it felt really good. The album had turned out as planned. I hadn't felt so good about Anvil in a while, probably not since *Forged In Fire*. At last we were finding ourselves again.

We didn't tour off the back of the album, instead we played festivals and odd gigs here and there, including in New York and Montreal. It was awesome showcasing a badass album of which we were totally proud, but the critics ripped into it because of the cover. I thought it was fucking ridiculous to judge the music by the album cover, but they couldn't come to terms with the fact that it had a bulldozer on it. Lips took it hard.

'I thought we were just trying to push the boundaries of what's acceptable on a heavy metal album, but maybe

I was wrong, Gaze. Maybe we should have used a tank instead of a bulldozer.'

'Or a locomotive.' Maybe we'd made the mistake of thinking that anything that was heavy and made of metal was acceptable on a heavy metal album. It seemed we were wrong to make that assumption. Locomotives and tanks were OK; bulldozers were not. Fuck knows why. I didn't understand humanity. 'Maybe a tank's OK because it represents accessible violence?'

'I get it: violence . . . heavy . . . metal – it makes sense,' said Lips. 'But put a bulldozer on your cover and it's like "Huh?" Maybe the problem is that a bulldozer comes from a construction site.'

'A construction site? So fucking what?'

'It's *con*struction, Gaze, not *de*struction.'

I pointed at the album cover. 'Actually, it's not construction. It's mining, so it's destruction.'

'It's just not a tank. They see caterpillar tracks and they think: It's gotta be a tank. Nothing else will do.'

'But it's close enough to a tank. And a tank would be too obvious. We're trying to push boundaries, Lips. And that bulldozer could level this building, so it's destructive.'

Fathoming the mentality of heavy metal fans was difficult. Hypnotic told us the album also wasn't liked because the bulldozer was yellow. It might have been the most significant marketing colour, but yellow was not acceptable to heavy metal fans. Red was preferred, apparently.

For our next album, *Still Going Strong*, we swung from the bright yellow pop-art-inspired cover of *Plenty Of Power* to classical imagery. *Still Going Strong* had a black and silver Atlas carrying an anvil on his shoulders. It was the first album for which Ivan didn't come to the studio for the recording. The few solos he contributed were all recorded at his home and added to tapes that we'd recorded in a Montreal studio. At least we saved on his recording and accommodation costs.

We didn't tour *Still Going Strong*. The Belgian company that had organized the previous European tours had collapsed. Our only European gig came out of the blue. Maybe it was the Greek image on the cover, but immediately after we released the album, we were invited to play a one-off gig in Athens. The promoter lost a fortune bringing us over from Toronto, but we had a totally awesome weekend visiting the Acropolis and playing the gig to a packed bar.

After releasing six albums in eight years through Hypnotic, our distribution deal came to an end at the end of 2003. The business was changing and they could no longer afford to distribute our CDs. Downloads were the way forward, so we had to self-finance our next album, *Back To Basics*, released in 2004. Massacre distributed the finished product in Europe, but put no money up front. With a very limited budget, the production suffered. *Back To Basics* was recorded like a demo. If we'd had the money to do it properly, it would have gone gold, of that I'm sure. We didn't tour the album and played only festivals and a handful of dates in Canada.

LIPS: In early 2005, we received the invitation to play at Ironfest. Having not been to Europe for a few years, it was a festival we totally wanted to play. But the really bizarre thing was that even before I opened the email I had a premonition that we were about to be asked to return to Italy. To make it even more spooky, weird things had been happening to me for some time. I had an overwhelming feeling that forces I couldn't explain were starting to control Anvil's destiny.

People I hadn't heard from in decades were suddenly appearing. I'd had a rash of emails from guys and girls I'd forgotten about years ago. One of them was from Marjolaine, a girl who befriended us at the first-ever Anvil gig in Quebec City. She became a good friend – nothing more, nothing less – then disappeared. Now, twenty years later, Marjolaine had got in touch to tell me she'd known me in a past life and that me and Robbo were about to become big stars. She also said some weird shit about concentration camps that I couldn't understand at the time.

Maybe the strange premonitions I was having were the result of a lot happening in the last year. My brother Jeffrey had been diagnosed with multiple system atrophy, a devastating degenerative neurological disorder that was like a more severe and faster-progressing form of Parkinson's. The onset of his illness left me feeling helpless in the face of something that was much bigger and more complicated than anything I'd previously encountered. But the biggest change in my life had happened a year earlier, when my father died. The ripples from the massive shock of his sudden and unexpected death were still spreading and maybe that was affecting my mood.

My father had always been in peak physical condition. He swam every day and was a big-time golfer, so it was a huge surprise when my brother Gary called from the hospital at six o'clock one morning with some bad news.

'You better get your ass over here fast. Dad's not well. It doesn't look good.'

'Whaddya mean?' I was confused. Dad was always so healthy.

Gary told me the story. After dinner in a restaurant the previous evening, Dad got indigestion. In the night, he'd vomited so hard that it tore open his oesophagus. Now he was in intensive care.

When I got to the hospital, Mom, my sister Rhonda

and Gary were waiting. As we hugged and looked at each other with the frightened stares of people caught in a crisis, the doctor came out to talk to us.

'I'm afraid he's not going to live. I'm very sorry.'

Surely this couldn't be true. We asked him how he could be so definite.

'Hardly anyone survives what's happened to your father. If he recovers, there'll be multiple complications and he's eighty-three . . .'

The doctor went on to explain what had happened. For the first few hours after my father arrived at the hospital, the medics couldn't work out what was the matter with him. After vomiting, he'd collapsed. By the time he was admitted, he couldn't breathe without the help of a machine.

Pushing a camera through a tube down his throat, they discovered his vomit had burst into his chest cavity. His stomach acid was digesting his lungs, heart and other internal organs. Even a few minutes' exposure to highly corrosive stomach acid was enough to do irreparable damage. That's why he couldn't breathe.

Dad's struggle for life didn't last long after the doctor spoke to us. A short while later, only nine hours after he'd first vomited, Dad was finished. It was over.

The suddenness of Dad's death was dreadful, but its most profound effect was that it felt like a road marker for me. Until Dad died, I'd never thought about my own mortality. Now I realized my son Averey would probably not see me reach the same age as Dad. My time suddenly seemed very limited and coupled to this realization was a disappointment that my dad would never see me achieve lasting success, if it ever happened.

It was only in the last year or so that Dad had fully realized what Anvil had achieved. Until then, his view had always been that our chance at success came and went, and that it was high time I woke up to my responsibilities. He didn't understand why I had to make music and why I was so dedicated to making it with Robb.

Then one day I told him about the trouble we were having with bootleg Anvil albums and how it dented our earnings. When he realized that we were sufficiently significant for someone to rip us off, Dad saw Robbo and me in a different light. It ignited something in my father like I'd never seen before.

'I'm . . . I'm . . .' Dad perked right up. 'I'm flabbergasted. Why didn't you tell me when it was happening? I would have hired the best lawyers in town. I would have helped you. Why didn't you tell me?'

It was a good question and I didn't have an easy answer. My father didn't know about it because, like many sons with their fathers, I never explained myself fully to him. Because of that, Dad thought I was a crazy guy who ought to get a real job and because of that he didn't fully grasp quite how revolutionary *Metal On Metal* had been at the time of its release. The bootleg albums changed all that. He'd got another indication a few months before his death, when he and my mother went into a music shop in Florida to buy me a guitar case. 'Your son made some classic music that will always be with us,' the shop owner told my dad. That impressed him.

So when Dad died so suddenly I was deeply disappointed that I'd not opened up to him earlier and that he'd gone to his grave with the injustice of his son being ripped off by bootleggers stuck in his craw. And I think that, like me, he felt guilty that the two of us hadn't communicated better over the years.

I knew that Dad's guilt at not giving me the credit that I deserved really bothered him. After he died I became convinced that Dad's guilt was driving his spirit to help me achieve the recognition and success that Anvil deserved. As soon as Dad passed away, I was seized by an overwhelming desire to be extremely prolific in my writing. When I started work on *Back To Basics*, I wrote three times as many songs as were needed. Now that Dad was gone I wanted to prove something to myself.

In the days after Dad's death, I decided that I was going to make a speech at his funeral. The speech was quite short, a simple remembrance of some of the things my father used to do, but preparing it made me think over our relationship. Dad wasn't an easy man. He had a very direct manner that made it difficult to cry on his shoulder when things didn't go to plan. He made his feelings clear when I moved in too young with Lee and he frequently told me I was an idiot when I did something he thought was stupid. Usually he was right, and most often his comments came from a good place: my father would have done anything for me. He just had a strange way of showing it. Whereas my brothers and sister were forever asking for things from my father, I never expected him to give me anything. I learned that lesson as a kid when, asking him for an ice cream, his response was succinct.

'Steve, you want money for an ice cream?'

'Yeah.'

'Go to work.'

That's the kind of guy he was. Sometimes he felt like being generous, but I knew not to ask him, so when he asked if I needed a car, I knew what to say.

'I don't know. I think I'm OK.'

'Whaddya mean you don't need a car? I'm gonna sell your mother's car. Why don't you take it?'

'Oh, OK.'

Dealing with my dad and the rest of my family's idiosyncrasies was the perfect training ground for becoming the lead vocalist of Anvil. Negotiating my family prepared me for putting up with everything I had to deal with to get someplace in the music business. As the third of four children, I'd learned how to deal with authority figures because I had not only my parents towering over me, but also two much older siblings. And as the older child of the second pair of children, I also learned the responsibility of looking after a younger person. Families and bands: both required the skills of rubbing along with other people and running with a gang. And it taught me there was no point in getting mad at other people when things didn't work out. David Krebs, Al Mair, Squirrely and Robb were all easy targets to blame for my failure to achieve success, but in each case there were things I could have done much better to stop them controlling my existence.

With all these thoughts going around my head in the wake of my father's death, maybe it wasn't surprising that I had a sense of cosmic forces coming together when the invitation came to play Ironfest and several old friends and fans contacted me out of the blue. Maybe some kind of protective or guiding force really was watching over us. The sense that big changes were in motion was so strong that it felt like a warm heat inside me. As nutty as it might seem, that terrified me. As we boarded the plane to Italy, I was freaking out. Once the flight was under way, I calmed down, relaxing over dinner and a movie. It was *The Terminal*, a Steven Spielberg film. At the end I idly watched the credits roll up the screen, my interest rising momentarily when I saw the name of the screenwriter. Sacha Gervasi, it said.

'Hey, Robb . . .'

'Yeah, man.'

'Ah, it's nothin'. I thought I saw something.'

It was too much of a coincidence. And anyway, I thought to myself, didn't Teabag spell his surname Gervase? I didn't think about it again. There was sleeping to be done.

The next morning, we were dropped at our hotel near the festival site. I walked up to a booth in the hotel courtyard, ripping hungry after the long journey.

'Anybody know where I can get something to eat?'

The guy inside the kiosk had his back to me. He turned around.

'Hey, Lips. How's it going, man?'

It was fucking Ronnie James Dio. I hadn't seen him since Anvil had opened for Dio more than twenty years earlier at Massey Hall in Toronto. Another blast from the past. It was way too much. Not only did I feel like my past was coming back to meet me, but I was realizing that I had a history that meant something to a lot of people. Ronnie had played thousands of gigs in his career, yet the two times that Anvil had supported Dio had clearly left an impression.

After sharing breakfast with Ronnie, I hooked up with Robb and we headed down to the festival. Walking into a backstage tent, we were on the hunt for some papers to roll a joint. Across the catering area we spotted a blonde girl wearing silver pants and a red jacket, rolling a cigarette.

'See that chick, Robbo? Get some papers from her.'

Sorted with the booty, Robbo and I hung out in the tent, eating hotdogs because we had the munchies. That's when Mike Flyntz from Riot came up to us to say that our time was about to come.

Like Robb I was unsettled by Mike's enthusiasm. For Robb it was the recognition he'd been seeking for years. But for me, it was more freaky. It matched the pattern of my premonitions. Just as I had instinctively known they would, everywhere I went people from my past were acknowledging Anvil's history.

The next day we played our set. It was a good audience and we smoked them. Afterwards we went back to our camper van dressing room. Ivan was smoking and drinking beer outside with the girl in the silver pants and red jacket we'd met the previous day, when there was a knock on the door of the van. Two guys with long hair were there.

'Hello!' The dudes had seriously thick Swedish accents. 'We met you guys many years ago.'

'Yeah? Who are you?' Robbo invited them into the van.

'We're Mats and Leif, the guitarist and bassist from Candlemass.'

'Oh . . . right.' They were playing on the same bill as us.

'We met you in 1982 on Carnaby Street.'

'What?' I couldn't believe it. 'Like . . . fuck. You mean you're the two Swedish guys that I signed the fucking autograph for on Carnaby Street?'

'Yeah. You remember?'

'Fuck yeah.' I was shocked. Another visitation from our past. 'So you became Candlemass?'

They told us how they'd followed us from Donnington to the Marquee and, on the morning after the first Marquee gig, had gone in search of us until they'd run into us on Carnaby Street.

'Fuck, that's when Sacha took us out to Carnaby Street.' I looked at Robb. 'Wow. I wonder whatever happened to Sacha.'

'Hey, yeah, Teabag, man.' Robb looked kind of misty-eyed. It was a conversation we'd have every five years or so. 'Teabag? Who knows what the fuck happened to him.'

Something was going on. Forces were pulling things together. I was sure of that as much as I knew my name was Lips. Maybe my grief for my father was heightening all my emotions, but it certainly felt way weird. Or maybe my father was watching over me and the unfairness of his untimely death was being balanced by some strange sequence of events. Whatever the causes, if I had any doubts that something bizarre was going on, those doubts were dispelled when I got home, opened up my computer and checked my email.

Hi! It's Teabag, the email said. *Haven't heard from you guys in years. How have you been? If anybody – Lips, Robb or anybody – is there, please email me back.*

ROBB: Within a few days, Lips was on his way to LA. My prison sentence for drugs possession meant I had border issues and had to stay at home. I gave Lips a little Anvil gift package for Sacha containing all our CDs. A few days later, Lips was back and telling me all about Teabag.

It didn't sound real. We'd last seen Teabag in Toronto in 1986, when we'd had the bust-up at the coke party. Ever since then I'd felt some guilt at the road we'd taken Sacha down when he was still a little kid, not yet twenty. Now Teabag was a highly successful dude in Hollywood. While staying in LA, Lips had gone to a guitar store with Sacha. It was just a day out, a chance to eye some cool instruments. As they were leaving, Sacha grabbed Lips by the arm.

'Hey, hang on a minute, I gotta go to the washroom. Why don't you wait in the car?'

Lips didn't think much of it. Ten minutes later, when Lips was wondering what the fuck was taking Teabag so long, Sacha walked out with a guitar.

'Here, man, it's for you. It's a gift.'

It was a totally cool semi-hollow guitar. Lips was blown away. It was the first guitar anyone had given Lips as a present since his bar mitzvah. To me it sounded like Sacha was just as eccentric and crazy as ever. I was really buzzed just hearing about it, but, being Robbo, there was only really one thing I wanted to know about: what Teabag thought of the Anvil music I'd given him in the gift bag.

'Fuck, man, he's really profoundly blown away by the whole feel that we're still here. Like we made all this music and we never stopped rocking.'

'Way, man.'

'Anyway, why don't you ask him yourself? He's coming up here in a few days.'

Two weeks later, Sacha arrived in Toronto. Lips picked him up from the airport and dropped him at his uncle Marty's place. The next day they picked me up from outside an apartment building. By the look on Sacha's face I could see he was shocked at the way I looked.

'Robbo, dude. How are you, man?'

'Not so good. Sometimes I feel like I died in about 1992 and I'm now little more than a walking ghost.'

'Dude, it's great to see you.' Sacha threw his arms round me. He was so full of energy that I realized what had become of me since we last saw each other. Teabag was still the same special dude, full of crazy ideas. I'd been like that once.

'Seriously. How are you, Robbo?'

'It looks like I'm here, but I'm not any more.' It was the truth. I had to say it. 'My spirit and soul are long dead.'

Seeing Sacha again made me realize just how broken I'd been by Anvil's many struggles over the years. When I'd last seen Sacha, we'd been at the top of our game. I was desperate to return to those days, but over the years maybe I'd forgotten how to get there.

Over the next few days, Sacha and I spoke about that night in 1986 when I'd last seen him at his mother's apartment. I told Sacha I felt responsible for taking him down a very dangerous path at an age when he didn't really know how to handle it.

'All that shit that you got exposed to through us, it led you there.'

'You have to dispel that idea for ever. I was on a journey of my own and you didn't make any difference to it. Way before I met you guys, I was using hard drugs. I was smoking grass with you when I was fifteen, but before that, I got into hard drugs at school. That's part of the reason I gravitated towards you guys.'

Sacha told me a story about being at Dingwalls, a rock club at Camden Town in north London in the early 1980s. He was watching the band when Lemmy walked in. Having partied with Lemmy and Girlschool on Lemmy's pink barge on the Thames, Sacha knew British metal's hardest party animal.

'I went up to Lemmy and I asked him for some heroin. And Lemmy got me by the scruff of the neck, twisted my shirt and pushed me up against the wall. "If I ever hear you asking for that again, I'm going to rip your head off. I'm going to kill you." I didn't get any that night, but I was looking for it way before I even met you guys.'

After the big bust-up in Toronto, Sacha's drug use became more excessive. He still managed to get a degree in modern history and he'd had some amazing jobs such as working for the Poet Laureate of England, Ted Hughes, but he was still getting wasted regularly.

As Sacha told his story about what he went through and what happened to him I started to feel: Fuck, I knew it, man, I knew it. What I had feared back in 1986, when Sacha went out of control in that Toronto apartment, had come true.

Fortunately Sacha was a smart dude and by the early 1990s he had started to realize there were all kinds of cool things he could be doing if he wasn't taking drugs and out of his head most of the time.

'I decided that I had to tackle a problem that I hadn't thought would ever become a problem. So I just made a decision. Simple as that. I realized that being on heroin wasn't going to help me do the things I'd always wanted to do.'

It was profoundly inspiring to hear Sacha say that, particularly as I was at times still haunted by my own personal demons.

'Listen, Robb. I made a decision, dude. It seemed to be more of a waste to let one's life go than to face the pain of dealing with what was clearly a solvable problem. Once I made that decision I never looked back.'

Having admitted his addictions, Sacha went into rehab. He sorted his life out and started to fulfil his potential. Less than ten years later, he was in a Lear jet with Steven Spielberg and Tom Hanks, discussing the script he was writing for *The Terminal*. If he could do it, maybe there was a chance for me and for Anvil.

LIPS: A few days after Sacha arrived in Toronto, I went over to his uncle Marty's apartment. As soon as I got there, Sacha asked me to sit down because he said he had something really amazing to tell me.

'I'm going to make a movie about you.'

I fucking flipped. Then I started to cry. Suddenly it all made sense. This was the big thing to which all the premonitions had been building up.

'My father sent you, didn't he?'

'Er . . . maybe, Lips. Maybe I feel his presence. I don't know.'

'I felt something was coming. And I think my father summoned us to come together. I don't know why, but I do know this movie is meant to be.'

'Let's not question it, Lips. Let's just go with it.'

We talked about the construction of the movie, but I couldn't get away from the feeling that all the co-incidences over the last years were connected and that Sacha's arrival was like an act of God or an act of destiny. Or maybe, I thought, he was carrying the spirit of Ashley Jarnicki. I didn't know anything for sure. All I knew was that weird shit was happening.

'It's gonna be a very personal film. It'll be about how the friendship between you and Robb has been stronger than anything the world could throw at you. But you have to realize that you guys are really really funny . . .'

'I know. I know. We are like the real-life Spinal Tap. I've said it to Robb dozens of times.'

'And you've got to be prepared to acknowledge that too, Lips.'

It was all cool with me. This wasn't some little video being made about us by some small-time producer. This was a Hollywood movie by one of the best buddies we'd ever had, someone who understood Anvil's history and loved us.

I realized then that this was the beginning of Anvil's big moment. The big break that for years I'd promised to Robb would eventually come. And it all made total sense. Everything we'd lived through happened for the purpose of making this movie. That was what it was all for. Since the day I stood in my parents' living room with that first guitar around my neck, I'd known that one day I'd be a star. I didn't know how I'd achieve that inevitable fate until Sacha said he was going to make a movie. Now it was hitting me like a slap in the face: Here it is, Lips. Wake up. This is the moment you've been waiting for. Your story is compelling. Everyone will want to know about it.

Hollywood was going to make a movie about Anvil. It was a fucking miracle. All we had to do now was convince Robb. We met with him later that day. Sacha and I told him about the plans for the movie. At the end, Robbo looked shocked. Profoundly shocked.

'Whaaat? You wanna make a movie about us? Why the fuck?'

'Gaze, man. It's gonna be totally awesome. This is what we've been waiting for. It was meant to happen.'

Sacha explained it would be a documentary that told

our story and followed our existence for a couple of years.

'OK, that sounds cool, man. Sure.'

'It's a Hollywood movie, Gaze. A documentary that you can see in theatres. Not just a DVD.'

'That means . . . wow . . . everybody. Like people watching me? This is beyond metal.'

'Yes. Exactly. Beyond metal.' Sacha was grinning.

'Come on, man.' Robb was starting to look sceptical. 'It's all good, but like who's gonna really wanna know about Anvil? They don't know our band. And who the hell is gonna care about me and Lips?'

'You guys . . .' said Sacha. 'Your story is compelling because it's about not giving up. It's about sticking to your dreams. It's about what friendship really means. It just happens that you're in a heavy metal group called Anvil that the world of heavy metal recognizes as one of the most influential and innovative bands of its era.'

'So how is this going to help the band?' said Robb. 'You know that for me it's all about the band and the music. That's all.'

'Well, Robbo, I don't know if it will help Anvil. All I can say is I will do everything in my power to make it help the band as much as possible.'

'Fuck, man, well . . . oh, all right.'

Relieved that we'd overcome Robbo's natural scepticism, my thoughts turned to the future. If this movie was going to be a success, we needed to be more active than we'd been in the previous few years. One of the reasons Anvil still survived beyond its heyday when many other bands would have imploded is that Robbo and I were prepared to settle for smaller tours, less prestigious producers and diminishing support from record companies. Other bands who had tasted success like us weren't prepared to scale back. But Robbo and I had always been convinced that if we reverted to what we did best, success would eventually return. And when that happened, we'd be ready for the world to accept us. We'd remained prepared every single day for nearly thirty years. All we needed now was something else to fall in place so that we had something to show the world.

Within days an email arrived from Tiziana Arrigoni, that chick who'd been hanging out and drinking beer with Ivan at Ironfest. It turned out that she was a booking agent and she was offering us a European tour. When I looked at the dates she was proposing – Italy, Switzerland, Germany, France, Austria, Belgium – I couldn't believe it. It was going to be the biggest tour we'd done in twenty years. And we'd be able to shoot it for the movie. Weird things were happening and I was convinced they were meant to be.

Sacha was thrilled.

'Fucking perfect! We'll bring the crew to Europe.'

'Yeah. Totally. Perfect.'

'OK, the first place we'll see you is in Prague.'

ROBB: A few days later we landed in Milan, where Tiziana was going to meet us with a tour bus that she told us would be paid for by the sponsor of Phantom X, the support band. But when we exited the terminal, there was no tour bus. Instead we were going to embark on the largest European tour in Anvil's twenty-eight-year history in two camper vans.

Standing beside them was Tiziana with a sheepish smile. One of the vans was already smashed up. She'd hit a fire escape shortly after collecting it from the rental company. The rigging was damaged and the awning was gaffer-taped to the side of the van. We hadn't even started the tour and we'd already lost our two-thousand-dollar deposit.

Usually we'd have a trailer, but Tiziana had over-looked that detail. Instead we crammed our instruments and amps into the corridor and bathroom of the camper, despairing that we were going to spend the next five weeks crawling over them to get into bed, cook a meal or move anywhere. My drums were stacked in the shower, which took quite some abuse, but not as much as the outside of the van.

In the first couple of days, Tiziana wedged the van against the roof and sides of a round-edged tunnel. With a terrifying scraping sound, the van came to a screeching halt. Then she put it in neutral on a slope and banged into a wall, which pushed the bike rack through the rear wall of the camper. Later on, she was forced to drive on to an icy snow-covered mountain road that was so narrow she had to scrape the side of the van along bushes and tree branches to avoid driving off a cliff. Her driving was so erratic that it made G5's bed fall apart while he was sleeping in it. Eventually, deciding that we'd already had so many incidents that, as G5 put it, 'by rights there's no fuckin' way we should be alive' and recognizing that Tiziana may have needed a rest, Robbo came to the rescue. I took over the driving.

As if our transport troubles weren't enough, we were making no money on the tour. Having secured deposits from many of the promoters, Lips arrived with a thick wad of notes. Two thousand dollars of it went immediately for camper-van deposits; we wouldn't see that again. Another eleven hundred went on hiring my drums, leaving us with next to no cash. We'd counted on living off the door money promised to us by promoters if we attracted a large crowd, but we had to spend whatever we earned on sorting out disasters and hiring hotel rooms when the schedule went wrong.

The biggest problem was the lack of promotion and marketing. Two days before the tour started, Phantom X had called to say they couldn't afford to pay for the hire of their camper or for their petrol. We agreed to cover their costs; in return they agreed that their record company would pay for all the tour promotion.

As soon as we arrived at the first venue, we realized the promise had not been kept. No marketing had been done. There were no posters, no flyers, nothing. And, unsurprisingly, there was no audience.

We contacted an exec at the record company.

'We can't afford to have your band supporting us because they're not paying for the fuel and you haven't paid for the promotion.'

'Your fuckin' agent-manager-bitch put the tour together using a map as a dartboard. You expect me to help promote that? Forget it. And I'm not giving you any money for gas.'

After that, we refused to take Phantom X with us to the next few gigs, which were in Scandinavia. We couldn't afford it and we weren't going to have anyone take advantage of Anvil. Meanwhile, Tiziana and Phantom X's manager took to fighting over who was responsible for each of the fuck-ups. It was like a heavy metal version of Jerry Springer with Tiziana and Phantom X's manager, a buxom Texan broad, ripping into each other every other day. Most of the arguments were about money. Others were about the logistics, which weren't Tiziana's strongest suit. But we played a lot of good gigs – sure, there were times when only a few hundred came to a ten-thousand-capacity venue, but that was business as usual for Anvil – and we only didn't get paid once. That was in Prague, where the promoter refused to pay us after we arrived late because we couldn't read the road signs. After we'd played a long set, he offered us plates of goulash in lieu of our fee. Lips went apeshit, following the promoter around the club, insisting on payment. Then a guy in a suit with short hair, glasses and an English accent appeared.

'Gentlemen, may I interject?'

The promoter looked pissed off. 'No, you may not.'

'I know but seriously, seriously, what I've got to say is very important.' This guy was persistent. And very drunk.

'Excuse me, who are you?'

The drunk English guy pointed at Lips. 'I'm this gentleman's legal representative for the purposes of this conversation and if you will just listen to me for one moment. For one moment.'

'Is he a lawyer?'

Lips shrugged. 'He's a friend.'

'Can you just listen to me for one moment?' He was totally slurring his words.

I was interested. 'I'd love to, man. I'd love to.'

'OK. Guys, Anvil is a name.'

I nodded. 'It is indeed.'

'We are not moving the way we should be doing by

having this argument. I love Anvil; I've loved Anvil since I was a kid. It breaks my heart to hear you have these conversations right here, right now. You know? We can do this. We can do Europe. We can do the States. We can do everything that we want to do. If, and here's the big if: everybody starts focusing on the big issue. And that's not the politics.'

Lips was starting to find this guy funny. 'What have you been smoking, dude? What is the big issue?'

'Listen. The big issue is getting Anvil marketed effectively. Which is not being done.'

Lips nodded. 'That's a major problem because if we're not being marketed, who's going to show up and see this?'

'Because you weren't marketed, you played in front of fuck-all people here tonight. You were screwed.'

'Right.'

'Let's be honest about this. Anvil should be playing in front of a thousand minimum people every night in Europe.' The lawyer dude pointed at himself. 'That's my opinion.'

'You're probably right.'

'And you are not. You've got to ask yourself why you're not doing that.'

Lips shook his head. 'I've been asking myself that for twenty-eight years.'

I interrupted. 'I can answer that in one word . . . two

words . . . three words: we haven't got good management.'

While the lawyer was trying to persuade us that we needed his services as a manager, next to us the support band was having a whine about their lack of money. We didn't have a problem with the guys in the band on a personal level. We liked them a lot, but their manager was giving us hell over budget problems that were of their making.

Lips spoke to their lead singer, who was asking for money. 'It's not my problem that you guys spent your money on your flight tickets to get over here and didn't provide any marketing support. We could have left you standing, but I did not have the heart to go: Fuck them. I couldn't do it, even though I didn't know who you guys were. I'm telling you: I don't know what the fuck to do. As it is I've got to go home to my wife penniless . . .'

'As do we,' said the guy from Phantom X.

'But what excuse can I have for going home in debt? Do I tell my wife I gave all my money to the support band?'

It was down to the same old cause. We didn't have a record company and without a record company's support, there was no proper marketing and we were out on our own.

Throughout it all, the film crew was circling like flies

around shit. In spite of their cameras and their microphones on booms, we soon forgot they were even there and got on with dealing with the stresses of being on the road or the enjoyment of being on stage.

For Anvil, the eccentricities of the tour were business as usual, but for some of the Hollywood boys and girls, it was too much. In the corridor of the Everest hotel in Transylvania, one of the production crew broke down in tears, unable to handle Anvil life any more. Sacha called the guy's parents before putting the twenty-seven-year-old kid on a flight home. He'd had a mental breakdown.

Events that were commonplace to us seemed extraordinary to the film crew. Like the moment during our gig at the Monsters of Transylvanian Rockfest when, during my legendary White Rhino drum solo, Lips slipped off to the side of the stage, tuned his guitar, sipped a drink and then groped down the back of his trousers to pop in his haemorrhoids. Popping out 'rhoids is a common professional injury for rock singers. All that grunting and screaming can push them out. There are many much more famous names – lead singers in some of the world's largest bands – who suffer the same affliction as Lips, but it was the first time anyone in the film crew had witnessed it. No wonder they watched open-mouthed.

Some of the things that went on, you couldn't make

up, like when Tiziana accused me of stealing money. So I fired Tiziana and she retaliated by saying that Ivan, with whom she'd been partying most nights, was now out of the band. The next day everything was back to normal. Status quo resumed.

As the tour progressed, we all wondered if we would ever work with Tiziana again. She had the heart and the passion for touring with a metal band and she was obviously dedicated to Anvil, but she was missing the organizational skills. Admittedly, it wasn't easy for her dealing with a commodity like Anvil. If we'd been a bigger band, we'd have had a tour bus and she wouldn't have had to drive campers, nor would she have wrecked them. But with Anvil, Tiziana had little choice but to do it the Anvil way. It was hardcore touring, totally different to the way any other band generally did Europe. The facts of Anvil life.

Near the end of the tour, Tiziana took me aside. We were sitting in the back of the camper.

'Would you mind if I marry Ivan? Do you mind, Robert?'

Me and Lips thought it was a bit fucking rushed, but we weren't going to say no. We didn't want to lose a guitar player when the best part of the tour was yet to come. A promoter in Greece had offered to pay for our flights to and from Europe, provided we came to play in Greece for ten days. He put us up in a great hotel and provided excellent meals for free. We put back on all the weight that we'd lost in the previous five weeks. The transport was organized and efficient. We got nights off between gigs to go sightseeing. It couldn't have been better and it was a great way to cap the shit of the tour we'd just been through. Totally awesome gigs packed with enthusiastic, energetic people. We finished on a high.

15 REDEMPTION

LIPS: When we got back to Toronto after the European tour, it was back to the same old routine of rehearsing, writing songs and playing local gigs, only this time it felt different. It wasn't just that a movie crew was following us everywhere. Things felt like they were getting better for us. I was convinced that the turnaround in the band's fortunes that I'd been promising brother Robb for so long was now starting to happen.

Maybe it was my fiftieth birthday party in 2006, a milestone for anyone but all the more awesome when you get to play a gig in your favourite bar to celebrate it. Dix came out and played 'Metal On Metal' and 'Forged In Fire' with us. G5 said it was weird, like watching someone else kiss his girlfriend, but it was cool to have Dix back for the evening. We asked Squirrely too, but he declined. The only time any of us had seen him since he left the band was when Robbo met him outside a strip club in the late 1990s. They'd had a drink, yakked a bit, and then parted, Robb thinking that little of the old Squirrely still remained.

A couple of days after my birthday party, the phone rang. It was Sacha. He was at the Texan house of Tom Araya, bassist and vocalist of Slayer, interviewing him for the movie.

'Lips, there's someone here who really wants to talk to you.'

Sacha passed the phone to Tom. 'An angel has come to help you, Lips.'

'Tom . . .'

'When I heard from Sacha, I knew that this is a very magical, special thing to get involved in. I not only want to be part of it – I am compelled to be a part of it . . .'

Tom went on to tell me why Sacha was an angel and why Anvil's fortunes were about to change dramatically.

'I don't know if I am ready for it, Tom.'

'What do you mean you don't know if you are ready for it? Lips, you have been trying for thirty years. You are more than ready. Your time has come.'

I was blown away. It was totally profound. Suddenly I realized I was not alone in thinking that strange forces were controlling my destiny. I hadn't spoken to Tom Araya in fifteen years and he felt the same way. I wondered what the fuck was going on, but stranger things yet were about to happen.

After coming back from tour, I'd admitted to myself that there was a good reason why many of our albums since *Forged In Fire* had not sold well. The production was not great. If Anvil was going to rise again like I believed it would, we needed much better producers, so I wrote to Chris Tsangarides, asking if he would help us record our next album, *This Is Thirteen,* and enclosed a demo tape. If CT said yes, it would be the first time we'd worked together since *Forged In Fire*, twenty-four years earlier.

A few days later, CT left me a message on my answer machine.

'Hey, Lips. It's CT here, man. I got the tape, dude. I'd like you to give me a call at my studio and we'll talk further. All right, dude.'

It was great to hear his voice again. I called him.

'I listened to the tape and I definitely think we've got something.'

CT now had a studio in the English countryside, he said, and it would be an honour for us to be the first band to record in it. We would need about thirteen thousand dollars up front to cover expenses.

We had an incredible opportunity to record an album with one of the world's best producers. At this time in our history it was nothing short of a miracle. The only problem now was finding the money. I had no idea from where I could get it.

I contacted our old buddy Cut Loose, a fan who'd been to more than three hundred Anvil shows over the years, to ask if he could set me up with a job at his tele-sales company. Sitting me in a booth with a phone and a bunch of sales leads, he explained the gig.

'Read the pitch word for word. That's what's gonna make you money here. The pitch is designed so that if a monkey could read, he'd make six hundred bucks a week.'

Cut Loose left me in a room full of people who were comfortable coercing other people into buying things they probably didn't want, their primary motto in life being ABC: always be closing. I was like a duck out of water. I'd been trained my whole life to be polite and the job did the exact opposite. I thought that if I adopted my Lips stage persona, I'd have no trouble doing it, but it turned out I was more honest than I thought. I made nothing.

Things were getting serious. I'd already remortgaged my home to finance the time off to go on the Europe tour. This movie was costing us money that we wouldn't have otherwise spent, but we regarded it as an investment in the future of Anvil. And we were all in this together. Ivan was behind on his mortgage payments and was risking foreclosure. G5 didn't even have a home. He slept in our rehearsal space or on buddies' floors. Nobody was being paid and all because of me. It was like a blind dedication. I was the one with the vision that we were going to make it now. Everyone believed in me – Lips will take us there – so I needed to deliver the goods.

For a year now, I'd been convinced Anvil was about to rise again. When I spoke to Robb about it, the choices we needed to make seemed clear to me. And after all our arguments and fights, our despair at each other's behaviour, our bitching and our disagreements, thirty years together boiled down to something simple: Robb was dedicated to me and I was dedicated to him. We believed in each other. No matter that we were now in our fifties and we'd been promising ourselves the same thing since we were in our teens; we were going to be rock stars. It was our dream. And I was going to make it come true. I just needed to find the money.

In desperation, I turned to my last port of call: my big sister Rhonda. Without questioning anything, Rhonda offered to lend me some of the money we needed. She could see it was a critical moment in my life and in the history of Anvil. She wanted to help. It was an incredible thing. Rhonda's only interest was to help me to be happy and successful. It proved what I'd always said: family is important shit.

Before leaving for England, I went to visit my mother. While at her home, I took a look at my favourite painting, a landscape of the coast and cliffs near Dover in the south-east of England. My dad knew I'd always liked the painting, ever since I was a kid, when he would tell me off for taking it off the wall to have a closer look. That afternoon, I took it down again, this time to have a look at the back to see when it was painted.

When I went to put the painting back on the wall, the nail on which it had hung for at least forty-five years was missing. Freaking out, I scoured the ground. I couldn't find the nail anywhere. Convinced it was a sign from my father that I shouldn't have touched the painting, I substituted a new nail and tried not to think anything more of it.

A couple of days later, we arrived at CT's place. The studio wasn't quite finished, so we helped CT with some carpentry and painting. One afternoon, G5 went for a walk. When he returned he held up his little digital camera.

'Lips, look at this.'

G5 showed me a picture on the camera's screen. It was my father's painting.

'How the fuck did you take that? When did you see the painting?'

'It's not a painting, man. It's the view over that hill.' G5 pointed out of the window. 'If you go down there and walk a bit, that's the view you'll see.'

It all made sense. CT's house was on the cliffs near Dover. But the coincidence was too much. The chances of us recording at a studio right above the scene in my favourite painting had to be infinitesimally small. Again I was convinced that some kind of weird force was bringing everything in our lives together.

The recording of *This Is Thirteen* started well. We were on a creative roll and had lots of ideas. The only weak link was Ivan. Before we left Canada, I'd asked him to come to rehearsals.

'The train is leaving the station, Ivan. Are you on board? We've got a chance to record with a great producer in England. Come and learn the songs so you can be part of this. We want you along with us for the ride.'

But Ivan didn't come, so I gave him demos of the songs to learn at home so he'd be prepared when we got to the studio.

At CT's we laid down all the base tracks, and then called in Ivan so he could add his solo sections. Standing on the floor with his guitar in his hand and the red light blazing, Ivan looked blank.

'I don't know what to play.'

Robbo and G5 had lost patience with Ivan some time ago, but I'd always stuck up for him. Now I'd had enough. 'I can't defend you any more.' It had been a long time coming, but that day marked the beginning of the end of the relationship between Anvil and Ivan.

It didn't help that we were stuck in the English

countryside for three months. G5 took to it immediately and made buddies with the guys at the local pub. But for Robbo, being away from a big city gave him cabin fever. He'd wake at five o'clock in the morning, get dressed and go out. We wouldn't see him again until the middle of the afternoon, almost twelve hours later. We wondered where he went. Then G5's pub buddies asked him what was going on with the tall guy dressed all in black walking through the cornfields shortly after dawn every morning. A couple of times they'd seen Robb nearly thirty miles away. He was covering some awesome distances. And sometimes when he returned, he was very despondent. Nothing was going to work, Robbo said. The album would be a failure; no one would want to see the movie; Anvil had reached the end. As for G5 and me, we were settling for crap.

'You're not working hard enough, man. And, Lips, you need to go to CT and tell him to hurry up.'

There was no end to Robbo's negativity. I'd never seen him so pessimistic. 'You guys are fucking around. CT thinks G5 is a shitty bass player.'

So I went to speak to CT.

'So G5's a shit bassist? What's that about?'

'Huh, what?'

'Robb said you thought G5 wasn't playing up to snuff and that you have to fix a whole bunch of parts.'

'What? I don't know what you're on about, Lips. All

we did was change the staccato part into some straight stuff because it sounded better.'

'Really?'

'Shitty bass player? G5's amazing. The guy's incredible.'

I was fucking raging. It didn't help that I'd had bad news from home about my brother's health and that we were having difficulty financing the recording. A tour of South America that Tiziana had promised us had fallen through, together with the twenty thousand dollars we'd bargained on from it to pay CT. So maybe I was more stressed than usual. And because of that I went to Robb and told him that CT had said he was talking shit about G5's bass-playing. I explained CT had wanted to rerecord G5's track to get a better sound, but I also made the mistake of saying I was worried that CT might be taking his time because he was worried he wasn't going to get paid in full.

Robb's response was simple and swift. He found CT and told him that I'd complained he was working too slow.

'You know what Lips thinks, man? Lips thinks that you're taking your time because you don't think you're going to get paid.'

Then Robb returned to where I was eating lunch.

'I just told CT everything you fucking said to me.' Lifting his feet up on to the table, he fixed me eye to eye. 'Now go deal with it.'

'Oh my fucking God. What the fuck have you said?' I had enough shit going on in my life without Robb picking a fight. 'You just fucking took a baseball bat to the beehive. What the fuck are you doing, man? Are you fucking nuts?'

Robb shrugged. 'You're fucking fired. Get yourself a new drummer.'

I ran back to CT. I found him in the studio.

'Listen, CT. If I had something to say to you, I would have said it to your face. I was simply venting my frustrations to Robb. I've got a lot of things going on.'

CT said nothing, so I babbled on.

'I understand why you work slowly and I respect that. You have to understand that I'm used to being put in a studio with like ten bucks and coming out with a recording. I'm used to getting things done really fast because I've had no choice.'

I apologized repeatedly and CT reassured me that no offence was taken. He'd seen this kind of thing many times before.

I left the studio and went into the washroom. When I returned, Robb was outside the studio, leaning against a counter with a smirk on his face.

'OK?'

I went fucking nuts. 'You fucking asshole.'

I realized he'd been hanging around to get the scoop on the damage he'd caused. I was raging that he'd broken my confidence. Grabbing Robbo by the collars of his leather coat, I pushed him up against some cupboards.

'Don't you realize? Don't you fucking get it? We're going for it. This is our big chance, Gaze. Do you understand the enormity of what has happened here?'

'Let it all out, Lips. Let it all out.'

'It's destructive, man. It's negative energy. What are you doing?' I couldn't understand why Gaze was trying to pull everything apart. 'You've got everything fucking going for you' – I was totally screaming now – 'and what are you doing?'

For a moment there was no response. It was like Robbo had switched off the lights and gone to bed. Then he spoke quite calmly.

'And everyone tells me that. You're right: I've got everything going for me. Everyone tells me that. Constantly.'

Here it comes, I thought. Robbo's usual line about how he'd be much better off in another band.

'Constantly. I agree with you. It's all I hear. So maybe—'

'So where are you going?' I was yelling so loud I was losing my voice. 'What are you doing?'

'I'm gonna go and pursue something a bit more satisfactory than what's happening with you. You push me away. I'm accepting your offer. I'm on to the next page.'

Robb walked out. As far as I was concerned it was over. I felt like I'd had enough. Anvil was over.

Watching Robb walk away from the studio, I couldn't understand it. When we'd been driving through Europe in the camper, we'd yakked for hours. Sitting in the space between the front seats while Robb was at the wheel, I'd told him everything that I thought was going to happen. I had the vision: the movie was going to change everything. 'I can see it already happening, Gaze,' I'd said. 'And you've got to really embrace it. Enjoy it. This is the ride up, man. We're going to make it big. On our terms at last.'

The tour was all part of that because we needed to be filmed doing it. 'We're making our own history, Gaze,' I'd said. 'You and me, brother, we're going to stand up and we're going to do it.'

Although Robbo didn't appreciate the spiritual aspect of what was happening, I'd managed to shake him out of his despondency for the simple reason that ultimately he cared deeply about Anvil and our music.

'If this helps Anvil rise, then what the fuck. I'm ready, man,' he'd said. 'I'm with you, brother. I've been waiting twenty-five years for this.'

ROBB: After I left the studio, I continued walking up on to the cliffs. I always liked to walk. That's why I was getting up early each morning. I was physically fit and walking is good for you. Getting away helped me to deal with the stresses of recording. I was uptight because I was concerned at our lack of finances and our slow progress. I was used to working for twelve hours a day, but we were doing only two. That was driving me out of my mind. I just wanted to get on with recording.

After Lips had vented to me about how slow things were going, I told him to go speak about it to CT. He did that and then when we got down to recording, I made a remark about something. It was nothing significant. Maybe it was about feeling excluded from the decision-making on the production or maybe it was about how something was being played. Whatever it was, it threw Lips over the edge. He snapped at the seams. He totally lost it, grabbing me, yelling at me, calling me all kinds of names and telling me he didn't want negative energy. I was one of the most positive forces in the whole fucking goddam thing. Way more negativity came from other people.

As I walked across the cliffs, I thought about our situation. Lips over-reacted. Lips went crazy. And, at times, he snapped. He was very emotional and he wore his heart on his sleeve. I'd seen it before. I loved the guy, but sometimes I felt he lived to hurt me, making me wonder exactly to what I was staying dedicated.

Back at our apartment, I waited for Lips to return. Eventually the door clicked open, then slammed shut.

'The first thing I want to say is sorry. OK?' Lips held out his hand to me.

'I would have liked to hear that when—'

'Just look at me. I want to talk to you, Robb. I'm sorry. I'm under a hell of a lot of stress. If I lose my temper . . . if anyone knows what I'm going through, you do.'

'I'm tired of being the fall guy. I really am.'

'I don't want negative energy around.'

That made me angry. 'Fuck you. I'm the most positive.'

'No. Negative energy is when you say I do half-assed takes and settle for it. That is a rude, underhanded, low blow. I could say the same thing about your takes, but I would never dare because I don't feel that way.'

Lips was still really angry. Standing over me and pointing, he was yelling, giving me no chance to defend myself.

CT arrived and tried to negotiate. Gradually Lips cooled off. And as had happened several times before, Lips's emotions flipped suddenly from anger to hurt and hyper-sensitivity.

'I'm hard to live with.' He looked hangdog as he conceded his position. 'I'm emotional. No doubt about it.'

'That's cool, man. I know that's what you are. But the bottom line is: Why am I your fall guy? Constant-fucking-ly.'

Lips's lower lip wobbled. 'Because I love you.' Tears welled in his eyes. 'You're my fucking brother, Gaze.' Rubbing his eyes, he looked totally upset. 'Who else can I fucking cry on their shoulder and say fucking shit to? Who else?'

I didn't know what to say. I felt I didn't have to say anything. I'd done nothing wrong.

'Who's the closest person I've got in the world?'

Lips was crying totally now and his lower lip was wobbling like Jell-O. 'Think about that! If I can't express myself or blow up at you, what have I got? You're the closest person I have.'

'Well . . . I . . . ah . . .'

'I'm sorry. I don't know what to say. I'm sorry, Gaze. I'm very sorry.'

'Fine . . . ah . . . I hear you.' Now I felt like talking. 'It's just there's been so much of it, man. Dude . . .'

'We're both stressed,' yelled Lips.

'I ain't stressed about nothing, man.'

'Well I am . . .'

'I get stressed when you start blowing it on me, dude. But otherwise, I don't get stressed. I'm going: Let's go, boys. Let's show the fucking world and some of those assholes that they're wrong. Who is the one always driving that machine? Robbo.'

CT gave us a lecture about putting our differences to bed and making the record 'the fucking dog's bollocks that I'm sure you will'. When he finished, Lips leaned over to me and threw his arms around my shoulders.

'I'm fucking sorry, man.'

We hugged, and then Lips spoke again. 'OK? We've got a long road ahead of us.'

We made up. I accepted Lips's apology and got on with things. It was typical unproductive dog crap. I had zero tolerance for it and it hurt. All I did was make a remark and it was valid to boot. I wasn't nitpicking. And Lips went nuts on me, like twenty-five years earlier at the *Forged In Fire* sessions, where we had a big blowout too. I suppose you could call this one our silver-anniversary fight.

The recording was soon over and it was time to leave for a new tour of Europe, booked again by Tiziana. Ivan and G5 had been so well accepted by the regulars at the local pub that they got us a ride to the airport in the church minibus.

Arriving at Copenhagen that evening, we were smack back into chaos. Everything was fucked. No one knew where we were meant to be going. All we had was the name of a hotel. Fortunately, Lips's wife, Ginny, was meeting us and she'd worked out which bus and train we needed to get to the hotel, but sadly Tiziana had left her briefcase, containing all the money and our itinerary, on the train.

With cash from Ginny, we got into Copenhagen,

while Tiziana went in search of her briefcase. We then spent half an hour walking the streets, pushing all our gear in shopping trolleys, looking for the hotel. Having found the hotel and offloaded our gear, we then went to the club at which we had a gig that night.

'No gig tonight, guys,' said the club manager. 'You're supposed to play tomorrow night.'

Day one of our tour and already the logistics were fucked up. The next night we were supposed to be playing at the Sweden Rock festival. It was Ginny's first time with us on a European tour and she was getting wound up at the lack of organization. When we got back to the hotel, Tiziana was there with her laptop. Lips went straight up to her.

'No fucking gig tonight. How are we getting to the Sweden Rock Festival?'

'I don't know. We'll find out.'

LIPS: It was a huge embarrassment to have Ginny see the disorganization we endured on the road. After a night of arguments, in the morning I contacted Sweden Rock and asked them to collect us. With one simple phone call, it was all sorted out. Life could be that simple, if you wanted it to be.

The gig at Sweden Rock was awesome. We were one of the first acts of the day and got a totally full-on response from the crowd, but had to leave quickly afterwards to get from the festival site at Sölvesborg to a gig in Motala, which Tiziana had assured us would be a two-hour train journey. Having not bought tickets in advance, Tiziana was confident we could buy them at the station. What none of us bargained on was that thousands of fans from the festival would all want to get on the same train. The tickets had sold out weeks earlier. Hot and sweaty from the gig and hauling our gear to the station platform under a blazing sun, we watched as the fans in front of whom we'd just played poured on to the train. Another fuck-up.

Two guys who'd been in the front row of the festival and a T-shirt-seller recognized us and offered to drive us the four hundred kilometres to Motala, which turned out to be five hours by car or six hours by train. A long way to go for a gig that paid just five hundred euros. The gig was good, but the next morning we had to get to Amsterdam. Again there was no forward planning from Tiziana. She hadn't worked out that the combination of a car and train from Motala to Gothenburg for a flight to Holland, followed by a train from the airport to Amsterdam would get us to the venue several hours after we were scheduled to play. We cancelled the gig, stayed the night in the Motala club-owner's flat, organized transport to get Ginny to Stockholm for a flight to Canada, and vowed that things would change.

After a couple of nights in Sweden, we flew to

Brussels, where we spent the night sleeping on the floor of the airport before flying on to Valencia, where we missed the train to Lorca, venue for our next festival gig. So much for the glamour of the rock 'n' roll lifestyle. And to make it worse, we were being followed by a film crew.

Robbo and I went for a walk in Valencia to decide what to do about Tiziana. After what we'd been through, I was losing patience. The one vital quality in a manager was organizational skill; Tiziana was passionate and dedicated, but so far she had shown very little of that. We did admit to ourselves, however, that she'd got us more gigs in the last two years than we'd played in the previous decade. That part was good, and her heart was in the right place, so we decided to ask her to make sure the rest of the tour ran more smoothly. Back at the hotel, we asked for a word.

'Tiziana, we can't go on like this. We need you to assure us that the rest of the gigs and travel will be better organized.'

'Tour is over now. Go home.'

'What?'

Tiziana was clearly upset.

'I gonna cancel everything. I tell German promoters you cannot come.'

'Tiziana, we are very grateful for everything you've done for us, but the transport is a mess. I think you underestimated it.'

We worked hard to reassure Tiziana that we wanted only one thing: a tour that ran to plan. Surely that wasn't too much to ask? Eventually Tiziana calmed down. For the moment, at least, we were still friends. She promised we'd seen the last of missed trains and planes, and for the immediate future we were happy to go along with her weird way of doing things.

Anyway, I had other, happier, things on my mind. When we went for the walk to discuss Tiziana, Robb had told me that he was now clean from drugs. He'd long ago started the journey and now he could safely say he'd kicked them for good. Maybe my dream that Sacha's movie would free all of us from our personal demons was coming true.

ROBB: A long time before telling Lips, I'd already made the decision to change my lifestyle of the previous thirty years, but I kept it quiet from him until I knew I could do it for sure. Even before Teabag came back into our lives, I'd decided to make fundamental changes. An inner voice had been gaining volume for some time. It had told me to look at my life closely and to realize that I had everything anyone would want.

I had a beautiful wife and a handsome kid. I played in a great band, with my awesome brother, Lips. I was a great painter. I wanted for nothing. My life was complete. Only one thing was missing: success with Anvil.

By that I meant true recognition of my talents – on a global scale – and proper financial reward. But other than that, I had a pretty complete little trip.

So when I asked myself why I hadn't achieved the success that Anvil and I deserved, I realized the answer was simple and staring me in the face. I could hear the voice telling me: Robbo, give that fucking shit up and everything is going to change. By the time we were in Valencia, I knew I'd reached that point.

On our second morning in Spain, I got up early. We were staying at a hotel near a beautiful beach fringed with palm trees. It was seven o'clock and I had the entire beach to myself. Walking along the water's edge as the Mediterranean quietly lapped the sand, I looked up at the sky. I felt like I was being watched. And for the first time in years I felt like I was totally clean.

'OK, man,' I shouted at the sky. 'You fucking happy? I did it. OK? I'm fucking done with it. It's all over. Are you fucking happy?'

I didn't know what I was trying to say. I just needed to communicate with that internal voice that had been telling me for a long time to change my ways. And I thought if I spoke to whatever was behind that internal voice, then I would have committed myself to my new way.

'You want me to make it? You want me to succeed? You want me to achieve what I've been fucking not getting? OK, man, I'm done with the poison. Come and get me because . . . because I'm ready for you.'

LIPS: After Lorca, we returned to Belgium to play a festival followed by a favour gig for a friend. We then travelled to Germany to play the Bang Your Head festival. All three gigs were awesome with great crowds. Then, after three months making the album at CT's studio and on the road in Europe, we returned home to mix *This Is Thirteen*. Six weeks later, in the summer of 2006, Ivan married Tiziana. Ivan had asked us to play at his reception, so we all turned out on his big day.

With no record company backing to distribute *This Is Thirteen*, all marketing and publicity was up to us. I sent or hand-delivered advance copies of the album to every outlet of which I could think: radio stations, promoters, magazines, fanzines. You name it, I sent it there. And it worked. A promoter in Japan heard the album and asked us to come over to play a festival. With the film crew still circling us, it seemed like serendipity. Twenty-two years earlier, Super Rock '84 in Japan had been the last great triumph for Anvil before Krebs turned his back on us; now we were returning to the scene.

Being back in Japan was a totally good experience, but when I saw that we were the first act on the festival bill, I panicked. We'd come thousands of miles to discover that we were playing at 11.35 a.m., a time of day when most fans were only just getting out of bed. Anywhere else I would have been happy to play in front of no one – I loved just to play – but Japan was different. The last gig we played in Japan was in a stadium packed with tens of thousands of people. It would be hard to see an almost empty arena as a reflection of how far we had fallen in twenty-two years. If Robbo and I were to be convinced that Anvil was on the rise again, we needed a hall packed right to the back with head-bangers freaking out at the power of our band.

After a night of broken sleep, we travelled to the arena. None of the audience had been admitted, and it was eerie and unsettling to look out at an empty hall. There was nothing to do but wait.

As the clock ticked down, our nervousness rose. We could tell people were entering the building, but we wouldn't know until the moment we walked out on stage how many of them were there to see us.

The moment arrived. A floor manager gave us the sign to move up to the stage and prepare to face our audience. In the quiet of our dressing room, deep underground and far from the stage, it was impossible to gauge the size of the crowd, but as we moved along the corridors and towards the stage, the crowd got louder. And then I heard something that I'd not experienced for a very long time, maybe not since the Heavy Sounds festival at Bruges in 1983.

'Anvil! Anvil! Anvil!'

With every step towards the arena, the chanting got louder until we ran on stage and were nearly knocked over by the force of the noise. Grabbing my Flying V, I looked round at Robb, gave him a nod and we kicked off straight into 'Metal On Metal'. The crowd went wild.

Right to the back of the arena, the hall was packed with headbangers all freaking out at Anvil. It felt as if the doldrum years had never happened and Squirrely and Dix had never become disillusioned, abandoning the Anvil fight. On the stage that morning, all the demons that had haunted Gaze and me in the twenty-two years since our 1984 heyday fell away. We loved it. It felt like it was well overdue, that somehow we belonged there. It felt like victory.

'What took us so long to get back here?' Robbo said to me the next day as we walked around a temple in Tokyo.

'Don't know, Gaze, but it feels like we've put a missing piece into Anvil's jigsaw.'

Japan itself hadn't changed much. It was the same millions of neon lights and crowds of people walking round. The streets were still spotlessly clean. But Robbo and I had changed a lot in the meantime. Returning to

Japan made me reassess my relationship with Robb after the fight at CT's studio and my concerns about his demons. I looked back at the journey we'd both travelled. We'd been together a long, long time through a lot of music and through a lot of hard times that life had dealt us.

Robbo and I hadn't always seen things the same way. There had been times when I felt like I was the only person in the band who was keeping the true spirit of Anvil alive, like in those disastrous days when Robbo wanted success at any price and followed Squirrely's lead. And I knew there'd been years when he felt like he was waiting for me to get my shit together. But our return to Japan was vindication that we were united and dedicated to each other more now than we'd ever been. Anvil was rising again and that was a fucking miracle. Knowing that Robbo had sometimes struggled with the way I behaved but always remained loyal made me love him deeply. Together we'd stayed dedicated to our vision that if we kept true to our beliefs, one day Anvil's time would come. We'd sacrificed a lot for that. Robbo or I could have taken off at any point, but we never did. We were true brothers.

It was also way cool to share Japan with G5 after he'd heard so much about our trips there in 1983 and 1984.

G5 loved it. He said it was one of the greatest weekends of his life. He loved all the weird things – the plates of plastic food on yellow dishes in the windows of restaurants and the huge enthusiasm and exotic dress of Japanese headbangers – but his most profound moment occurred as we came off stage after the gig. We were all buzzing and freaking out after the awesome reception of the Japanese crowd. Then I turned to G5.

'Hey, Dix, man. That was like totally fucking awesome, wasn't it?'

G5 looked at me dumbfounded. Then I realized what I'd said.

'Oh God. Sorry . . . I can't believe I did that. I'm so sorry, G5, man.'

I felt awful. Ten years playing with G5, the ultimate, perfect replacement for both Squirrely and Dix, and I'd called him Dix now. But G5 was smiling and shaking his head.

'Lips, man. That might be the nicest thing you ever said to me.'

I knew exactly what he meant. 'Yeah, absolutely, brother G5.'

16 VICTORY

ROBB: Everything was good from the moment we arrived in Japan. The only downside was that it was the last time we played with Ivan. But in the end that turned out to be a good thing, too. Maybe it was some kind of Buddhist karma, but Japan was where I finally got Anvil the way I wanted it.

We both felt that Ivan had been unreliable for some time. If it had been up to me and G5, we would parted ways with Ivan earlier, but Lips always wanted to give him another chance. Now, after years of extending friendship, brotherhood and unity, we decided that the gig in Japan was a good chance for Ivan to go out on a high.

We returned from Japan in October 2006. The following June, we got a phone call from Ivan. 'I want to come and collect my gear.' It had been sitting unused in our studio for more than six months. In the meantime, *This Is Thirteen* had come out without a picture of Ivan on the back. He was credited for only the few short solos that he contributed.

While Ivan's gear was sitting in our rehearsal space, Lips had booked a show in New York. It focused our minds on what to do about Ivan's replacement. Lips wanted to recruit his teenage bandmate, Gary Greenblatt. It would be like reforming Gravestone, he said. But although he often talked about how much he missed playing in a band, when faced with an offer, Gary declined. Likewise another childhood friend of Lips.

Since shortly after G5 joined Anvil, I'd been convinced we would be better as a power trio, the likes of which the world had never seen. A while ago, Jethro from the days of the New Jersey Metal Militia had called Lips.

'Lips, man, I just woke up from a dream. You guys are a three-piece. You're going to make it. But you've got to get rid of Ivan.'

'OK, Jethro. Whatever. Have a talk to Robbo.'

So Jethro called me. 'Why don't you get Lips to make the band a three-piece?'

'What the fuck do you think I've been telling him for the last fuckin' ten years?'

Five years after joining the band, G5 started to agree with me that Ivan's guitar was adding nothing to Anvil.

But Lips was always the hardest one to convince. Anvil had always been a four-piece, he said, so what would the fans think if we became a trio? I knew it would work, but Lips was not so sure.

'OK,' said Lips. 'This will be our experiment. We've got this New York show and we'll just go do it as a three-piece.'

From the moment we started to rehearse for the show, I knew it was going to be awesome. Without Ivan, we found we could play songs that we hadn't played for years.

The gig was at L'Amour in Brooklyn, scene of the most disastrous gig in Anvil's history, when Squirrely had taken control of the band and we alienated our entire fan base by playing Squirrely compositions such as 'Good Love Gone Bad'. This night, however, was different. We didn't tell anyone that Ivan had left. Neither the promoter nor the fans. Nobody noticed that he wasn't even in the band until we were on stage. In front of an audience of diehard woodworkers and hypercritical motherfuckers, we went down a storm. Afterwards everyone told us that the new Anvil was the best we'd ever been. It was fucking amazing.

The club owner came over.

'Yeah, you pulled a fast one on me tonight there, boys. You said you were a four-piece. You were lucky I liked it and you went over all right.'

As we packed up the gear, put it in the van and drove to our hotel, Lips was smiling.

'That was great. Everyone loved it. I'm sorry, guys. You were right. We should've been doing this for a long while now.'

I could see the emotion, happiness and relief in his face. It had been worrying him that there was no back-up guitar behind him. And he was concerned about what the diehards would say. But now he was beaming. 'Like . . . fucking wow. It went over really well.'

I was hugely relieved that Lips was convinced at last.

'For the first time since *Forged In Fire*, Gaze, I feel total confidence,' he said. 'If we were ever again in a situation like just before the Philly Spectrum, everyone would go to bed on time. We'd all take things seriously so that the next night when we played the biggest gig of our lives and all the record labels were watching, one of us wouldn't be puking behind the stacks. It's cool to have the confidence that everyone is giving everything they've got and no one trying to pick up a girl in the front row.'

By removing Ivan, we'd gained so much. Our sound was clearer and harder than ever. We felt like a new band with everyone banging hard. G5 came to the fore, everyone could see his totally brilliant musicianship and we could hear the bass as a separate instrument. Its percussiveness was apparent to everyone. We were cooking. And now there would be no looking back.

LIPS: In the summer of 2007, we played a short European tour as a trio. Eight gigs over eight nights in five different countries.

We organized the tour ourselves and it went off without a hitch. We arrived on time, well rested and well fed for every show. Touring had never been so easy or so enjoyable. The only dark cloud was the news we heard on the tour that Philip Harvey had died. According to Denise Dufort, Girlschool's drummer, Lord Phil had killed himself. Suddenly those days of partying with Teabag at his big house in Marylebone seemed a very long time ago.

After the tour we started work on *Juggernaut Of Justice*, our fourteenth studio album. The name was inspired by Sacha's movie, which was being edited in Hollywood at the time. Even before it was finished, it was having a healing effect. Robb had kicked hard drugs, the band was totally united and we were playing better than at any time in our history. The sun was coming out after a long period of darkness.

As I saw it, Sacha and Robbo had slipped into quicksand together. Sacha got out first and when he made something of his life, he came back looking for his friends and he rescued Robbo.

Sacha's movie was nearing completion and towards the end of the year I travelled frequently to Hollywood to work on it. Robbo and G5 would pester me with questions about the movie every time I returned to Toronto. It was weird seeing myself on screen and it made me very self-conscious for a while. G5 joked that it damaged me pretty good and there was some truth in that. Having a movie focus on certain aspects of our personalities to the exclusion of others made it seem to me that Robbo and I were characters in our own lives. I hadn't noticed how often Robbo said 'Anyway, that's what I was thinking' until I'd watched the movie several times. Then I realized he said it all the time. I also became much more aware of our facial expressions and gestures than I'd ever been. The weirdest thing was hanging out with Robbo and G5 after watching them on screen. I'd feel like I was hanging out with actors from a movie, not buddies in my life. When Robbo cracked a joke, I even said to him, 'You're just like that guy in the movie.'

In November 2007, Sacha organized a screening for us at his house. It was the first time that Robbo and G5 had seen the movie. At the end of it, Robbo was very quiet. G5 was beaming with pride. 'We look pretty good,' he said. 'I don't know if we look that good in person.'

Robbo asked if he could watch it again immediately. He sat on his own, smoking a joint. When it was finished, he went up to Sacha.

'Wow, man. This is pretty impressive storytelling. I need to watch it again.'

Robbo sat through it a third time, then he shook Sacha's hand and hugged him.

'OK, man, I understand what you're doing, Sacha. It's totally awesome.'

All year, Sacha and his team had been working towards submitting the movie to the Sundance Film Festival. It was the largest festival of independent American movies and I'd assumed that Sacha's movie would be a shoo-in. Then Sacha told me that already more than eight thousand movies had been submitted for 2008, of which only about 120 would be selected for screening. With the Anvil movie too late to enter into competition, Sacha had requested an extension for submission for it to be shown outside competition. It was quite a shock to me when I heard that Sundance might not accept it.

'What? You mean we're not going to Sundance?'

Sacha gave me one of those what-planet-are-you-living-on looks. 'No. We're just telling you it's not for sure.'

'What the fuck will it mean if we don't get in?'

'Well, it'll mean a lot of bad shit, Lips.'

I thought all Hollywood movies were shown at Sundance, no matter how good or bad. I felt like a bomb had been dropped on me.

'OK, Lips,' said Sacha. 'I want you to take a DVD of the movie over to the head of the submission committee.'

'Me?'

'Yeah.'

'Like . . . oh fuck.'

Robbo, G5, me, Sacha, our amazing producer Rebecca Yeldham and everyone who had worked on the movie stood in a circle in Sacha's living room. We passed the DVD around and everyone kissed it. Then we all shook hands, had a drink of wine and I got in a car. A short while later we were at the submission guy's house in Beverly Hills. I knocked on the door.

'Hey, cool.' A young guy stepped out of the front door. 'Hey, Lips, how's it going? Thanks.'

I handed over the DVD and that was it – until a couple of days later when we heard that everyone on the submissions committee lost their shit when they saw the movie. Our movie was straight into the festival, they said, and they all wanted CDs of our music for their kids. Fucking crazy.

ROBB: Flying to Utah early in the New Year for the Sundance festival with Jane-o was the first time the two of us had ever been on a plane together and we almost didn't make it. Because of my drugs bust twelve years earlier, I needed to go through secondary screening at the airport to get into the States. It took a lot longer than we anticipated. Running as fast as we could to get to the shuttle that would take us to the plane, Jane-o and I arrived only seconds before they closed the doors.

Every year, before the opening night of Sundance, two movies are selected for a special screening in front of the volunteers who work at the festival. In 2008, the Anvil movie was one of those movies: a huge honour. Late that night, we all entered a movie theatre to watch it with a big audience for the very first time. I was totally psyched to see this movie in front of strangers. I thought it was the coolest movie I'd ever seen, but I needed to know that it was going to work in front of people who didn't know us and who weren't necessarily metal fans.

Also, this wasn't a usual audience of people who'd paid for a ticket. Those types of people usually want to like what they see because they're eager for a return on their money. These guys were given free tickets and could show up if they felt like it or not.

When we arrived at the theatre, it was packed. Except for those directly involved with it, no one in the world had seen the movie. Yet the buzz around the movie was already so strong that the Sundance organizers had been forced to put on a second volunteer screening.

Feeling like our fate was in the hands of a bunch of total strangers, we sat down to watch the movie. Within the first few minutes, everyone around us appeared to be totally engaged with it. *Anvil! The Story of Anvil* was working. Twenty minutes into it, I noticed that nobody had left. At the end, it got a standing ovation. That's when I knew some sick magic was going on; it was a profound wow-there's-something-happening moment. The movie had worked.

The next morning, dozens of volunteers who had attended the screening were walking around Sundance wearing Anvil hats. Sacha had given away free hats so that whenever festival-goers asked the volunteers which movie they should see, many of them would recommend the Anvil movie. By the afternoon of the first day, all six screenings of the movie over the next week had sold out and others were being added to the schedule. By the middle of the week, Anvil was all over Sundance as thousands of people sported Anvil buttons. For a band that had been obscure for more than twenty years, it was kind of weird.

The night after the volunteer screening was the premiere. Paparazzi were waiting outside, their flashes popping as we walked into the theatre. It felt unreal and very exciting. Scott Ian turned up with the guys from Anthrax. Tom Araya from Slayer was there. At the end of the screening, everyone in the audience of six hundred stood up and clapped. Waiting at the side of the theatre, Lips looked at me.

'This is fucking weird. We're getting a standing ovation and we haven't even played.'

Trevor Groth, a senior programmer at the festival, announced our names and we walked out on to the stage in front of the screen. Over the whoops and screams, the clapping got even louder. Me and Lips had never had people clap at us for just standing there, for being us. But for me, the biggest thing was when I saw Jane-o crying. Some of it was tears of relief that the movie wasn't the disaster I had convinced her it would be. And some of it was tears of joy that Anvil's majesty had been recognized at last. It was a profound moment for Jane-o and me, one that changed my wife's life and her outlook on a lot of things. It had been a long ride for the two of us; suddenly those thirty years made sense.

When we went outside, crowds of people were jostling us with their cameras and wanting to buy our CDs. We sold out completely and then went for a dinner organized by Sacha for our families at a Chinese restaurant. Jane-o, my son Tyler, Lips's family, including his sister Rhonda who lent us the money to make *This Is Thirteen*, and the families of Sacha and his producers were there. Many of those people had often wondered if anything was ever going to come of me and Lips, of Anvil and of the movie. Now they could see for themselves why Lips and I had always stuck together and why the movie was so special.

At the end of the meal, Lips stood up to make a speech. He spoke about how he hoped that our families would now see us for who we really were and that they'd realize we were not just reckless dreamers, but responsible, determined and very focused rockers.

'You can't give up your dreams,' Lips said. 'If you give up your dreams, you give up yourself. Making music is what I do best, so if I gave it up, I'd be giving up what I'm best at.'

He thanked everyone in the room, particularly Sacha. When he got to me, he said: 'Robbo, you said to me if they make a film about us and it's successful and we become famous, then we'll be famous because of the movie, not our music.'.

Turning to the rest of the room, Lips went on. 'And I said to Robbo: "Wake up, man. The only reason there is a film is because Sacha became a fan of our music when he was fifteen. If it wasn't for the music, there would be no movie."'

Later in the week we played a gig at a little club on Main Street in Park City. We already knew Scott Ian was going to join us on stage for 'Metal On Metal' and we'd heard that Slash would be at the club until around eleven thirty that night, but that he needed to fly back to Los Angeles then.

When we didn't even go on stage until slightly after eleven thirty, I thought there was no chance that Slash would play with us, but kept on looking into the wings at the side of the stage in the hope he might be there. After Scott played 'Metal On Metal' with us, Sacha came on stage to thank Scott and the crowd. At the end of his speech, he made an announcement.

'Hang on, there's a bloke just showed up that wants to get on stage with Anvil.'

I looked over and there was Slash. Fucking surreal. He walked on stage, shook hands with G5 and Lips, said hi, and ten seconds later he had a guitar over his shoulder and was playing 'Cat Scratch Fever' with us. Totally awesome.

I went to every screening of the movie that week, mainly so that when I left the festival I'd be convinced that at long last our luck was going to change. I wanted to leave no stone unturned in my efforts to ensure the movie was a success.

By the time we left Park City and the Sundance Film Festival was over, there was a feeling of mania around the movie. Sacha kept calling it a phenomenon and it seemed like he was right. *Anvil! The Story of Anvil* wasn't just a good movie. It was a burning fire.

Back in Toronto, our focus returned to finishing the record and gigging whenever we could. Sundance had changed a lot of things. My mood was more positive than it had been for twenty years. Already we had more attention on us than in our entire career.

The story was powerful and it had opened a lot of eyes to Anvil.

Three months later, the movie was shown in front of a home crowd at the Hot Docs festival in Toronto. We did dozens of interviews and the press was totally overwhelming.

I was standing in front of the theatre talking with two enthusiastic Anvil fans, shooting the breeze, when a third person walked in front of the two other guys. While I continued talking to the fans, the third guy stood absolutely still, saying nothing, just staring at me. It was kind of freaky, so I ignored him.

'What does a guy got to do here to get some attention?'

As soon as I heard his voice, I recognized it.

'Fucking . . . Squirrely? Sorry . . . I didn't recognize you, man.'

Seeing Squirrely again after such a long time was like meeting a total stranger. He'd changed a lot and he acted like he never knew us. His answers were very quick, very dry and fast. He'd certainly changed horses.

Squirrely looked completely different. Gone was the long hair, making him look much older, like someone who had never been a rocker, who was very conservative. He could have landed from another planet. It blew me away.

I sat beside Squirrely during the screening at the Elgin Theatre, a big old-time theatre. It was like being on Broadway in New York. It seated twelve hundred people. We had several rows of family and friends. Squirrely laughed a lot, so I thought he liked it. Certainly the rest of the crowd were captivated from the first minute. Later on, however, the crowd reacted in a way we hadn't experienced at Sundance. Maybe it was because they were a home crowd, but this time Fraser Hill, the director of A&R at EMI Canada, got booed when he appeared in the movie saying 'We've got to be able to give you guys what you deserve' after listening to half a track from *This Is Thirteen*. And then when Frazer's email to Lips was shown on screen – *After careful consideration, we've decided that your album isn't what we're looking for* – the abuse got stronger.

'Fuck you, asshole,' was one of the comments shouted out.

That became a pattern at many later screenings. Fraser was only doing his job – he actually says good things about Anvil in the movie – but he was seen as the face of the establishment in a movie about two people refusing to bow to convention.

After the screening the movie got a two-minute standing ovation. We played a show the following night at the Bovine Club in Toronto. It was packed. We totally rocked.

LIPS: Two minutes is a long time to stand in front of an audience on its feet, clapping the movie in which you feature. It went on and on and on. And as Robbo and I stood there, not believing what we were experiencing in our home town, where twenty-five years earlier we'd struggled to move up from the Yonge Station to the Gas Works, I looked at Robb. My brother Gaze was crying, the first time I'd seen tears from him for a very long time.

The change in Robb since he first saw the movie at Sacha's house – and particularly since Sundance – was amazing. He no longer looked like the living dead. He smiled and cracked jokes. Looking now at Robbo, who had not laughed for twenty years, was like seeing a neglected, barren tree that for the first time in decades had blossomed and might bear fruit. Over the years, Robbo had become too frightened to hope that he might be able to make things better for himself and for Anvil. The movie had banished that fear and given him a mountain of new belief in the future.

The response at the Los Angeles Film Festival in June 2008 far exceeded anything we'd experienced so far. Again the movie got a standing ovation. When it had quietened down, Sacha went up to the microphone at the front of the theatre. He was holding a piece of paper.

'I want to read everybody part of an email I got today.' Sacha read a raving review, which said the movie was 'the best documentary I've seen in years'.

'At the end,' said Sacha, 'it says: "Yours truly, Michael Moore."'

The god of American documentary-makers had heaped fulsome praise on Sacha's movie. The audience went nuts.

Sacha went on to say that Michael Moore had invited us to the film festival he'd founded in Traverse City, vowing he wouldn't shave off his beard or cut his hair until every last ticket was sold for the *Anvil! The Story of Anvil.*

After the LA screening, we played a gig at Sacha's house. It was outdoors and summer. It felt awesome and it was crowned at the end of the week when the movie won the audience award when it was shown in late June.

In early July we flew to Ireland for the Galway Film Fleadh. Again the movie went down a storm and won the best documentary feature prize. The only weird thing was when a woman journalist came up to us.

'Great movie, but it's a spoof, right?'

'Hey, we're real all right. I'm Lips and this is Robb.'

'It can't be real. It's too good. You guys are actors.'

'I tell you we're not.' Robb got out his passport. She looked at it and saw his name was Robb Reiner.

'You Hollywood guys can get fake ID anywhere.'

In mid-July, we hit the west coast for the San Francisco Jewish Film Festival, where I had another of my weird premonitions. Waiting for instructions about being collected from our hotel, I pulled out my cell-phone and looked at it.

'Call me. Call me. Call me.' I was hoping I could prompt whoever was making arrangements to call at that moment. I was just about to put the phone back in my pouch when it rang.

'OK . . . OK . . . cool.' Feeling slightly freaked I answered it. It was the person arranging our collection. I listened and then passed on the instructions to Robb.

'That was her. She just called me from a light-grey-interiored car.'

'*What?*' Robb looked at me very strangely.

'Yeah, I could see her talking to me. I could see the inside of the car.'

We left our room, went downstairs and out of the hotel to where the car was waiting. I opened the door. The interior was light grey, just as I had seen it in my mind's eye.

On the Friday we were in San Francisco, we were invited to Shabbot dinner, something neither of had been to since childhood. We immediately fitted in. The people were open and loving to us. Over dinner, the weird feeling I'd had earlier in the day returned. I realized that the only reason Robbo and I were at this Jewish religious celebration before a Jewish film festival was the miracle of Robbo's dad surviving the concentration camps. I'd only become aware of Robb's father's history when I heard his mother mention it in the movie. Robb had never told me about it before that. As we listened to the recitation of *kiddush* and the blessing of a *challah* loaf, it suddenly all seemed very clear to me. I nearly flipped out about it, but managed to wait until the end of the dinner, when I took Robbo outside.

'Gaze, man. Think about it: what are we doing at the Jewish Film Festival?'

Robbo looked at me kind of blankly as I explained my thoughts. I told him about how shortly before Sacha got in touch, I'd received an email from Marjolaine and how she'd said something weird about concentration camps figuring in my future.

'OK, man, whatever.'

'No, Gaze. I want to know. Why are we here?'

For the first time, Robbo told me how he felt about what his father had experienced, and about how his father had always avoided flaunting his background because of the hatred he'd lived through. And how Robb grew up hiding his background because that's what his father taught him to do for self-preservation.

We talked for a long time about how he repressed his heritage and a lot of himself in the process. I was fascinated by the way his family had denied its own history. Why was it such a secret? What had gone on?

'My dad just wanted better for his kids,' said Robb. 'He wanted to leave it all behind and ensure that, God willing, it would never be put on to his children.'

From San Francisco, we moved on to Traverse City in Michigan. We were all psyched up about meeting Michael Moore and the chance to play gigs at several clubs. Michael Moore had made a promo clip hyping the movie and exhorting people to see it. Before the first showing, about a thousand people were lined up all the way around the building and down the street, a total holy-fuck! moment.

Backstage, as the first showing was nearing its end, Robbo, G5 and I were waiting with Michael Moore. He told us he really meant it when he said it was the best documentary he had seen in years. Then we started talking about Michigan and Detroit rock, Grand Funk and Cactus. He had been really into them when he was younger. He talked about how much the movie was happening and said he would be a foot soldier in the Anvil army, spreading the word.

Sacha had just called me on my cellphone when Michael Moore asked Robbo a question.

'You guys got plenty of merchandise to sell after the movie?'

'Yeah, we brought fifty shirts and fifty CDs.'

'That's it?'

We explained we couldn't bring more than that across the border.

'Give me that phone.'

Michael Moore grabbed my cellphone.

'It's great to have the guys here, Sacha. The only thing I'm pissed at is I've got a thousand people who want merchandise, and these guys didn't have the balls to bring hundreds of T-shirts and CDs.'

We didn't have time to argue it with Michael Moore. In the auditorium, the people were giving the credits a standing ovation. As the credits reached the part at which I said, 'The music lasts for ever, but maybe the debt does too,' we pulled a black sheet off Robb's drums and I hit the first chord of 'Metal On Metal' on my guitar. The crowd were already standing, but when they saw us emerge, their arms went up in the air as one. They went apeshit.

The screaming was so loud I couldn't hear the amps when I stepped off the front of the stage. The only way I could keep in time was to watch the stick in Robb's hand hitting his drums. It felt like the Beatles. The crowd was drowning out the music. It was so intense. And then it took a step towards the surreal when Michael Moore appeared at the side of the stage to watch. As we started rocking out, Michael Moore started headbanging, giving it full fucking force.

It was hard to believe what this movie was doing to people.

After playing a few songs, we stopped for a question-and-answer session. Grabbing the microphone, Michael Moore started to speak about the movie.

'I want everyone here to thank God that Robb's father survived Auschwitz, otherwise the world would never know of speed metal. Without Robb and Lips, there would be no Anvil. Without Anvil, there would be no speed metal.'

Robbo and I both looked at each other. We were both in shock. Robbo and I were totally headfucked.

In September we were in France for the Deauville American Film Festival. Whereas all the other festivals were for film fanatics, Deauville attracted seriously rich socialites from all over the world. Before the festival dinner, Robbo was told he was going to be seated next to some cougar, a wealthy old lady from New York.

'I don't sit next to anybody. They sit next to me,' he said as we made our way to our table in a big ballroom with chandeliers hanging and more cutlery on each table than all of us had at home.

Everyone was dressed up in serious penguin suits or long dresses, all except Robbo and me in leather. Members of the Rothschild family were at the next table, looking over at us. Dressed as rockers, we knew we didn't belong there. When we sat down, the cougar started chatting Robb up over rich food that neither of us could eat. She was infatuated with the movie. Another acolyte at Anvil's altar.

In September and October, the film picked up some more awards for best documentary feature at the Calgary and Edmonton film festivals. We didn't attend those festivals. Instead we went to Oslo and Prague, where again the movie received standing ovations and we played awesome gigs, before arriving in Britain for the London International Film Festival, the most surreal of all our festival experiences.

With a long red carpet, a bank of paparazzi on stepladders behind crash barriers and Keanu Reeves as the special guest to introduce the movie, it felt like a Hollywood premiere. But the strangest thing of all was standing on the red carpet with Keanu and my brothers on one side of me, and on the other side, Sarah Brown, wife of the Prime Minister of Britain.

Standing in a line and smiling in the face of the photographers' lights flashing so fast and furious that it became like a single continuous light, I whispered to G5: 'Can you believe this shit?'

'If they weren't here' – G5 nodded towards Sarah Brown and Keanu Reeves – 'we might have had a grey carpet and a couple of disposable cameras.'

Turning to Sarah Brown, I did the metal salute – middle and ring finger held down by my thumb and my forefinger and little finger up like horns – at the cameras.

'You gotta make the metal salute.' I fully expected Sarah to follow my lead.

'No, I won't do that.'

We played a few songs on the stage after the credits rolled. Again everyone was already on their feet before we appeared, but still it was a surprise and we kicked ass. Then, after the picture of us had appeared in almost every London newspaper the next morning, we had a day of the press coming in for eight or nine hours. It was good preparation for our appearance at the *Classic Rock* awards in London a week later.

Ross Halfin, the photographer who'd shot me stark naked on the balcony outside my motel room in 1983, got us invited to the awards after he'd seen the movie. It said something about how Ross felt about the movie, because he doesn't offer to do favours lightly. He wanted to get me naked again for some pictures he was taking at the ceremony, but I refused. At fifty-two, I didn't think my naked body would help us sell many records. And anyway, a full-page of Ross's picture of me from 1983 would be in the copies of the latest issue of *Classic Rock* that would be displayed on every table at the dinner.

We turned up in a car outside the Park Lane Hilton hotel in London. Again there was a red carpet and a bank of photographers, although this time it was understandable as the rock aristocracy were in full attendance. Having never been to an awards ceremony before, we didn't know what to expect. Entering the ballroom to find everyone mingling, we glanced around. Within seconds our mouths were wide open and they didn't close again for the rest of the evening.

The first person we spotted passing by was David Coverdale of Whitesnake. Grabbing both of our hands, he grinned.

'I know you fuckers.'

It was twenty-four years since Super Rock '84 in Japan, but from the way Dave said it, we could see that he remembered exactly who we were.

Robbo tapped me on the shoulder, pointed and whispered.

'Lips, that's fucking Jeff Beck.'

'I know.'

'There's Ron Wood. Lips, that's fucking Jack Bruce, man.'

'It fucking is, too.'

Robb pushed through the crowd with me behind him until he got to Jack Bruce. Robbo put out his hand.

'Hi, I'm Robb Reiner from Anvil.'

'Hey, man. I've heard of your band.'

I knew exactly what Robbo was thinking: I'm not supposed to hear that from your mouth.

Extending my hand to Jack Bruce, I said hello. Jack grabbed my face between two large hands and looked into my eyes. 'I love you.'

A man whom I'd adored since I was a teenager, the man who sang 'Sunshine Of Your Love' with Cream, smiling at me was out there beyond anything I'd ever experienced.

Later on, after dinner, Robbo was standing at the back of the room when Ozzy Osbourne, one of our ultimate idols, came walking towards him. The last time either of us had seen Ozzy was in the dying days of Sabbath at Niagara in 1978 and I'd watched amazed as Ozzy threw off the depression and exhaustion I'd seen backstage to put on an awesome performance. Determined not to let Ozzy pass him by without seizing a chance to say hello, Robbo stood directly in his path and stuck out his hand. Before he could say his full name, Ozzy interrupted him.

'Fuck off, man. I know who the fuck you are, Robb. I love your fucking movie, man. It's fucking awesome. It's unbelievable, man.'

Another totally wow moment, but I knew nothing about it until I got a tap on the shoulder. I looked around and Robbo was standing there with the person who'd tapped me.

'Fuck me, man. It's fucking Ozzy.'

Peering over his little blue glasses with a warm look

in his eyes, he grabbed my outstretched hand between both of his hands and shook it.

'I love your movie. It's fucking great. I wish you all the fucking luck and take care.'

Later, when Ozzy accepted his Living Legend award, he went off on a tangent about Tony Iommi. It sounded like he was missing his buddy. That night, Ozzy was receiving an award that recognized a history that Ozzy shared deeply with Tony. Listening to him speak, we couldn't help wondering if the Anvil movie had made Ozzy think about the friendships formed in bands and what happens when you turn your back on those bonds. Later, when Ross called us aside to take some photographs with Ozzy, Robbo leaned over to him.

'It was beautiful what you said about Tony.'

Ozzy didn't say anything. He just smiled and nodded.

We took another set of pictures with Slash and then I spotted Ron Wood.

'Come on, Ross is going to take a picture. Come on, man, just one fucking picture.'

'Yeah, no problem.'

Ron even did the Lips wide-lipped grin. A total fucking geezer.

Looking around at all the stars in the room, I didn't feel in the slightest bit jealous of their success, fame and recognition. Like any of them, we got to record an album every couple of years and play gigs whenever we wanted. Robbo and I didn't have the global recognition, the fame and enormous financial riches of most of the other musicians in the room, but we had something much more valuable that not one of them – not Jack Bruce or Ron Wood, not Ozzy or David Coverdale – could say they had. Robbo and I were still rocking with the brother that we'd met when we were kids and first hatched dreams of making music our lives. We'd always been united by our music and as soon as I slammed my guitar and Robbo hit his drums, we were back in that basement beneath his father's house, dreaming of making it big and vowing to rock together for ever.

As we were leaving the *Classic Rock* awards, I stopped Robbo and pointed back into the room.

'Pretty fucking amazing, eh, Gaze? You and me in the same room as all those rock stars.'

'Awesome, Lips. Totally awesome.'

'It's been quite a year, bro. An amazing train ride.'

Robbo smiled. 'Yeah, man. Totally.'

'And the train is taking on coal right now, brother. We're going to have a great time, man. We're about to go through the best time we ever had.'

'Hey, I'm with you, brother.'

'And if we could reverse the train all the way back to 1977, would you board it again?'

'Lips, it's been awesome. We didn't have to change or

compromise anything to end up here. The music did it and that's a beautiful thing.'

'Yeah, Gaze. But would you get on again? The same train, the same journey, everything we've been through and with me again? Because I would. You know that, Gaze, man.'

'Totally. Every day of it. I'd be with you every mile and every footstep along the way, brother. And I'll keep on going with you all the way down the track. You know I will. Rockin' together for ever.'

Acknowledgements

Steve 'Lips' Kudlow would like to thank: Ginny, Ashley, Jasmine and Averey for their loving support and being the family I've always dreamed of having; Maxwell and Toby Kudlow for being devoted and loving parents; Glenn Gyorffy for his true determination, tenacity, talent and being our amazing bass player and a best friend; Sacha Gervasi for being the truest friend anyone has ever had, more worthy of being a brother; Rhonda Gibson for being my big sister who I love with all my heart and her husband Robbie for his generosity and great sense of humour; Jeffrey and Linda Kudlow for their belief in me, and Gary Kudlow for his love and support; Bob, Paul and Rita Schenk for family support; Chris (CT) Tsangarides for his excellent production and close friendship; Jackie Wallace and Vickie Merrilees for family support; Ian (Dix) Dickson for his years of dedication; Dave (Squirrely) Allison for the years of hard work; Sebastian Marino, Mike Duncan and Ivan Hurd for their work on our music; Jethro (Iron-fist) Hirsch for his endless help and friendship; Millie Gervasi for being our best friend's mom and being so cool; Claudine and Geza Gyorffy for their love support and hospitality and being G5's parents; Phil and Aeda Kosoy for their love and support; Colin (Mad Dog) Brown and Chris (Cut Loose) Hillis for years of head-banging friendship; Lee Burton, Gary Greenblatt, Jay Weiss, Bruce Hartley, Ashley Jarnicki, Marty Hoffman, Mark Grossman, Chemo, Richard Blackman, Mike Mayer, Les Brown for the early years of fun; Tom Smith for his crazy friendship; Black Metal (Ray Wallace) for his help on numerous occasions; Paula Danovich; Drew Masters; Danko; Ron Budreau for being our Canadian promo help; Peter Makowski and Ross Halfin for their continued support; Bob Muldowney for his great metal attitude and deep respect; John and Mark Gallhager, and the Hound of Hasselvander (Raven) for great memories; Jon and Marsha Zazula for the Route 18 experience and introducing us to Jethro; Paul O'Neill and David Krebs for making Super Rock '84 in Japan a part of our history; Bob Kellher for his fun post-Aerosmith antics; Rockin' Ray Dill, Metal Joe for opening your hearts and homes to us; Pete Perrina for his help when we come to 'The City'; Kenny from NJ for his help during crisis; Sebastian Maer for being at Loud

Park '06; Lemmy Kilminster, Brian Robertson, and Little Philthy for an experience of a lifetime touring the UK in '83; Belgium headbangers for being there for ever; Scott Ian for his honesty and good will; Tom Araya for his spiritual insight and turning me on to the Secret; Slash for his generosity and great attitude towards us; Lars Ulrich for his beautifully accurate insight; Gary Braniff (Brick) for being the almighty soundman and great friend; Kenny McNeil for his work with us; Barry (Bess Ross) Rosenberg for being there when we needed him; Tom Treumuth and Bruce Longman for their hard work during the nineties; Girlschool for being our friends; Ronnie James Dio for the party we had in Italy '05; Shmier for his attitude toward us; Candlemass for our continued friendship since '83; Jon Bon Jovi, Ritchie Sambora and Tico Torres for the memories of Super Rock '84; Michael Schenker for letting us use the film clip; Barbara Schenker for sharing some memories of Brugge with us at The Underworld Camden; Tony Iommi and Ozzy Osbourne for years of inspiration; Twisted Sister for being good to us and giving us respect; Bazz for help when we really need it in the UK; David Waring and Sue from Kingsdown where we always feel welcome; Rina Elfassi for helping us when in England; Ray Pike for his help in staying in tune when in England; Mike Sky for his help in entering the USA and some of the best sound we have ever had; John

Leverdingen for introducing me to Ginny and being Beast's best friend; Sandra Hawkins for putting up with Beast; Bob Morgan (Guitar Guru) for fixing my guitar; Tom Dirtman Orange for his views on life; Chris Soos for the finest photography and for having the belief in Anvil; Rebecca Yeldham for her great point of view and contribution of time; Jeff Renfroe and Andrew Dickler for their amazing editing work; David Norlan for the best chord progression I've heard in years; Matt Dennis, Brent, Ray Dumas and Jeremy for their contribution of time, effort and abilities; Lauren McClard for her hard work; Mick Southworth; Laurence Gornall; Lucy Fleet; Ailsa Scott; Liberty Frazer for all the dedication and belief in Anvil; Robert Uhlig for his open ear and great job putting it straight to paper; Sarah Emsley and Nick Robinson for making this book possible.

Robb Reiner would like to add his thanks to everyone thanked by Lips and also send his thanks in particular to: Jane-o (my life-long loving and totally supportive partner, who has been with me through all. Always love you!); Tyler (for being there and making my life complete, love you); William Reiner and Eniko Reiner for all the years of love and support (I love you); Andrea, my sister; Cozy Powell (inspiration and for giving me your time); Doug 5 (for being that crazy friend); John Tempesta; Thomas Hertler (for many years of belief and support); Robert Greenwald (for the hemp and cotton).

Sacha Gervasi's acknowledgements:

Without Bruce Robinson's *Withnail and I* I wouldn't have become a film maker, without Rob Reiner's *Spinal Tap* I wouldn't have had a film and without the brilliant Steve Zaillian I wouldn't have had a chance. Thanks to one and all.

Anvil and I would also like to thank our irrefutably excellent producer Rebecca Yeldham, whose passion and soul infused the film with more fun, truth and beauty than any of us deserved!

Lastly, to Sean 'Barnstormer' Barney, for pouring petrol into the engine day after day and never complaining once.

Credits